India, Vietnam and the Indo-Pacific

This book delves into the examination of bilateral relations between India and Vietnam in the 21st century and how the Indo-Pacific as a geopolitical construct lends itself to the improvement of their engagement.

With the rise and increasing assertiveness of China, the slow growth of the United States, the resurgence of Japan, and the oscillating role of ASEAN as a multilateral organization, the Indo-Pacific has emerged as a theatre of international geostrategic competition. This book studies these changing geopolitical realities and new evolving strategic configurations, while addressing political, economic, defence, and strategic aspects of the relationship along with the role of China and the US in facilitating ties. India's Act East Policy that was upgraded from the Look East Policy – one of the main drivers for India's increasing presence in the Asia-Pacific region – is also examined in this volume.

An important intervention in the study of international relations, this book will be indispensable to students and researchers of maritime studies, security studies, politics and international relations, geopolitics, and Asian studies.

Pankaj K Jha is Associate Professor, Jindal School of International Affairs (JSIA), O P Jindal Global University, Haryana, India. He was previously Director (Research) of Indian Council of World Affairs. He has also worked as Deputy Director of National Security Council Secretariat, India, (2012–2013) and been closely associated with national security apparatus in India. He was a visiting fellow with Centre for International Security Studies, Sydney University, Australia, and Institute for South Asian Studies, Singapore. He has authored over 60 articles that have been published in books as well as refereed and non–refereed journals. He is regularly quoted in International Newspapers/Magazines such as *Nikkei Asian Review, South China Morning Post, Bangkok Post, Gulf News* and *International Business Times,* etc. He has authored two books: *India and China in Southeast Asia: Competition or Cooperation* (2013) and *India and the Oceania: Exploring Vistas of Cooperation* (2016).

Vo Xuan Vinh is Deputy Director, Institute for Southeast Asian Studies (ISEAS), Vietnam Academy of Social Sciences (VASS), Hanoi. His research focuses on India's foreign policy, India's Look East/Act East Policy, India–ASEAN and India–Vietnam relations, political, security and international relations in Southeast Asia, the East Sea/South China Sea disputes, and politics of Thailand and Myanmar. He has presented research papers in national and international conferences in various countries. He has also contributed articles in international journals such as *Maritime Affairs, Journal of Himalayan and Central Asian Studies*, and *World Focus*. He is currently conducting research on maritime issues in Southeast Asia, India's Look East/Act East Policy, democratization process in Myanmar and Thailand, and international relations in Asia-Pacific.

India, Vietnam and the Indo-Pacific

Expanding Horizons

Pankaj K Jha and Vo Xuan Vinh

LONDON AND NEW YORK

First published 2020
by Routledge
2 Park Square, Milton Park, Abingdon, Oxon OX14 4RN

and by Routledge
52 Vanderbilt Avenue, New York, NY 10017

Routledge is an imprint of the Taylor & Francis Group, an informa business

© 2020 Pankaj K Jha and Vo Xuan Vinh

The right of Pankaj K Jha and Vo Xuan Vinh to be identified as authors of
this work has been asserted by them in accordance with sections 77 and 78 of
the Copyright, Designs and Patents Act 1988.

All rights reserved. No part of this book may be reprinted or reproduced or utilised
in any form or by any electronic, mechanical, or other means, now known or
hereafter invented, including photocopying and recording, or in any information
storage or retrieval system, without permission in writing from the publishers.

Trademark notice: Product or corporate names may be trademarks or
registered trademarks, and are used only for identification and explanation
without intent to infringe.

British Library Cataloguing-in-Publication Data
A catalogue record for this book is available from the British Library

Library of Congress Cataloging-in-Publication Data
Names: Jha, Pankaj, author. | Vo, Xuan Vinh, author.
Title: India, Vietnam and the Indo-Pacific : expanding horizons /
Pankaj K Jha and Vo Xuan Vinh.
Description: Abingdon, Oxon ; New York, NY : Routledge, 2020. |
Includes bibliographical references and index.
Identifiers: LCCN 2020001658 (print) | LCCN 2020001659 (ebook)
Subjects: LCSH: Regionalism--Indo-Pacific Region. | India--Foreign
relations--Vietnam. | Vietnam--Foreign relations--India. | India--Foreign
relations--21st century. | Vietnam--Foreign relations--21st century.
Classification: LCC DS450.V5 J43 2020 (print) | LCC DS450.V5 (ebook) |
DDC 327.540597--dc23
LC record available at https://lccn.loc.gov/2020001658
LC ebook record available at https://lccn.loc.gov/2020001659

ISBN: 978-0-367-11030-7 (hbk)
ISBN: 978-0-429-28187-7 (ebk)

Typeset in Sabon
by Taylor & Francis Books

Dedicated to our respective spouses and children:
Ms Kavita, Apurva and Kiara
and
Ms Bac, Kien and Quyen

Contents

	Preface	viii
	Acknowledgements	xi
1	India, Vietnam and the Indo-Pacific security architecture	1
2	The Indo-Pacific construct and utility of 'new' derived regions	18
3	India's Act East Policy and Vietnam	33
4	Political convergence in the context of the Indo-Pacific	53
5	Enhancing strategic understanding and developing defence cooperation	66
6	Ensuring peace, stability and security in the South China Sea	77
7	Developing trade and economic ties	88
8	India, Vietnam and ASEAN regionalism	106
9	The China factor in India–Vietnam relations	118
10	The US factor in Vietnam–India relations	131
11	Conclusion	145
	Index	152

Preface

In geopolitics, there are no permanent friends or enemies but only national interests, which define priorities for any country in terms of foreign policy, and calibrate their strategic outlook over a period. During the Cold War, better relations between any two countries developed on the terms of three major criteria that included ideological underpinnings, historical pasts and, lastly, the Non-Aligned Movement (NAM). There have been four major debates, which have been going on simultaneously in the international system. Firstly, whether the power bloc politics would make the world secure or insecure. Secondly, whether a nuclear war was an impending threat. Thirdly, are there any other models of development apart from capitalism and communism? Lastly, whether the Non-Aligned Movement would emerge as the unique embodiment of South–South unity or would wither away because of the geopolitical magnetic fields of the two power blocs. The end of the Cold War defined a new order but also led to problems such as nuclear proliferation, economic and trade wars, and increasing problems related to poverty and population. Further, issues like global warming, climate change and many other non-traditional security issues drew attention in the international discourse. Regional security became a major issue with new internecine and intra-regional disputes having limited international impact, and the influence of foreign actors in national discourse became more pronounced.

Bilateral relations between any two countries are determined by the convergence of interests in strategic, economic, cultural, political and social domains. However, in the case of India and Vietnam, this convergence germinated out of an anti-colonial struggle, closeness with the erstwhile Soviet Union, and the resilience of the two societies to emerge out of long periods of imperialist oppression. A connection between the two societies emerged because of the recognition of each other's freedom struggle and the unique respect between the leaders of the two countries. The foundation of these ties holds imprints of the influence of Indic civilization in the Vietnam cultural and traditional ethos. This was a result of the influence of Buddhism from India. However, the strand of Buddhism propagated in Vietnam has more Tibetan influence. Vietnam's Cham civilization, and the existence of practicing Cham Hindus in Vietnam, shows the deep umbilical cords that existed between the two civilizations. Vietnam has made sincere efforts to

Preface ix

preserve the historical artefacts, temples, Buddhist stupas and the remnants of Buddha. The cultural influence helped in sustaining ties and relations even in the modern age.

India–Vietnam ties have transcended the usual diplomatic formalities primarily related to the establishment of diplomatic relations in 1972, and have ventured into the strategic and economic domains. The two developing economies, having large populations and relatively skilled labour, found new horizons for developing and promoting their economic growth. The two countries had unpleasant colonial pasts. Vietnam suffered the aggression of France and the United States, while at the same time countering Chinese aggression. India, on the other hand, suffered more than two centuries of British imperialist oppression. Both countries, however, have found able leadership to guide the nations, and relatively stable relations, which were unaffected by the change in the global order from bipolar, to unipolar, to a more futuristic multipolar world. The two nations have found valuable convergence and understanding related to the regional security, economic development, free trade, and investment, development in social sector, cultural values, and traditions, and common heritage in terms of Buddhism, religious heritage and artefacts. The fundamentals of development, poverty alleviation and the generation of employment were additional areas of convergence.

While the two countries have addressed the challenges of growth and development, there have been other areas of cooperation. These included changing the regional order, with the US relegating itself to the sidelines while China made inroads into the regional order. However, this tectonic change has brought about its own share of problems with regard to military and naval skirmishes, as well as the issue of the South China Sea galvanizing opinion against the peaceful rise of China. India has catapulted itself into the league of major regional players and has been actively taking part in multilateral negotiations, as well as developing strategic and defence ties with other ASEAN members. India is perceived as a balancer, or the swing state, in the major power struggle against China.

This book could not have come at a more opportune time, when the Republic of India and the Socialist Republic of Vietnam have completed a series of events to celebrate the 45th and 10th anniversaries of the establishments of full diplomatic relations (1972) and their Strategic Partnership (2007) respectively. The 21st century witnessed the increasing assertiveness of China, the slow growth of the United States, the re-emergence of Japan with the aspiration to be a normal power, and the oscillating role of ASEAN as a multilateral organization. Furthermore, the emergence of non-security problems, especially in the maritime domain, have made the Asia-Pacific a true theatre of international geostrategic competition in the 21st century. The evolving context of the Asia-Pacific has made India–Vietnam relations, which have been nurtured for several centuries and strategically embedded in the Cold War, deepen and expand significantly. The bilateral linkages to a strategic partnership and a comprehensive strategic partnership in 2007 and 2016 respectively were seen as mature moves between the two countries.

x *Preface*

There have been books, articles and other kinds of short commentaries on the relations between India and Vietnam released for decades. However, another book, jointly written by an Indian scholar and a Vietnamese scholar, could bring some more perspectives into the context of an evolving Indo-Pacific architecture. The two authors of the book do not have an ambition to chart out the whole history of the relations between India and Vietnam; instead, we focus on the broader context of an evolving Indo-Pacific region in the 21st century as a background for the bilateral relations between the two countries. Topics of bilateral cooperation fields of discussion in this book include: (1) India–Vietnam political relations; (2) Exploring defence and strategic convergences; (3) Cooperation in ensuring peace, stability and security in the South China Sea; and (4) Developing trade and economic ties. Other factors with influences on India–Vietnam relations, such as ASEAN, the United States and China, will also be analysed in this book. India's Act East Policy, upgraded from the Look East Policy – one of the main drivers for India's increasing presence in the Asia-Pacific region, and for the upgrade of India–Vietnam relations – is examined. As the scholars who have been conducting research on India–Vietnam relations for many years with heart and love, we hope to bring to the readers of the two countries (and others) more aspects of their bilateral relations.

On the occasion of the birth of the book on 'India, Vietnam and the Indo-Pacific', the authors would like to express their deep thanks to scholars and experts from India and Vietnam, whose research has been a source of reference and encouragement for the writing of this book.

Acknowledgements

The authors would like to acknowledge the guidance and help provided by those academic and policy luminaries who have been working in the field of India–Vietnam relations, and this includes diplomats, strategic thinkers, academics and the new generation of young scholars. This relationship has been nurtured by the respective ambassadors, commercial counsellors, technical consultants and trade and industry associations. We would like to express our gratitude to all those people who have worked within their official commitments, and cultivated informal interactions to build our relationship.

The authors would like to thank the publisher for showing a keen interest in the manuscript and bringing out the refined version in a very short time.

New Delhi and Hanoi
Pankaj K Jha and Vo Xuan Vinh

1 India, Vietnam and the Indo-Pacific security architecture

Southeast Asia, as a region, has been witness to a global power struggle between major powers. It was used as a strategic staging post by multiple colonial powers, such as France, the Netherlands, Portugal, the US and Britain, to sustain their presence in the geopolitically sensitive region of Asia and expand their trade linkages. The developments in Vietnam, Indonesia, Malaysia and Myanmar were testimony to such a power struggle. In Vietnam, the division of the country into North and South Vietnam, and the three Indo-China wars fought by the Vietnamese with major powers such as France (1954), the US (1975), and China (1979) manifested the importance of Indo-China. Subsequently, efforts were directed to contain the surge of communism and maintain control by western colonial powers after Japan's withdrawal from South Asia in the post-war phase. Indonesia had its own struggle with Dutch and Portuguese colonial powers to maintain control over its 17,000 islands and the surrounding archipelagic waters of the country. The accessions of East Timor and Papua were examples of this struggle. Malaysia witnessed the withdrawal of British troops from the country and declared independence. However, even after Malaysia became independent, Britain played a critical role in keeping the country protected from communist insurgents. Lastly, Myanmar, which had seen the military rule for the major part of its history after independence from British rule, failed to maintain the democratic fundamentals which were seen as an increasing reflection of West-imposed order. Within Southeast Asia, organizations were formed to build an anti-communist edifice, bringing together like-minded countries which were wary of the influx of communism in the region. The evolution of an anti-communist front came in the form of ASEAN, which was transformed in the late 1960s into an inclusive and consensus-based organisation. The regional organization was meant to address the core challenge of communism, while at the same time maintaining the Asian value of consensus building.

The question of peace and stability in Southeast Asia has always defined the trajectory of ASEAN-centred multilateralism. This was demonstrated in the development of security alliances across the region, such as the Southeast Asian Treaty Organization (SEATO), the Five Power Defence Agreement (FPDA), and a more moderate visiting forces agreement between the US and the

2 The Indo-Pacific security architecture

Philippines. Barry Buzan had talked about the security complexes,[1] but even before his prognosis, Asia was always a geopolitical lab for different permutations and combinations which have defined the strategic scenario of the Asian continent.[2] From ideological underpinnings, which subsequently evolved to that of regional consensus making, ASEAN's evolution was guided by geopolitical compulsions and economic preferences. The precursor was the formation of security alliances and thereafter regional security architecture to create loose cooperative security structures.

Regional security architecture was meant to promote trust among the countries, and address common concerns related to security.[3] The expansion and fusion of the Asian and Pacific regions led to the formation of new terminology, as the region became known as the Asia-Pacific. The integration of contiguous regions was signalled through terms such as 'Asia-Pacific' in the early 1990s, and therefore, as a corollary to such thinking, new constructs such as the Indo-Pacific were coined to denote larger geopolitical interest areas. The vast Indo-Pacific region encompasses regional theatres such as South Asia, Southeast Asia, East Asia and Oceania, and these regions need stable community building and regional dialogue processes. A few scholars, such as Chengxin Pan, have stated that owing to the growing anxieties of the US, Japan, Australia and India about China's rise in Asia, the Indo-Pacific region is a contrived super-region, acting as a strategic hedge[4] to counter Sino-centric regional order.[5] It is neither a neutral nor a cooperative construct, instead, it is a loose flexible collective security arrangement. For select Indian strategic thinkers,[6] it was the bedrock of India's expanding relationship under the Act East Policy which now covered a huge swathe of territory, from the East China Sea to the South Pacific Ocean. For countries in Southeast Asia, including Vietnam, it meant subscription to US-imposed order, and therefore there has been hesitation, but not a complete discarding of this concept.

The region of Southeast Asia has always been a microcosm of great power rivalry, as well as ideological conflict between communism and capitalism. The anti-imperialist struggle by the Asian nations have made them adverse to capitalism, but at the same time, the institutional and governance mechanisms were borrowed from the colonial masters in the post-independence phase. This has been true in the case of most of the independent nations in South and Southeast Asia. With most Asian countries becoming independent in the early 1940s to late 1950s, the alliance formation and the regional security organization have always defined national and regional priorities. This was witnessed with the formation of the Association for Southeast Asia (ASA) in 1961, which included countries such as Malaysia, Thailand, and the Philippines.[7] Following this association were two defence groupings, which were more defence-oriented alliances. This included the Five Power Defence Agreement (FPDA),[8] and the continuing Southeast Asia Treaty Organization (SEATO). SEATO (1954–1977)[9] was a defence alliance supported by the US, which was joined by Thailand, the Philippines and Pakistan. However, this organization was not effective in consolidating the American stance and supporting American activities during

The Indo-Pacific security architecture   3

the Vietnam conflict. In 1971, nearly four years after the formation of ASEAN, the Five Power Defence Agreement (FPDA) came into force. One major reason was Britain's withdrawal from East of Suez (after the Suez crisis), which made the former Southeast Asian colonies, particularly Malaysia and Singapore, anxious about their security and stability. The new geopolitical dynamics encouraged Britain to terminate its security frontier located East of Suez, and this was reflected in the 1967 British Defence White Paper. Britain made it clear that it would not be involved in the security of the region beyond East of Suez, and this was further compelled by the circumstances which had dogged the regional security scenario in Southeast Asia, with the strengthening of the communist party movements in the region, including in Myanmar, Malaysia, Indonesia, and the Philippines. Indonesia–Malaysia *Konfrontasi* (1963–1966) further added to the tensions between newly independent nations of Southeast Asia. Subsequently, right after the formation of ASEAN, the FPDA was seen as a transitory arrangement to facilitate the military and defence capability building of Malaysia and Singapore.

With the announcement of the gradual withdrawal of British forces in January 1968, British troop withdrawal from Malaysia and Singapore was to be completed by the year 1971. This announcement impacted Australia, which perceived an active British interest in European affairs, Britain's enhancement of trade ties with its European neighbours, and changes in its domestic policy (in particular, immigration from Asian countries) as signs of Britain's retreat from Asia. Australia thereafter focused on its interests in Malaysia–Singapore.

In April 1971, Australia, Britain and New Zealand signed the Five Power Defence Arrangement with Malaysia and Singapore.[10] The subsequent years saw Soviet intervention in Afghanistan, the third Indochina war, and the resolution of the Cambodian crisis. A new code of conduct for regionalism in the region derived from the emergence of ASEAN as an organization, which facilitated the emergence of ASEAN consensus (better known as the 'ASEAN way'), economic cooperation, and community building that specifically stressed non-interventionist principles. The phased expansion of ASEAN membership and a staggered method for the inclusion of major powers as dialogue partners gave birth to new institutions, such as the East Asian summit, and increased acceptance of the concept of the Indo-Pacific. The inclusion of the US in the East Asian Summit consolidated this concept. However, at one point in time, the East Asian Region was also thought of as a possible alternative, but this would have brought China into the configuration. It would be pertinent to note the utility and evaluation of the regional constructs.

The Indo-Pacific in historical discourse

At any point in history, geopolitical imaginations and constructs have been superimposed on geographical features and outlines to create military commands, trading ports, commercial economic zones, and military theatres. This has served purposes of navigation, grading of threat, port identification, and

4 The Indo-Pacific security architecture

military strategy. This does not undermine bloc politics and the balance of power, which, to a large extent, were based on these geopolitical nomenclatures, with clearly demarcated spheres of influence and projection of military might. In the 1920s, the concept of the Indo-Pacific was promoted by German strategic thinker Karl Haushofer.[11] The Indo-Pacific was known as a contiguous marine region for biologists. This region witnessed the movement of marine organisms, and an identical oceanic ecosystem across Indian and Pacific oceans. The zoologists have been researching animal and wild life gene sampling across this region, while botanists have documented marine flora and fauna. Geologists have been studying oceanic features, and anthropologists have presented distinct similarities between the physical features of the Pacific islanders and Asians. In all these studies, the Indo-Pacific was a reference point. A few anthropologists geographically mapped the migration patterns from Asia and other continents, including Africa, to the Pacific over long periods of time. This has helped in drawing links between civilizations across the Indo-Pacific region. However, in geopolitical discourse it had not garnered the expected attention. The Indo-Pacific construct gained political traction in the late 2000s, when it was felt that the Asia-Pacific needed to include India and the Indian Ocean to be more inclusive and create a cooperative sphere between democracies and like-minded nations. It is now widely resonating as the fulcrum of new geopolitical realities.[12] Since 2011, the usage of the term 'Indo-Pacific' has increased manifold, with references from the political and defence leaderships of Australia, the US, India and, to a limited extent, Japan.

Many geographic regions have flexible geopolitical boundaries. As a result of this, sub-regions such as the Greater Mekong sub-region, the Bay of Bengal community, and the emergence of selective membership organizations, such as BRICS (Brazil, Russia, India, China, and South Africa), have defied all logic related to regionalism which has been more geographically based. BRICS as an *à la carte* institution depicted the structures based on economic priorities, geopolitical compulsions and as an alternative to Western regionalism concepts. As a result, geography and, more particularly, political geography, gained traction and evolved as a new area of study in global politics. The political geography has anchored itself in classical geopolitics and critical geopolitics. In the two cases of sub-regional institutions and *à la carte* multilateralism, latitude and longitude become irrelevant, and are replaced by the geopolitical ambitions of other emerging powers.[13]

Karl Haushofer, in his discourse about geographical and strategic constructs, referred to the *Indopazifischen Raum* ('Indo-Pacific region/space') as the fusion of the two regional constructs, and noted that:

> the geographic impact of the dense Indo-Pacific concentration of humanity and cultural empire of India and China, which ... are geographically sheltered behind the protective veil of the offshore island arcs' of the western Pacific and Bay of Bengal, offshore island arcs through which they are now both actively and competitively deploying.[14]

Furthermore, the trade and cultural routes between the Indian and Pacific Oceans had been reflected in the archaeological studies and historical data. The new construct of the Indo-Pacific had relatively more Oceanic flavour in comparison to the Asia-Pacific, but also in rediscovering, forging and strengthening cultural and historical links between the mainland and island communities. The debate over the viability and utility of the Asia-Pacific and Indo-Pacific has been widely debated but, for both India and Vietnam, the Indo-Pacific seemed more appropriate because it was inclusive of both the countries as equal stakeholders, and integrated the two into emerging geopolitical calculations.

In the international discourse concerning China, there are two issues which are widely debated: the strategic expansion of Chinese military, in terms of military bases like Djibouti, and their island reclamation activity in South China Sea; and China's growth story, catalysed by economic diplomacy and integrated supply chains. However, in the international political economy, economic diplomacy has increasingly been viewed from a strategic prism, thereby giving rise to the notion of comprehensive strategy. Nevertheless, there is a dichotomy between the two – while the earlier aspect shows the differing perception of China's rise, the other is the modulated impression of the economic growth of China as perceived by each country. The major factor in China's growth story has been the proportional increase in its international clout. The transformation of China from an isolated command economy to one of the largest market forces in the world in a space of three decades is unparalleled in history.[15] However, while economic diplomacy acted to China's advantage, it also created disparities within society, as well as created a negative balance of trade with most of the Asian economies. In addition, most trade was carried out from the eastern coast and some, though comparatively less, from the south-eastern land routes. However, the lack of land interconnectivity and infrastructure, as well as domestic compulsions, have undermined trade and investment potential. There is still much unexplored potential within the southern area and the Indian Ocean region.

There are apprehensions about China's approach towards the Indian Ocean and the South China Sea, mostly propagated by Western strategists, through concepts like the 'String of Pearls' strategy, and China's 'assumed' revisionist tendencies. This is where a clash between the two schools of thought – namely neo-realism and neo-liberalism – takes place. In order to sustain their economic momentum, both India and China were looking for room in the South and Southeast Asian region to cultivate their economic clout. One way of doing so is through soft power. Soft power is defined by Joseph Nye as 'the ability to get what you want through attraction rather than through coercion'.[16] According to him, this power can 'be cultivated through relations with allies, economic assistance, and cultural exchanges'. He argues that this can result in 'a more favourable public opinion' and credibility abroad.[17] Neo-liberalism also supports this template for enhancing cooperation and confidence building. Neo-liberalism, however, is facing doubt with regard to increasing protectionism and non-tariff barriers. Robert Keohane and Lisa

6 The Indo-Pacific security architecture

Martin have noted that 'for better or worse, institutional theory is a half-sibling of neorealism'.[18] Both neo-realism and neo-liberalism start from the assumption that the absence of a sovereign authority that can make and enforce binding agreements creates opportunities for states to advance their interests unilaterally, and makes it both important and difficult for states to cooperate with one another. States must worry that others will seek to take advantage of them; agreements must be crafted to minimize the danger of double crosses; the incentives that operate when agreements are signed may be quite different when the time comes for them to be carried out, and both promises and threats need to be made credible. Thus, it will take some disentangling to isolate the areas in which there are important disputes between neo-realism and neo-liberalism.[19] In this context, the debate about the Asia-Pacific and the Indo-Pacific becomes all the more relevant. While the Asia-Pacific includes China, the Indo-Pacific selectively excludes China.

Asia-Pacific or Indo-Pacific: discourse about the region

Geography has been a decisive factor in the political, commercial, and strategic relations of the nation state. At a strategic level, maintaining balance of power among littoral, island nations and continental countries has been a decisive element in the rise and fall of states. The geographic locale of a country and its military might have also been determinants of the prospects of peace and war. From a purely defensive and strategic point of view, whether a country had purely continental power, devoid of any sea access, or was a maritime nation with strong navy defined security outlooks throughout history. The comprehensive topography of a battleground has often influenced the outcome of any skirmish or the conflict itself. However, a nation's global influence and utility is often decided by the strategic vantage point bestowed on it by its geography and location.[20]

The discourse about preference for the Asia-Pacific or the Indo-Pacific germinates from the fact that despite being a part of the Asia-Pacific, India was somewhat ignored in its power and economic configuration. The eminence of India in regional politics, and the important role that it now plays in global politics because of its nuclear power status, fourth largest standing army and above-average annual growth of six to seven per cent, has established India as an important stakeholder in the Asia-Pacific. As a result, India's inclusion gave birth to the term Indo-Pacific. Further, reference to the Indian and Pacific Oceans as one continuous, strategic space has made littoral countries become important stakeholders. Littoral countries of the Indian and Pacific Oceans need to be seen as one community but this has not been the case. Australia's Indo-Pacific construct starts from the east of the Indian Ocean, primarily the Bay of Bengal, up to the western limits of Pacific Ocean. Indonesia also subscribes to the same geographic space. The resultant effect has been the relegation of the Indian Ocean Rim Association as an ineffective multilateral organization because it involves littoral countries around the Indian Ocean, given its slow growth and the lack of economic and business agenda. The basic element of the strengthening of any construct is increasing references to that geopolitical imagination in speeches, and evolution of multilateral structures defining that construct and increasing subscription from the interested stakeholders and countries.

The new geopolitical construct does have a strategic imprint. With the military modernization of China, many analysts have stated that a 'hidden objective of this is to drive out the US from the western Pacific'.[21] According to one of the 2020 projections, the Chinese navy would have developed expeditionary capability and a brown navy 'far seas' (*yuan hai*) capability. This enhanced capability would facilitate its power projection 'from the northwest Pacific to the East Indian Ocean', and by 2050 the objective is to develop a blue navy having 'far ocean' (*yuan yang*) capability.[22] This emerged as a possible challenge to the US hegemony, which, because of the US' involvement in various theatres in Libya, Afghanistan and Iraq, was seen as an overextended and overstretched power. As a result of this, East Asia became a less important region in US geostrategic calculations.

Since the end of the Second World War, the US has adopted a grand strategy to support its global hegemonic ambitions. Three basic assumptions have supported this ambition. First, the US policy makers believe that 'multipolarity' is intrinsically unstable and have therefore supported the hegemonic stability theory to justify their thinking. With the demise of the Soviet Union, this long-standing goal was achieved and unipolarity was seen as the natural equilibrium for sustained peace and regional stability. Since the early 1990s, the US strategy has been to prolong the country's 'unipolar prerogative' by containing any possible challenge to its global hegemony and countering the rise of potentially hostile regional powers. Secondly, the US had identified three regions – Western Europe, East Asia, and the Middle East – to focus on intensively to preserve its strategic and economic superiority.[23] As a result of this soft balancing, offshore balancing and alliance formations came to be seen as panacea to the long term challenges. Thirdly, in order to preserve its economic superiority, the US would have to create other production centres, which could then challenge the economic superiority of China. As a result, captive market strategies and non-tariff barriers were used as a policy. Ashley Tellis, in his analysis of the Indo-Pacific, has opined that involving a transregional concept which generates policies builds a strategic framework of reference in the making of regional security apparatus:

> The Indian Ocean is going to be increasingly integrated with the Western Pacific. In fact, the concept of Indo-Pacific is not as fantastical as one would have thought a decade or two decades ago, because … economics and politics will combine to push a much tighter integration of these two ocean spaces than before.[24]

This spatial perspective combines the Indian and Pacific Oceans, especially the eastern Indian and western Pacific oceans, with the South China Sea as a further

8 *The Indo-Pacific security architecture*

overlap. From this comes the second theme, Indo-Pacific regional security convergence, a degree of softer strategic balancing by India and the US in relation to the Indian and Pacific Oceans.[25] In modern times, geography has rested on a secure theoretical foundation. Classical geopolitics (coordinates defining the location in a region) overlaps with critical geopolitics (projecting perceptual aspirations, expectations, and uncertainties in a region).[26] In the modern discourse, the Indo-Pacific has gained much traction and currency. However, the Indo-Pacific construct is not a new concept. As discussed earlier, Karl Haushofer mentioned the *Indopazifischen Raum* in his synthesis of the two regional constructs.[27] This geopolitical imagination was propounded in the late 1920s and early 1930s. He said that:

> the geographic impact of the dense Indo-Pacific concentration of humanity and cultural empire of India and China, which ... are geographically sheltered behind the protective veil of the offshore island arcs of the western Pacific and Bay of Bengal, offshore island arcs through which they are now both actively and competitively deploying.[28]

Furthermore, the trade and cultural routes between the Indian and Pacific Oceans has been reflected in archaeological studies and historical data.

In international politics, in order to demarcate its growing clout, every major power outlined its areas of influence, dominance, and acceptance. India, having graduated from a regional power to one of the emerging powers, tried to engage countries in its extended neighbourhood, such as West and East Asia, Africa, and Central Asia. Indian foreign policy based on Nehruvian idealism also fostered neo-realist thinking. India's engagement with Israel and Southeast Asian nations was one such transition of the foreign policy, and the genesis of a new strategic understanding. As a result of this, Indian foreign policy adopted a 'concentric circles' approach (inner orbit to outer periphery), and foreign policy objectives adhered to an 'immediate to extended' neighbourhood paradigm. John Mearsheimer has argued that in an international theatre, nations are evolving, seeking and pursuing all potential advantages. This quest for hegemonic power is constant and unending. Therefore, drawing analogies from historical evidence, Professor Mearsheimer argued that the US–China relationship has the potential to become more intense and unpredictable during the twenty-first century. He points to the fact that both countries have critical interests in the Indo-Pacific region. However, in the immediate future, their interests will not run analogously. At some juncture, both countries will struggle to define their hegemonic role in the Indo-Pacific region. According to Mearsheimer, 'China might emerge as the key to the regional stability in northeast Asia in the future, if not all of the Indo-Pacific region'.[29] In the Indo-Pacific construct, with increasing rates of piracy and terrorism, the challenge of keeping the Sea Lines of Communication free for navigation and shipping would be the paramount objective of major powers.

Oceans have been instruments which have facilitated trade and commerce between distant continents and nations. However, a negative aspect of developing trade having high transactional value was that this led to security issues related to the protection of cargo, and even the human lives of those onboard. The four oceans (Indian, Pacific, Atlantic and Arctic), and their adjoining continents and landmasses, have been catalysts in various security and cooperative institutions, such as the Indian Ocean Rim Association (IORA, earlier known as IOR-ARC); collective security and alliance systems, such as the North Atlantic Treaty Organisation (NATO), and regional cooperative forums like the Pacific Islands Forum (PIF) and the Asia-Pacific Economic Cooperation (APEC). In November 2011, the US Secretary of State Hillary Clinton outlined the new US strategic approach towards the Asia-Pacific region in her article titled 'America's Pacific Century' in a web magazine.[30] However, the article strongly advocated for the necessity of addressing challenges in the Indian and Pacific Oceans in a composite manner. The two oceans have economic and geopolitical relevance, and are of contiguous strategic importance. Secretary Clinton's essay unambiguously clarified the reasons for the US to refocus its energies toward the Asia-Pacific and explained the strategic relevance of the Indo-Pacific region.[31]

Along with these regional and transregional institutions, the increasing nontraditional security challenges such as migration, piracy, natural calamities and other environmental hazards forced nations to upgrade their naval capabilities. This served their traditional security role. However, a struggle to secure resources and energy supplies led to debate about alignments and new coalitions such East Asian Security, Asia-Pacific Security, and Indo-Pacific security complexes. The more recent construct of the Indo-Pacific generated discussion about the possibility and consequences of different security complexes having geopolitical and geostrategic ramifications. In the current context, the multilateral organizations have become more inclusive and endeavour to build consensus on regional developmental, trade and security issues. This triggered a debate regarding whether multilateralism would outline security constructs or vice versa. Following the evolution of geopolitical constructs and multilateralism discourse, the conceptualisation of the Indo-Pacific, even though not articulated as such, echoed in the works of the well-known strategic thinker K M Panikkar. Panikkar has alluded to the strategic relevance of Yemen (Socotra Island) and Straits of Malacca as the two arcs for India's strategic thinking.[32] Later, Indian Prime Minister Jawaharlal Nehru articulated a new objective of the Afro-Asian unity as an invective against imperialism and apartheid. This objective resonated during the Afro-Asian conference in 1947. Subsequently, the Non-Aligned Movement (NAM) outlined a new idea to mobilize South–South co-operation, thereby fashioning the third bloc. In the first half of the 1990s, 'Asia-Pacific' was a new term which laid the foundation of the Asia-Pacific Economic Cooperation (APEC).

The relevance of ASEAN as a regional multilateral institution stems from India's efforts to recalibrate its foreign and trade policies, which were later

10 The Indo-Pacific security architecture

found to be in sync with the Indo-Pacific region. In June 2008, the then Prime Minister of Australia Kevin Rudd remarked which he had earlier reiterated in Japan and Indonesia that there was a need for 'a vision for an Asia Pacific Community' (APC).[33] He proposed a regional institution, which would span the entire Asia-Pacific region including the United States, Japan, China, India, Indonesia and the other states: 'A Regional institution which is able to engage in the full spectrum of dialogue, cooperation and action on economic and political matters and future challenges related to security'[34] was growing more important and acceptable in the regional discourses. For Prime Minister Rudd, the proposal for a new regional institution was propelled by the European Union and was primarily meant to 'encourage the development of a genuine and comprehensive sense of community whose habitual operating principle is cooperation'.[35] Australia had earlier played a significant role in the formation of APEC in the early 1990s (although ignoring India as a member); it had developed acumen for the development of multilateral security 'architecture'. Even though this initiative was criticized, the key question was whether the initiative had the capacity to encapsulate the interests of major Asia-Pacific powers, who had entrenched themselves in the diverse regional security institutions. These arrangements included the APEC, the ASEAN plus Six, the East Asia Summit (EAS), the ASEAN Defence Ministers Meeting plus (ADMM+) and the Extended ASEAN Maritime Forum. For example, Southeast Asian states were, for the most part, well attached to ASEAN, APEC, Japan to APEC and EAS, and China to the EAS. These 'architectures' were competing among themselves to become more relevant and important, a fight which was potentially intensified by the Kevin Rudd proposal.[36] Subsequently, Hatoyama proposed the East Asian Economic Community, which was an abridged version of the Kevin Rudd proposal with a few inclusions and exceptions.

In more recent times, many strategic thinkers, as well as the policy think-tanks of countries such as Australia and Indonesia, have shown preference to the Indo-Pacific concept. The then Indian Prime Minister Manmohan Singh had articulated India's stance. The 'Indo-Pacific' was outlined as a new prototypical concept for enhancing cooperation in the region. With reference to the 'quest for stability and peace in the vast region in Asia that is washed by the Pacific and Indian Oceans', the Indian Prime Minister had noted Japan as their preferred partner.[37] It is yet to be seen whether the idea will outline new arrangements or be annulled by countries of the Indian and Pacific Oceans.

Outlining the Indo-Pacific construct, India's Maritime Strategy has also developed in the last one and a half decades. Primary areas of interest include the following:

> ...choke points leading to, from and across the Indian Ocean, including the Six-degree Channel, Eight/Nine-degree Channels, Straits of Hormuz, Bab-el-Mandeb, Malacca, Singapore, Sunda and Lombok, the Mozambique Channel, and Cape of Good Hope and their littoral regions.

The Indo-Pacific security architecture 11

In the same document, India's secondary areas of maritime interest are outlined as:

> the Southeast Indian Ocean, including sea routes to the Pacific Ocean and littoral regions in the vicinity;
> the South and East China Seas, Western Pacific Ocean, and their littoral regions.
> the Southern Indian Ocean Region, including Antarctica.[38]

From an entirely naval point of view, interpretations have been made that the Indian Ocean Naval Symposium and Western Pacific Naval Symposium should synchronize to address issues in an all-inclusive manner. Further, coordinated patrols along the choke points and critical sea lanes might address the issues of piracy and armed robbery, and create deterrence for the non-state actors operating at high seas. While India is incrementally subscribing to the Indo-Pacific construct, the articulation from Vietnam is still in the evolutionary phase. There is a need to build on a political understanding about this transregional construct.

Asia-Pacific or Indo-Pacific: choices for India and Vietnam

As has been seen, until recent years, India adopted a conservative policy regarding the concept of the Asia-Pacific. However, the divisions between the different regions of Asia are becoming less distinct. India is emerging as a significant player in the security dynamics of Southeast Asia and, to a lesser extent, in Northeast Asia and the South Pacific. The separation of Asia into different regions of strategic interaction was at its clearest between South Asia and Northeast Asia. This is well illustrated by the trajectory of the India–Japan relationship. Through much of the twentieth century, Japan saw its own strategic space, even in its most extended form, as effectively ending at the Indian border where the Japanese army halted in 1942. For 50 years after independence, India was preoccupied with security threats in South Asia and its own attempts to achieve predominance within that region. It is only recently that India and Japan have made common cause. The end of the Cold War and India's reach for major power status also forced it to end its passive approach towards Southeast Asia.[39]

The idea of a 'Concert of Powers' spanning the Pacific and Indian Oceans is interesting. In recent years, there has been increased discussion about a Concert of Powers in the Asia-Pacific, as a way of engaging with China as a responsible member of a new strategic order.[40] The idea harks back to the first half of the nineteenth century, when a 'concert' of four or five European powers explicitly took collective managerial responsibility for the security of Europe. This was seen as a way of mitigating competition between them, and reducing the risk of unintended conflicts. It required major powers to accept that role. A rising India would seem to be an essential member of any such concert in Asia, although as former NSA Shivshankar Menon had implicitly acknowledged, India may only have the necessary credibility if the managerial scope of such a concern extends to the Indian Ocean.

12   The Indo-Pacific security architecture

The conceptualization of the Asia-Pacific and Indian Ocean regions as a strategic whole could also be a two-edged sword for India. Such an approach would certainly legitimize a much greater role for India in the Asia-Pacific. The development of a working concert of major powers with a focus on maritime security would also involve a much more multipolar Asia, and require India to concede a role to China in the Indian Ocean region that it has never before conceded. India might be forced to give up any dream of the Indian Ocean being 'India's Ocean'. While the United States is facilitating the development of India's relationships in the Asia-Pacific, it could also act as an implicit inhibitor of India's role in the region. The United States may see some benefit in Sino-Indian strategic rivalry, and may even at times encourage that rivalry, at least in the Indian Ocean. However, there may be circumstances in which the United States could come to regard India as a destabilizing factor in regional security (for example, in the case of conflict in the South China Sea). It is difficult to imagine India being able to take a substantial direct security role in the Asia Pacific in the face of strong opposition from the United States.[41] India's vital role in the South Asia and Indian Ocean region has been acknowledged in the US Quadrennial Defence Reviews. The US Quadrennial Defence Review (QDR) has also listed India as a friendly country which should undertake responsibility in securing the Indian Ocean, and this categorically means that, in a regional context, India has to elevate itself to being more than a south Asian actor.[42] The QDR states:

> As the economic power, cultural reach, and political influence of India increase, it is assuming a more influential role in global affairs. This growing influence, combined with democratic values it shares with the United States, an open political system, and a commitment to global stability, will present many opportunities for cooperation. India's military capabilities are rapidly improving through increased defence acquisitions and these now include long-range maritime surveillance, maritime interdiction and patrolling, air interdiction, and strategic airlift. India has established its worldwide military influence, through counter piracy, peacekeeping, humanitarian assistance, and disaster relief efforts. As its military capabilities grow, India will contribute to Asia as a net provider of security in the Indian Ocean and beyond.[43]

Military presence on islands in the Indian and Pacific Oceans has been enhanced of late, in conjunction with the growing importance of the Indo-Pacific region. This is certainly true of the US air base on Diego Garcia in the Chagos Archipelago, as well as India's island territories of Andaman & Nicobar and Lakshadweep, and also for France in the Réunion. The naval and logistical bases built by China and Japan in Djibouti show the need for Asian powers to project power into the Indian Ocean. Many other islands that are now being seen as strategic outposts and integrated into the defence planning of other countries include Seychelles, Mauritius, Sri Lanka, the Maldives, Yemen's Socotra, Oman's

The Indo-Pacific security architecture 13

Masirah Island, and Australia's Cocos (Keeling) Islands.[44] Australia, in its 2013 Defence White Paper, has alluded to strengthening its naval facility at Darwin, clearly projecting it as the conjunction point between the Indian and Pacific Oceans. The US, being cognizant of the utility of the Darwin base, has agreed to station its troops in Darwin. India has also strengthened its Joint Command in the Andaman and Nicobar islands, and is upgrading its jetties and runways. In the past, Indonesia Foreign Minister Marty Natalgewa has talked about the Indo-Pacific Treaty. In 2018, ASEAN also started debating subscription to the Indo-Pacific concept, and deliberations have started in this regard.[45]

For Vietnam, the choice between the Indo-Pacific and the Asia-Pacific has already been reflected in a number of policy papers and official statements. Its preference is the inclusion of India in the Asia-Pacific, therefore the Indo-Pacific becomes all the more relevant. In its Defence White Paper released in 2009, Vietnam identified four major security challenges: (1) the impact of the global financial crisis on Vietnam's economy and the danger of 'further lagging behind' other regional states; (2) the threat of 'hostile forces ... to incite violence and separatism' in order to undermine domestic stability; (3) disputes over sovereignty, sovereign rights and jurisdiction over the territories in the East Sea (South China Sea), and (4) non-traditional security issues (specifically illegal trafficking of weapons and drugs, piracy, organized transnational crimes, terrorism, illegal migration and immigration, environmental degradation, climate change, and epidemics).[46] Vietnam's foreign minister, during his visit to India in 2013, stated that there is a need for India to participate in the affairs of the region and undertake a proactive role. He said:

> In this regard, ASEAN in general and Vietnam in particular always view India with great respect and as an important partner. India naturally has a formidable presence in the Indo-Pacific by virtue of its size, its economy and its willingness to assume a greater role on the world stage.[47]

He further expounded:

> ...bearing that in mind, I think we should have an ever broader view that Asia-Pacific and South Asia are interlinked into what is called Indo-Pacific. There are today many proposals, ideas, concepts and initiatives that promote linkage between South Asia with East Asia and the Pacific. This reflects a reality that we all share a common prosperity, our destinies are intertwined. And ASEAN plays the crucial role as the bridge linking our regions, as the threshold for India to enter Asia-Pacific.[48]

For Vietnam, it seems that Indo-Asia-Pacific is the preferred term for the country, while subscribing to the geographical outline of the Indo-Pacific.

In international discourse, security and economics define the state of global affairs. While security alliances such as NATO are still seen as relevant in select theatres, strategic and defence cooperation agreements, which include both

14 *The Indo-Pacific security architecture*

traditional security concerns (including maritime security), are carefully designing new, flexible cooperative structures. The security alliance has become, to a certain extent, a passé, while strategic partnerships and other flexible arrangements have become the preferred choice. This can be attributed to the increasing economic interdependence which has been experienced all across the globe. Economic organisations and forums are also becoming influenced by strategic preferences, with the US supporting the Trans Pacific Partnership (now that it has withdrawn from the organisation). China advocates for the Free Trade Agreement of the Asia-Pacific (FTAAP), with market access and investment as the dividends of the trade, and regional economic agreements. The Indo-Pacific as a construct still lacks the multilateral structure to support itself, and the closest structures are the East Asia Summit, APEC and the G20. However, out of these, two (EAS and G20) are rather loose formations in which discussion and collaboration are more of a voluntary nature.

Faced with the predicament of supporting the structures from both a security and an economic point of view, the choices for India are rather limited. In the case of security, India does have a defence cooperation agreement with a majority of the nations in the Indo-Pacific region, but the binding commitment is missing. Furthermore, the objective and the agenda for such a construct are missing. Comprehensive security through formal alliance structures is missing. In such a situation, India must carefully build on its strategic choices and economic preferences. So far, India has not fully subscribed to the Indo-Pacific concept because it is still vague and in nascent stages. Further, it is increasingly seen as a counter-China strategy. Though the Indo-Pacific as a geo-political imagination is increasingly relevant, it is still a very calculated and calibrated move for India to engage in any counter-China strategy. India is acting as a swing state. On one hand it is a participant in the Quadrilateral initiative (US, India, Japan and Australia), but on the other hand, it has avoided antagonistic statements against China, as these have certain regional and global costs. From a purely naval point of view, there are views that the Indian Ocean Naval Symposium and Western Pacific Naval Symposium should coordinate together to address issues in a holistic manner. This would help in the coordinated patrols along the critical sea lanes, as well as choke points, to address the issues of piracy and armed robbery at high seas, and act as a deterrent for the non-state actors operating at high seas.

In the end, one can say that the two constructs define different aspects of regions and interaction across societies, strategic communities and economic zones. It has been seen in the past that the Pacific Economic Cooperation Council (PECC) has given birth to the Asia-Pacific Economic Community, which might give birth to the Indo-Pacific Economic Community. It still would be premature to look into the Asia-Pacific and the Indo-Pacific, but the struggle for subscription and the problem of accommodation between rising powers, as well as the debate about the unipolar and multipolar order, might define the utility of the two constructs. It would, however, depend to a large extent on which construct includes India and which does not, as India is a stakeholder

The Indo-Pacific security architecture 15

which cannot be denied its rightful place in regional and global architecture. Vietnam has few reservations regarding the Indo-Pacific term, as it is already enmeshed into the Asia-Pacific, and has expressed that India should be included in the Asia-Pacific regional security structure. However, given the sensitivities involved with regard to any anti-China alliance, the two countries want security without antagonizing the dragon.

Notes

1 Buzan, Barry. 1991. 'New Patterns of Global Security in the Twenty-first Century', *International Affairs*, 67(3): 432–433
2 Buzan, Barry. 2012. 'Asia: A Geopolitical Reconfiguration', https://www.ifri.org/sites/default/files/atoms/files/barrybuzanengpe22012.pdf (accessed 24 October 2015)
3 Buzan, Barry. 1988. 'The Southeast Asian Security Complex', *Contemporary Southeast Asia*, 10(1): 1–16
4 Scott, David. 2008. 'The Great Power "Great Game" between India and China: "The Logic of Geography"', *Geopolitics*, 13(1): 1–26
5 Pan, Chengxin. 2014. 'The "Indo-Pacific" and geopolitical anxieties about China's rise in the Asian regional order', *Australian Journal of International Affairs*, 68(4): 453–469
6 Mohan, C Raja. 2012. *Samudra Manthan: Sino-Indian Rivalry in the Indo-Pacific*. Washington, DC: Carnegie Endowment for International Peace. Bajpaee, Chietigj. 2014. 'India–South Korea Relations and the Emerging Regional Architecture', *Strategic Analysis*, 38(4): 442. Chacko, Priya. 2012. 'India and the Indo-Pacific: An Emerging Regional Vision', *Indo-Pacific Governance Research Centre Policy Brief*, 5. http://www.adelaide.edu.au/indo-pacificgovernance/policy/Chacko_PB.pdf (accessed 21 October 2017). Menon, Shivshankar. 2013. 'Speech at the Book Release of Samudra Manthan: Sino-Indian Rivalry in the Indo-Pacific', March 4. http://www.orfonline.org/cms/export/orfonline/documents/Samudra-Manthan.pdf (accessed 22 October 2018)
7 Pollard, Vincent K. 1970. 'ASA and ASEAN, 1961–1967: Southeast Asian Regionalism', *Asian Survey* 10(3): 244–255
8 Five Power Defence Arrangements (FPDA). https://www.globalsecurity.org/military/world/int/fpda.htm (accessed 12 February 2019)
9 Southeast Asia Treaty Organization (SEATO). 1954. https://history.state.gov/milestones/1953-1960/seato (accessed 12 February 2019)
10 Bristow, D. 2005. 'The Five Power Defence Arrangements: Southeast Asia's Unknown Regional Security Organization', *Contemporary Southeast Asia*, 27(1): 1–20
11 Cited in Scott, David. 2012. 'The "Indo-Pacific"—New Regional Formulations and New Maritime Frameworks for US-India Strategic Convergence', *Asia-Pacific Review*, 19(2): 85–109
12 Pan, 2014: 454
13 Scott, 2012: 85–86
14 Haushofer, Karl. 2002. *An English Translation and Analysis of Major Karl Ernst Haushofer's Geopolitics of the Pacific Ocean*, tr. Lewis Tambs and Ernst Brehm. Lampeter: Edwin Mellor Press: 141
15 Lanteigne, Marc. 2009. *Chinese Foreign Policy: An Introduction*. London: Routledge: 9
16 Nye Jr, Joseph S. 2008. 'Public Diplomacy and Soft Power', *Annals of the American Academy of Political and Social Science*, 616(1): 94–109
17 Nye Jr, Joseph S. 2004. *Soft Power: The Means to Success in World Politics*. New York: Public Affairs: 105
18 Keohane, Robert O, and Martin, Lisa L. 1999. 'Institutional Theory, Endogeneity, and Delegation', *Working Paper Series 99–07*, Weatherhead Center for International Affairs, Harvard University: 3

16   *The Indo-Pacific security architecture*

19 Jervis, Robert. 1999. 'Realism, Neoliberalism, and Cooperation: Understanding the Debate', *International Security*, 24(1): 43–44

20 Dibb, Paul. 2006. 'Is strategic geography relevant to Australia's current defence policy?' *Australian Journal of International Affairs*, 60(2): 247

21 Ding, Arthur S. 2009. 'China's Growing Military Capability in Search of a Strategy', *The International Spectator*, 44(2): 95

22 Commander of the US Pacific Command, Adm. Timothy Keating, during his visit to China for dialogue over China's manufacture of aircraft carriers, was asked by senior Chinese naval officials about the possibility of the US force withdrawing to east of Hawaii, leaving the Pacific west of Hawaii to China. Keating, Paul. 2008. 'The US is concerned about China's development of aircraft carriers; avoiding to become a threat', *China Times*, 19 December 2008. http://news.chinatimes.com/2007Cti/2007Cti-News/2007Cti-News-Content/ (accessed 24 July 2012). Li, Nan. 2009. 'The Evolution of China's Naval Strategy and Capabilities: from "Near Coast" and "Near Seas" to "Far Seas"', *Asian Security*, 5(2): 144–169

23 Layne, Christopher. 2009. 'America's Middle East grand strategy after Iraq: the moment for offshore balancing has arrived', *Review of International Studies*, 35: 5

24 Scott, 2012: 85–90

25 Ibid.: 86

26 Ibid.: 87–89

27 Loc. cit.

28 Haushofer, 2002: 141

29 Quoted in Doyle, Randall. 2014. *The Geopolitical Power Shift in the Indo-Pacific Region: America, Australia, China and Triangular Diplomacy in the Twenty-First Century*. Washington: Lexington Books: 22

30 Clinton, Hillary. 2011. 'America's Pacific Century'. *Foreign Policy*, https://foreignpolicy.com/2011/10/11/americas-pacific-century/ (accessed 3 March 2020)

31 Ibid.: 24

32 Jha, Pankaj K. 2017. 'Defining Contours of the India–Korea Strategic Partnership: Political and Economic Parameters', *Studies in Comprehensive Regional Strategies Collected Papers (International Edition)*. KIEP Studies in Comprehensive Regional Strategies 16-15: 9–88.

33 Frost, Frank. 2009–2010. Australia's proposal for an 'Asia Pacific Community': issues and prospects, 1 December 2009, no. 13. (accessed 4 February 2020)

34 Smith, Gary. 2010. 'Australia and the rise of India', *Australian Journal of International Affairs*, 64(5): 570. Frost, Frank. 2010. Australia's regional engagements in East Asia and the Asia Pacific. https://www.aph.gov.au/About_Parliament/Parliamentary_Departments/Parliamentary_Library/pubs/BriefingBook43p/regionalengagements (accessed 3 February 2020)

35 Rudd, Kevin. 2008. 'Address to the Asia Society AustralAsia Centre, Sydney: It's time to build an Asia Pacific Community' 4 June. https://pmtranscripts.pmc.gov.au/release/transcript-15947 (accessed February 4 2020)

36 Ibid.: 571

37 Ministry of External Affairs, Government of India. 2013. 'Prime Minister's address to Japan–India Association, Japan–India Parliamentary Friendship League and International Friendship Exchange Council', Prime Minister's Office, May 13, 2013. https://www.mea.gov.in/press-releases.htm?dtl/21754. (accessed July 30 2016)

38 Loc. cit.

39 Brewster, David. 2012. *India as an Asia Pacific Power*. London: Routledge: 156

40 Bell, Coral. 2007. 'The end of the Vasco da Gama Era: the next landscape of world politics', Sydney: Lowy Institute for International Policy, Paper No. 21: 2–5

41 Brewster, 2012: 160

42 US Department of Defense. 2010. *Quadrennial Defense Review Report*. Washington DC: US Department of Defense, February: 60

43 Loc. cit.
44 Event Report. 2015. International Conference on 'New Directions in Indian Ocean Studies', Feb 26–28. http://www.icwa.in/pdfs/creports/2014/ReportonInternationalConference.pdf (accessed 12 July 2016)
45 Yulisman, Linda. 2019. 'Indonesia wants Asean to be axis of Indo-Pacific strategy', *The Straits Times*, January 10, 2019. https://www.straitstimes.com/asia/se-asia/indonesia-wants-asean-to-be-axis-of-indo-pacific-strategy (accessed 12 February 2019)
46 Tung, Nguyen Vu. 2010. Vietnam's Security Challenges: Hanoi's New Approach to National Security and Implications to Defense and Foreign Policies, at http://www.nids.mod.go.jp/english/publication/joint_research/series5/pdf/5-8.pdf (accessed 24 February 2020)
47 Pham Binh Minh, Minister of Foreign Affairs of the Socialist Republic of Vietnam. 2013. 'India–Vietnam Relations and Regional Issues', Sixth Sapru House Lecture: Sapru House: New Delhi. 12 July
48 Ibid.

2 The Indo-Pacific construct and utility of 'new' derived regions

With the end of Cold War, the strategic preferences of many countries underwent changes. India and Vietnam were also influenced by the birth of a unipolar world led by the US. Accordingly, the two nations recalibrated their position towards the US, while at the same time maintain good relations with China, the emerging superpower. Therefore, the two countries have looked into the proposed Indo-Pacific construct as a concept which could serve their national interests in the future. However, the Indo-Pacific as a 'geopolitical region' or an 'acceptable strategic space' has generated academic discourse, and a lingering scrutiny about the feasibility and utility of such a derived concept. The term 'contrived' has been used, because for many political commentators and strategic experts it was a contrived construct to meet certain ends.[1] Geography has become increasingly vital, and spatial perceptions as well as geopolitical outlines have become instrumental in the formation of multilateral institutions as well as Karl Deutsch's concept of 'security communities'. While power bloc politics had come to an end, the concept of the buffer state and strategic space is becoming increasingly redefined. This could also be attributed to the relatively slow increase in numbers of nuclear powers (five nuclear powers and three *de facto* new entrants – India, Pakistan and Israel – to the nuclear club) and the limits that were posed with regard to missile development and nuclear proliferation. Restrictions on the export of delivery systems (such as Inter-Continental Ballistic Missiles and other multiple delivery systems) have restricted access to critical technologies used to enhance a country's military strength. The rise of China on the global stage was a demonstration of its emergence from a regional player in East Asia to a global power through export-led growth and military modernization. While regions were important to define the expanse and strategic reach of a major power, the discourse has now shifted to derived regions in the study of international security and economic spheres. This helps in terms of the exclusion and inclusion of a few countries in such derived regions.

The growing recognition of the role of uneven development and regional transformation in the dynamics of modern entrepreneurship has encouraged discourse about spatial constructs as well. In such a context, regional differences have assumed a relatively central role.[2] However, the understanding and

The Indo-Pacific construct and 'new' regions   19

deliberation about the formation of a 'region' is contested. At times, regions have been subsumed, and at times divided along the geopolitical and geostrategic lines. In 1973, Thomson acknowledged 21 different characteristics which defined the international geopolitical environment.[3] Despite the 'renaissance of region' debate, and regional processes in the early 1990s, there is a relative scarcity of literature about how to define a region. There is also, to a large extent, debate about the parameters with which to evaluate a region, and its relevance in literature related to international relations. Despite this predicament, a large volume of literature remains concentrated on discussing the genesis of the region. This includes geopolitical approaches or cultural behavioural methods. This debate provides legitimacy to the rise of the regional powers, and the international relations theories (neo-realism and liberalism).[4]

In this discourse, the geopolitical approach defines regions in relation to their external environment. Geography, natural strategic landmarks, continental and oceanic fault lines along with mountain ranges, river course, watershed and maritime borders define the new parameters. The new parameters have also led to the evolution of strategic spaces, separate to the concept of buffer zones. The neo-realist concept in global affairs weighs these attributes, and the relevance of buffer zones. According to the neo-realist concept, 'a region's only significance lies in its relevance and role in conjunction with the great power strategies' for meeting their objectives and long term strategic goals.[5] This clearly has repercussions for the theorization and conceptualization of the role of regional powers, as most realist approaches categorize states from a global perspective as great/big, middle or small powers. This, to a certain extent, ignores the regional perspective, where the middle and even small powers might have significant influence within their respective neighbourhoods.[6]

The second concept describes a region in terms of the cultural-behavioural aspect. It emphasizes the importance of cultural homogeneity, developed mutual economic or security interdependencies among nations, and the historical and social descriptions that distinguish a region from outsiders.[7] This understanding resonated in the liberal-institutional philosophy, and the mechanisms involved are recognized, for instance, in Karl Deutsch's and other scholars' research on 'security communities'.[8] The societal level, rather than geographic constructs, is the basis of regional refinements and outlining regional perimeter. The communal nature of the region's history has also gained traction. While internal cohesiveness and other determinants, along with a common regional identity, can be important elements of any region, one must be vigilant about building an underlying requirement for harmony and an almost pre-determined progression towards integration and supranationalism into the concept of a region.[9]

Barry Buzan and Ole Waever[10] illustrated the way in which regions could nevertheless be defined by looking at internal dynamics in their discussion of regional security complexes, in which the notion of cultural homogeneity is replaced by a focus on regular patterns in both amenity and enmity.[11] The third concept derives from the constructivist thinking in IR theory. According to this

20   The Indo-Pacific construct and 'new' regions

concept, regions are to be understood to be dependent by necessity, or questioned and unstable, and their boundaries to be characteristics unable to be explained without reference to be ideas, norms and structural power that develop in and are reinforced by the region-building processes.[12] Empirical analyses that adopt a region-building approach are thus above all interested in how regions are defined and how they have come to be understood as 'natural'.[13] Political action and entrepreneurship, for example, but also discursive powers, are used to make certain political and cultural similarities or economic transaction patterns more relevant than others in the formation of particular regional identities: in other words, actors try to enact a definition of the region that makes them central to interactions within it.[14] The academic discourse questions whether the Indo-Pacific would be able to sustain itself as a new region, or was just a transitory lexicon.

The Indo-Pacific: is it a 'derived' or 'natural' construct?

Since ancient times, oceans have been facilitating trade and commerce between distant shores. These sea-lanes have contributed to flourishing merchandise trade, commerce and energy transactions among the sovereign nations. However, the increased volume of trade has been encountering issues related to the security of the cargo and even the protection of human lives. The Oceans (Indian, Pacific, Atlantic and Arctic) and adjoining landmasses have helped to define multilateral organizations such as the Indian Ocean Rim Association (IORA, earlier known as IOR-ARC); alliance systems such as the North Atlantic Treaty Organization (NATO), and regional forums like the Pacific Islands Forum (PIF). Along with these regional and transregional institutions, increasing challenges from piracy, natural calamities and other hazards forced nations to upgrade their naval capabilities – not only in terms of their traditional security role, but also to provide security against non-traditional threats. This competition to secure resources and energy supplies led to the conceptualisation of new coalitions and alignments, such the Asia-Pacific Security, the East Asian Security and Indo-Pacific security complexes. The relatively new construct of the Indo-Pacific has created a larger debate about the outcome and viability of such security complexes which has geopolitical and geostrategic implications. In contemporary times, multilateral institutions are also becoming more inclusive and strive to build common consensus on regional security and developmental issues. As a result, a debate has started over whether multilateralism would define security constructs or *vice versa*. However, if one looks into the geographic expanse of the Indo-Pacific, which runs from the Indian Ocean to the western periphery of the Pacific Ocean, then it is a slightly larger area than the Asian and African continents put together in geographic terms.

The 'Indo-Pacific' construct first resonated in the writings of the legendary strategic thinker K M Pannikar. Panikkar made references to the Yemen (Socotra Island) and Straits of Malacca as the two anchorages for India's

The Indo-Pacific construct and 'new' regions   21

strategic thought.[15] Subsequently, the Indian Prime Minister Jawaharlal Nehru defined a new construct of Afro-Asian unity as a tirade against anti-colonialism, anti-imperialism and anti-apartheid, and organised a conference defining this construct. Subsequently, the Non-Aligned Movement (NAM) defined a new construct to galvanise South–South cooperation, thereby creating a third bloc. In the early 1990s, 'Asia-Pacific' was new terminology which defined the formation of the Asia-Pacific Economic Cooperation (APEC).

In more contemporary times, a few strategic thinkers, and countries such as Australia and Indonesia, have shown a subscription to the new concept of the Indo-Pacific.[16] The then Prime Minister Manmohan Singh had also outlined the preferred strategic choices for India and highlighted the Indo-Pacific as a new paradigm for enhancing cooperation in the region. Alluding to the 'quest for stability and peace in the vast region in Asia that is washed by the Pacific and Indian Oceans',[17] the Indian leader listed Japan as their preferred partner. Earlier, during the India–ASEAN Commemorative Summit in 2012, the then Indian PM had also alluded to the term 'Indo-Pacific'. According to Rory Medcalf, the 'Indo-Pacific' terminology was referred to in the 1950s to discuss decolonisation, and was again alluded to in the 1960s and 1970s.[18]

The term remerged as a consequence of Michael Richardson's paper in 2005, which argued that the inclusion of Australia, India and New Zealand as members of East Asia Summit (EAS) reinvigorated the concept of the Indo-Pacific region.[19] The term 'Indo-Pacific' later found increasing reference in Australian foreign policy discourse, especially in speeches by Australian leaders and strategic analysts. However, the concept is still in its infancy and its applicability and utility in wider security concepts is still debated and discussed. The US also adapted to this new lexicon, albeit with apprehension, proclaiming that ensuring security in the Indo-Pacific region would be a challenging task for the United States and liberal nations.[20] The US has repeatedly endorsed the concept as the fulcrum for developing regional economic and security structures and ignoring this need would result in greater uncertainty, insecurity and instability. It even changed the nomenclature of its Southeast Asian security initiatives under the Indo-Pacific template:

> The US House Armed Services Committee has recommended in May 2018 under National Defence Authorization Act (NDAA) 2019 to rechristen the Southeast Asia Maritime Security Initiative as the Indo-Pacific Maritime Security Initiative and proposed to include India as a covered country.[21]

Given the rapid progress that has been witnessed in the region, it is expected that with its progressive economic growth, military clout, and political resilience, the Indo-Pacific is incrementally emerging as the powerhouse of the world. Within this region, there are different forms of governance and development, which can be witnessed in the form of liberalism, authoritarianism, and even totalitarianism. Moreover, with the large number of Global Commons in this geographic construct, increasing cooperation as well as competition would make it a

22 The Indo-Pacific construct and 'new' regions

geopolitical and strategic area of importance. Michael Auslin, in his report 'Security in the Indo-Pacific commons', stated that the Indo-Pacific's unique physical outline makes the balance of regional security most vulnerable in its 'commons': the open seas, air lanes, and cyber networks that link the region together and to the world.[22] Given the importance of the Indo-Pacific commons to the continued prosperity and stability of the region, the policy objectives of the United States and its Indo-Pacific allies and partners have been to:

- ensure accessibility for all nations to the Indo-Pacific commons;
- dissuade or manage conflict in the commons;
- preserve credible military capabilities that could act as a deterrent and even overcome the most likely regional threats;
- support the liberal-democratic norms that will assist in propagating freedom and promote cooperative behaviour.[23]

The overarching goal of this approach is to supplant a security environment that augments stability and development without the use of American or allied military power. The interests of the United States and its allies and partners are primarily aimed at pre-empting any disorder that would trigger political strain or conflict, negatively affect global economic activity, or hamper the access of any nation to the rest of the region and globe for political or military reasons. However, as a result of China's military modernisation in particular, the United States and its allies are apprehensive of maintaining their regional superiority of forces numerically or, eventually, qualitatively. The comprehensive build-up of Chinese military power is projected as a reason for the broader geopolitical expansion of Chinese influence, providing the means necessary to achieve regional acceptance of Chinese aims, however those may be defined in the future. At the same time, security in the Indo-Pacific region must not be reduced to hedging against China's rise or limited to attempting to shape Chinese behaviour, but rather must be focused on the Indo-Pacific commons as a whole. Therefore, America's strategy has three parts: an enhanced, superior, forward-based US presence in the region; an innovative new approach to allies and partners; and a political goal of helping create a more liberal Indo-Pacific region. This geopolitical imagination would outline the existing multilateral arrangements in the region and whether the concept would define new arrangements or would be negated by countries of Indian and Pacific oceans.

Geo-Political constructs and their utility for regional players

In the strategic and economic spheres, partnerships happen between any two countries depending on their defence and security complementarities, while in the economic domain the mutual economic benefit in terms of division of labour and the development of interdependence through complementary production, value chain and non-competitive products helps in forging links. However, in the contemporary international discourse, strategic and economic

The Indo-Pacific construct and 'new' regions 23

links have become so enmeshed into one another that every strategic link needs to develop more synergies in the economic sphere, while the same holds true for every economic link. In fact, many regional and international economic cooperation initiatives have merged the differences between strategic priorities and economic links. Issues which were deliberated two decades ago did not hold water when it came to the marginal utility and the enlargement of partnerships spanning the political, economic, strategic and cultural domains. It is interesting to note how the strategic outlook of countries such as India and Vietnam have now expanded to adapt to the derived region of the Indo-Pacific. India alludes to the Indo-Pacific, but Vietnam still addresses the region in a few statements as the Indo-Asia-Pacific. This means that Vietnam does look to include India in the Asia-Pacific, while India proposes to create a fusion of the Indian and Pacific Oceans.

Within ASEAN, there has been discourse with regard to culture, religion and politics as the foundation of new regions. In the case of the mainland Southeast Asia, while the major players in ASEAN (which include Thailand, Singapore, Indonesia and Malaysia) have earned their dividends with regard to greater interaction with the entire Indian sub-continent but particularly mainland southeast Asia, the CLMV countries have not been able to convert the free trade agreement and the other related services agreement into mutual benefit, given their low economic base as well as relatively poor developmental status. Among the developing economies, such as CLMV, there are four levels of engagement which have been the foundation of the interaction between the two regions particularly between South Asia and Southeast Asia. If one analyses the historical interactions between the two civilizations, the imprints of Indic influence, as well as Hindu and Buddhist culture, are visible in different parts of mainland Southeast Asia. The one particularly defining element in the relationship is with regard to the limits of the influence of Theravada Buddhism, wherein Cambodia is seen as the outer limit of the Theravada influence, and Laos and Vietnam have adopted strands of Tibetan Buddhism (Tantric and Shamanic) which is more of an amalgamation of Mahayana and Bonism. The reincarnating Lamas is another important aspect of differentiation between Indian and Tibetan Buddhism. The basic differences between the two are in terms of rituals and norms, as well as the practices adopted by the two different strands of Buddhism. Buddhism spans the larger Pacific region across countries such as Japan and Korea. The interaction between the two practiced forms of Buddhism has, at times, led to a synthesis of norms and rituals, while on another level there has been a latent struggle for supremacy. Therefore, the Indo-Pacific does have a religious imprint embedded into it.

The second aspect of interaction between India and Southeast Asian countries, more particularly Indochina countries, has been primarily focused on strategic and defence engagements. Further, between India and Myanmar, military exchanges have been regular, but there have been jarring phases, such as when Aung San Suu Kyi was given the Nehru Award for International Understanding in 1995 when the two armies were conducting counter-insurgency operations.

24 *The Indo-Pacific construct and 'new' regions*

Myanmar has now started high-level defence visits and their sailors and even naval aviation pilots are getting regular training in Indian establishments. The high command of the Myanmar army is keen to develop the army as a truly professional army, with a larger role in defence and international peacekeeping operations. Cambodia and Laos also get defence equipment from India, and Indian Defence forces conduct special training modules for the Cambodian armed forces. Among the four countries, only Myanmar does not have the political commissar system, while Vietnam and Laos have imbibed it within their military training hierarchy. While these institutional and structural differences have not created any major problems, because of their military equipment deficit, Cambodia and Laos have not yet been included into the bilateral military exercises and high level interaction mode. The interactions have been substantial but sporadic. While Vietnam has emerged as an important strategic partner, the other three countries have not been accorded that special status. The third important foundation for interaction between India and Vietnam has been the Mekong–Ganga Cooperation (MGC), and in the future the BIMSTEC (in which there was a proposal to include Vietnam) would increase engagements . The two institutions – MGC and BIMSTEC – are still in the development stages, but with an increased number of member countries, these sub-regional initiatives might become important .

The fourth level of interaction has been through the ASEAN institution, in which most of the CLMV countries were given deferred timelines for the implementation and ratification of most of the institutional arrangement regarding free trade and investment. India and ASEAN have a 'Strategic Partnership', but how it will benefit CLMV countries is matter of conjecture. In addition, Indian diaspora have at times facilitated P2P linkages between countries but because of the relatively fewer number of people of Indian origin staying in CLMV countries, the Track II interactions have been less. CLMV nations, who are relatively new members of the Association of Southeast Asian Nations (ASEAN), share a number of similarities, although they differ in the size of their markets and their economic priorities, among other things. While Vietnam, for example, has achieved high levels of economic development, per capita income and industrialization, the other members of the group still have low per capita income and limited human resources.[24] Similarities between CLMV nations include their primarily agro-based industries, transition economies, high poverty incidence rates, insufficient infrastructures, and institutions that are still too weak for a shift to the market economy. Although CLMV nations have enjoyed a certain degree of macroeconomic stability in recent years, and are considered one of the fastest-growing economies in the region, unemployment and underemployment still persist. CLMV nations are still facing huge challenges in fighting poverty, narrowing gaps in wealth among the population, and addressing development gaps within the regions. Although each CLMV nation faces different development constraints, CLMV as a whole has huge potential for future development, which will depend on individual country efforts and support from development partners within and outside the Southeast

The Indo-Pacific construct and 'new' regions 25

Asia.[25] For both India and Vietnam, the Indo-Pacific becomes a vehicle of convergence. Further, the Indo-Pacific was not only proposed as a strategic construct, but also an economic possibility encapsulating the economic institutions working in South and Southeast Asia. For India and Vietnam, the Indo-Pacific fuses the two regions of South and Southeast Asia together under an overarching region.

Structural evolution and synergies within the Indo-Pacific region

While launching the Look East policy, India focused on economic liberalization and export-led industrialization, drawing inspiration from the new tiger economies of Southeast Asia. While the four tiger economies (Singapore, Thailand, Indonesia and Malaysia) had relatively better growth trajectory, the rest of new entrants to ASEAN, particularly Cambodia, Laos, Myanmar and Vietnam, needed the benefits of ASEAN regionalism. The CLMV countries became members of ASEAN by the year 1999. At the Fourth ASEAN Informal Summit, held on 22–25 November 2000 in Singapore, the ASEAN Leaders agreed to launch an Initiative for ASEAN Integration (IAI), which gave direction to and sharpened the focus of collective efforts in ASEAN to narrow the development gap within ASEAN, as well as between ASEAN and other parts of the world.[26] The IAI Work Plan for CLMV focused on the priority areas of infrastructure development (transport and energy); human resource development (public sector capacity building, labour and employment, and higher education); information and communications technology; and promoting regional economic integration (trade in goods and services, customs, standards and investments) in the CLMV countries.[27] Given the fact that the Indochina region was relatively underdeveloped, attention was focused on the CLMV region and in this regard the possibilities of enhancing trade and investment possibilities were explored.

Within the CLMV region, there have been concerns raised with regard to the deferred integration of the region into the larger East Asian regionalism. Under various institutional processes, most of these countries are found as wanting in terms of economic development, infrastructure, trained manpower and regular power supply. However, the whole outlook regarding the inclusion of these countries in different institutional frameworks changed, starting with ASEAN. The four countries joined ASEAN in a staggered way: Vietnam joined in 1995, followed by Myanmar and Laos in 1997 and Cambodia in 1999, paving the way for their inclusion in the booming regional economy. Cambodia's inclusion in ASEAN effectively paved the way for the end of its international isolation and facilitated its participation in both the Regional Comprehensive Economic Partnership (RCEP) and the ASEAN Free Trade Agreement (AFTA). Its accession to the WTO in 2004 acted as a catalyst for its membership in the ASEAN Economic Community (AEC).

Vietnam initiated the *Doi Moi* (economic reforms programme) in 1986 with an objective of developing a socialist-oriented market economy. Vietnam undertook incremental liberalization of the equity markets, easy procedures for

26 The Indo-Pacific construct and 'new' regions

FDI, structural reforms of financial institutions, and tried building a large manufacturing base. Myanmar, which was previously ostracised from the international community, got included in the regional value chain with the incremental lifting of sanctions since 2014, and increasing foreign direct investment, which became more intense. At one point, Myanmar was having lot of FDI from Europe and the US, following the general elections which were held after nearly three decades of military rule. The rise of Aung San Suu Kyi and her party – the National League for Democracy – as well as negotiations and a conciliatory approach towards minorities and ethnic communities living in the peripheral regions of Myanmar, created the necessary structure for further integration of the reclusive country into the ASEAN regional economic framework. Laos was also showing signs of revival with a demonstration of willingness to diversify its economy. In the political sphere, with the exception of Vietnam, other economies enjoyed benefits owing to increasing Chinese investment and an expansion of the regional value chain. Vietnam being one of the claimant countries in the Spratly Islands dispute meant it had to weather an assertive Chinese posture. In 2007 there were tensions between China and Vietnam in the disputed islands, which led to demonstrations and anti-Chinese protests within Vietnam. The loss of property and Chinese investment did create fissures between the two countries. Further, Vietnam wanted to build ties with strategically relevant countries, and this included India and Japan. Indian participation in BIMSTEC (with the Thailand initiative) was aimed to connect India to Southeast Asia, and the inclusion of Myanmar and Thailand showed this intent.

The Bay of Bengal Initiative for Multi-Sectoral Technical and Economic Cooperation (BIMSTEC)

BIMSTEC was envisaged as a regional organization by the Bangkok Declaration on 6 June 1997, comprising seven member states (India, Myanmar, Nepal, Bangladesh, Bhutan, Sri Lanka and Thailand) lying in the littoral and adjacent areas of the Bay of Bengal and constituting a contiguous regional unity. In the initial stages, the precursor to BIMSTEC was 'BIST-EC' (Bangladesh, India, Sri Lanka and Thailand Economic Cooperation). With the admission of Nepal and Bhutan at the 6th Ministerial Meeting (February 2004, Thailand), the grouping was rechristened as 'Bay of Bengal Initiative for Multi-Sectoral Technical and Economic Cooperation' (BIMSTEC).[28] The forum was aimed to develop trade and economic linkages, while at the same time working on social, technical and economic aspects of cooperation. The inclusion of BIMSTEC ministers in the BRICS summit in 2015 by India clearly showed that India wanted to engage its eastern neighbours, and also prioritize it in the larger scheme of things. It was seen particularly as a snub to the Chinese proposal of BCIM, which, although it was endorsed by Prime Minister Modi during his visit to China (May 2015), is yet to see tangible movement. The other organization which connects India to

The Indo-Pacific construct and 'new' regions 27

this region is the Mekong–Ganga Cooperation Initiative, which is now transformed into the Mekong–India Economic Corridor.

Mekong–India Economic Corridor (MIEC)

India's urge to counter the increasing Chinese dominance in the region, led to the proposal of the MIEC, with the purpose of increasing cultural and historical interaction, along with exploring trade and investment complementarities with the Indo-China region. The development of the Kaladaan Multi Modal Transport Project and the trilateral highway were built on the premise that the two projects would enhance trade and investment between Northeast India and Southeast Asia. However, the two projects took more than 15 years to complete, with parts of the projects still in limbo. Mekong–India connectivity has been envisaged as a constituent of India's obligations under the Asian Highway Network. The United Nations Economic and Social Commission for Asia and the Pacific (UNESCAP)-sponsored trans-Asian railways would further enhance connectivity between the two regions. MIEC would help in connecting Indian manufacturing with the ancillary industries in the CLMV region, as well as those in Thailand. This corridor also fits into the Indo-Pacific corridor envisaged by the US government. The Indo-Pacific construct works to the benefit of both India and Vietnam, as the Indo-Pacific corridor fuses the two regions – South and Southeast Asia – together.

The Indo-Pacific Economic Corridor (IPEC)

Another important aspect of India's Act East policy and its stress on enhancing trade and connectivity with its Eastern neighbours was the US government. interest in the Indo-Pacific Corridor, as well as the need to counter the Chinese One Belt One Road (OBOR) project in the region. The US had given indication for financial support to be given for connectivity and infrastructure projects in Southern Asia. The Trump administration, drawing inspiration from Hillary Clinton's speech in July 2011 at Chennai, revived the New Silk Road (NSR) initiative, and further alluded to importance of the Indo-Pacific Economic Corridor, which would connect South and Southeast Asia. This has also been endorsed as a specific project by US aid agencies. It clearly states:

> ...vision of an Indo-Pacific Economic Corridor (IPEC), the U.S. government will undertake activities to promote greater regional economic connectivity in Asia. USAID, in collaboration with the U.S. State Department will implement a two-year, $1.86 million project to: foster economic growth in South Asia and promote regional trade; enhancing the business environment and increase private sector competitiveness in the region; on economic issues engage the private sector, particularly regional trade, in South Asia and between South and Southeast Asia and encourage stronger economic integration between South and Southeast Asia, engaging regional institutions and international financial institutions as appropriate.[29]

28   The Indo-Pacific construct and 'new' regions

Given the fact that multiple stakeholders are emerging in the CLMV regions, it is likely that these regions would see strategic manoeuvres, as well as investment from different sources.

Developing infrastructure and growth linkages under the Indo-Pacific

Even though China has been propagating that the One Belt One Road project does not pose any threat to any country, it is designed with China in the centre, aimed to facilitate its trade and also tacitly build its strategic periphery, thereby using other countries as mere tools. Moreover, the maps that are being circulated among the international media and China's own internal maps are starkly different. In the internal maps that are circulated, both Hambantota and Gwadar are listed as critical ports, while enlisting the ports in Myanmar and Cambodia as Chinese ports. The Silk Road Economic Belt and the Maritime Silk Route do have a strategic angle to them, but given the fact that China is increasingly being assailed as a revisionist power and criticised for taking assertive stance in the East China Sea and South China Sea, the strategic angle has not been debated. However, within coastal and landlocked provinces, there are serious disparities in economic growth and development. The popular feeling in the landlocked provinces of China is that India and the Southern Asian region are very important for their growth, and connectivity should be improved even at the cost of giving certain concessions.[30] The complete details of the implementation of and trade under the One Belt One Road initiative are yet to come out, both in international discourse and Chinese documents. Nevertheless, China is still falling short of convincing others as to how the One Belt One Road initiative would yield equitable dividends for all, and not just for China. Amid ambiguities, one thing is clear for China – the Maritime Silk Road and the One Belt One Road initiatives would serve Chinese interests better in the long run. However, that should not deter the countries of the region from engaging with China in deliberations regarding the proposed One Belt One Road initiative.

In Chinese aid documents (2011 and 2014), special references have been made to development and infrastructure projects in the Indochina region. This includes the building of bridges, connecting roads and better infrastructure. However, most instances of Chinese aid and assistance are locked loans, which means that only Chinese equipment could be bought from those loans. While India and Japan are also looking towards Indochina and there has been an incremental influx of investment in the region, the problem is that of basic infrastructure, particularly in Myanmar, Cambodia and Laos. The slow development of the Sittwe and Dawei ports has left much to be desired, as it was felt that with regard to environmental clearances and developing critical support infrastructure around ports, the response of the Myanmar government was slow. However, with the development of these two ports, more connectivity and economic opportunities would emerge. Further, the blue economy is also gaining momentum as, with the exception of Laos (which is landlocked), the other three

The Indo-Pacific construct and 'new' regions 29

countries (Cambodia, Vietnam and Myanmar) of CLMV are looking for the possibilities in this regard. Further, the discourse in different forums, such as BIMSTEC and MIEC, also need to focus on developing the much desired shipping and freight network. The role of fisheries and increasing the localised yield would also serve the food security objectives of the region. India is keen to work along with the Mekong River Commission (MRC) to emerge as a joint voice against China's dam-building projects in Mekong and Brahmaputra. CLMV countries are already part of the Mekong River Commission, in which China is an observer, but it would be appropriate if a trilateral initiative between China, Bangladesh and India could coordinate with the Mekong River Commission. While these are only a few suggestions, it would be prudent to look into the possibilities that India envisages with regard to the CLMV countries including Vietnam, and the India–ASEAN Action Plan provides for that.

In the India–ASEAN Action Plan, special mention is made with regard to their objectives, and the plan states it will:

> support ASEAN's efforts in narrowing the development gap within and between ASEAN Member States through the implementation of IAI Work Plan II and its successor documents, as well as alleviating poverty and promoting sustainable development in order to realize the ASEAN Community and regional integration.[31]

The document adds it will also:

> continue to support CLMV Countries, in the implementation of the IAI; continue to support the less developed countries of ASEAN, including CLMV Countries, in wider areas, among others, human resources development, rural household electrification programmes, information technology curriculum and IT teacher trainings, and further increase the number of fellowships and scholarships; and explore cooperation on the establishment of a rural development research institute in Cambodia, Lao PDR, Myanmar and Viet Nam by India.[32]

This clearly amplifies India's objectives of capacity building and developing congenial atmosphere for Indian investment. With regard to connectivity, the same action plan outlines that it will:

> …work closely to promote physical connectivity in the region by completing the missing links between South and Southeast Asia, including, but not limited to, expediting the completion of India–Myanmar–Thailand trilateral highway and extension to Laos and Cambodia; developing a new India–Myanmar–Laos–Vietnam–Cambodia highway; and encouraging private sector participation in the development of roads and railways and relevant logistics networks.[33]

30   The Indo-Pacific construct and 'new' regions

With regard to promoting tourism, these four countries were among the first to be granted e-visa schemes, which was followed by 'Visa on Arrival' schemes for the tourists from these four countries. There is a need to integrate the development initiatives of the northeast region with complementary economic projects undertaken by India across the CLMV region. This would help in building linkages and better understanding among the two regions.

India's approach towards Southeast Asia would be incomplete without the engagement of the CLMV countries. Its approach towards Oceania, through policy instruments such as the Forum for India Pacific Islands Co-operation (FIPIC),[34] shows that its priorities in mainland Southeast Asia and Oceania converge under the Indo-Pacific concept. India's various partnerships – its strategic partnerships with South Korea and Australia, and global security partnership with Japan – have defined the new periphery of its policy, which coincides with the expansion of the Indo-Pacific. Similarly, Vietnam's interactions and developmental partnerships with Australia and Japan also in a way projects Vietnam's global outlook. However, Vietnam and India's outlooks are inclusive even with regard to newly derived region of the Indo-Pacific. The Indo-Pacific has been an evolving concept, but the possible benefits of the construct would be enjoyed by India and Vietnam. Of late, the reflections from the leaderships of the two countries also project the possibility of working together within the Indo-Pacific in the future.

The US, for its part, has also made it clear that the Indo-Pacific was and would remain a priority for the US administration. The US vision for the Indo-Pacific region was reflected in speeches made by 'Secretary of State Mike Pompeo and the then Defense Secretary Jim Mattis during their visits to Southeast Asia in 2018 that it is central to the US Free and Open Indo-Pacific (FOIP) strategy'.[35] It will also help in facilitating maritime trade and promoting commerce: 'US security and prosperity have depended upon free and open access to the Indo-Pacific region.'[36]

> [The] US had announced in 2018 new initiatives to promote fair and mutual trade and mobilize larger private investment. President Trump signed in October 2018 the BUILD Act which enhances U.S. development finance capacity to USD $60 billion. In November 2018, the U.S., Japan and Australia signed a trilateral Memorandum of Understanding on development finance cooperation in the Indo-Pacific.[37]

Further, the US has promoted transparency and better cooperation through initiatives such as the Indo-Pacific Transparency Initiative to help secure nations' autonomy, combat corruption, attract increased private investment, and protect them from foreign coercion. It is stated to invest more than $400 million, for cooperation among allies, partners, and regional institutions, such as ASEAN and the APEC.[38] The interesting aspect is that the initiative does allude any foreign coercion indirectly. This is in contrast to Chinese OBOR initiative or aid offensive to the authoritarian regimes in the region.

Notes

1 Strategic experts and scholars such as Michael D Swaine, Ian Hall, Nick Bisley, etc. For details, see Swaine, Michael D. 2018. 'Creating an Unstable Asia: the US "Free and Open Indo-Pacific" Strategy', *Carnegie Endowment for Peace* 2. http://carne gieendowment.org/2018/03/02/creating-unstable-asia-u.s.-free-and-open-indo-pacific-strate gy-pub-75720 (accessed 12 January 2019); Hall, Ian. 2018. 'The Case for a Free and Open Indo-Pacific', *The Wire*. https://thewire.in/diplomacy/free-and-open-indo-pacific-dona ld-trump-foreign-policy (accessed 12 January 2019); Bisley, Nick. 2012. 'China's Rise and the Making of East Asia's Security Architecture', *Journal of Contemporary China*, 21(73): 19–34

2 Hettne, Björn and Söderbaum, Fredrik. 2010. 'Theorising the Rise of Regionness', *New Political Economy*, 5(3): 457–458. Hettne, Björn. 2006. 'Beyond the "new" regionalism', *New Political Economy*, 10(4): 543

3 Thompson, William R. 1973. 'The Regional Subsystems: A Conceptual Explication and a Propositional Inventory', *International Studies Quarterly*, 17(1): 89–117

4 Prys, Miriam. 2012. *Redefining Regional Power in International Relations: Indian and South African Perspectives*. London: Routledge: 14

5 Ibid.: 15

6 Loc. cit.

7 Loc. cit.

8 Vesa, Unto. 1999. 'Prospects of Security Communities: On The Relevance Of Karl W. Deutsch's Contribution', *Peace Research*, 31(1) (February 1999): 18–25

9 Prys, 2012: 15. Hettne, 2006: 543

10 Buzan, Barry, Wæver, Ole and De Wilde, Jaap. 1988. *Security: A New Framework for Analysis*. London: Rienner Publishers: 19–21. Buzan, Barry and Wæver, Ole. 2003. *Regions and Powers*. Cambridge: Cambridge University Press

11 Buzan and Weaver, 2003: 45. Prys, 2012: 15–16

12 Prys, 2012: 16

13 Neumann, Iver B. 1992. 'Regions in International Relations Theory: The Case for a Region-Building Approach', Research Report 162. Oslo: Norwegian Institute of International Affairs: 58. Prys, 2012: 16

14 Neumann, Iver B. 2003. 'A Region-Building Approach', in Fredrik Söderbaum and Timothy M Shaw, eds, *Theories of New Regionalism*, London: Palgrave Macmillan: 160

15 Panikkar, Kavalam M. 1945. *India and the Indian Ocean: An Essay on the Influence of Sea Power on Indian History*. London: G. Allen & Unwin Limited: 95. Paul, Joshy M. 2011. 'Merging Security Architecture in the Indian Ocean Region: Policy Options for India', *Maritime Affairs: Journal of the National Maritime Foundation of India*, 7(1): 28–47

16 Thinkers such as C Rajamohan, Harsh V Pant, Rory Medcalf and David Brewster have alluded to support for this concept while talking to the author.

17 Prime Minister's address to Japan-India Association, Japan-India Parliamentary Friendship League and International Friendship Exchange Council. 28 May 2013. https://www.mea.gov.in/press-releases.htm?dtl/21754/Prime+Ministers+address+to+ JapanIndia+Association+JapanIndia+Parliamentary+Friendship+League+and+Inter national+Friendship+Exchange+Council (accessed 6 February 2020)

18 Medcalf, Rory. 2015. 'Reimagining Asia: From Asia-Pacific to Indo-Pacific', *ASAN Forum*, 26 June 2015. http://www.theasanforum.org/reimagining-asia-from-asia-pacific-to-indo-pacific/ (accessed 24 April 2018)

19 Tyler, Melissa Conley and Shearman, Samantha. 2013. 'Australia's new region: The Indo-Pacific', *East Asia Forum*. 21 May 2013, http://www.eastasiaforum.org/2013/05/ 21/australias-new-region-the-indo-pacific/ (accessed 4 May 2018)

20 Scott, David. 2012. 'The "Indo-Pacific"—New Regional Formulations and New Maritime Frameworks for US-India Strategic Convergence', *Asia-Pacific Review*, 19

32 The Indo-Pacific construct and 'new' regions

(2): 85–86. Haushofer, Karl. 2002. *An English Translation and Analysis of Major Karl Ernst Haushofer's Geopolitics of the Pacific Ocean*, tr. Lewis Tambs and Ernst Brehm, Lampeter: Edwin Mellor: 141. Doyle, Randall. 2014. *The Geopolitical Power Shift in the Indo-Pacific Region: America, Australia, China and Triangular Diplomacy in the Twenty-first century*. Washington: Lexington Books: 22

21 'Congressional move to rename US Pacific Command as Indo-Pacific Command', *The Economic Times*, Press Trust of India, 4 May 2018. http://www.economictimes. indiatimes.com/articleshow/64034427.cms (accessed 4 May 2018)

22 Auslin, Michael. 2010. 'Security in the Indo-Pacific commons: toward a regional strategy', *AEI Paper & Studies*. https://www.thefreelibrary.com/Security+in+the+Indo-Pacific +commons%3A+toward+a+regional+strategy.-a0247225758 (accessed 24 May 2018)

23 Loc. cit.

24 Sotharith, Chap (ed). 2008. *Development Strategy For CLMV In The Age of Economic Integration*. IDE-JETRO. http://www.eria.org/uploads/media/Research-Project-Report/ RPR_FY2007_4_Executive_Summary.pdf (accessed 28 May 2018)

25 Loc. cit.

26 Initiative for ASEAN Integration (IAI) Work Plan for the CLMV Countries. http:// www.aseansec.org/pdf/IAI_doc1_6904.pdf. (accessed 28 May 2018)

27 Loc. cit.

28 BIMSTEC Background, at http://bimstec.org/overview/ (accessed 31 May 2018)

29 Indo-Pacific Economic Corridor, Phase II: Assessment of Non-Tariff Barriers in South Asia, Asia and the Middle East Economic Growth Best Practices (AMEG) Project Chemonics International, Inc. Task Order No. AID-OAA-12–00008, 14 July 2016. http://pdf.usaid.gov/pdf_docs/PA00MBPK.pdf (accessed 23 March 2018)

30 Author's interaction with academics from Yunnan University and Guangzhou University. Further interaction at the Institute of Indian Ocean Economies, Kunming.

31 Plan of Action to Implement the ASEAN-India Partnership for Peace, Progress And Shared Prosperity (2016–2020). http://asean.org/storage/images/2015/August/POA_ India/ASEAN-India%20POA%20-%20FINAL.pdf (accessed 23 March 2018)

32 Loc. cit.

33 Loc. cit.

34 India-Pacific Islands Sustainable Development Conference to enhance cooperation between India and Pacific Island Countries. 12 May 2017. https://mea.gov.in/p ress-releases.htm?dtl/28460/IndiaPacific_Islands_Sustainable_Development_Conferen ce_to_enhance_cooperation_between_India_and_Pacific_Island_Countries (accessed 12 February 2019)

35 Parameswaran, Prashanth. 2018. 'ASEAN and the U.S. Indo-Pacific Strategy', 16 October 2018. https://www.wilsoncenter.org/blog-post/asean-and-the-us-indo-pacific- strategy (accessed 12 February 2019)

36 White House. 2018. 'President Trump's Administration is Advancing a Free and Open Indo-Pacific through Investments and Partnerships in Economics, Security, and Governance', 18 November 2018. https://www.whitehouse.gov/briefings-statements/p resident-trumps-administration-advancing-free-open-indo-pacific-investments-partner ships-economics-security-governance/ (accessed 12 February 2019)

37 Loc. cit.

38 Loc. cit.

3 India's Act East Policy and Vietnam[1]

India's Act East Policy came with BJP leader Narendra Modi, who won the 2014 election in India. After officially winning the elections in May 2014, Prime Minister N. Modi participated in the ASEAN–India Summit, and the East Asia Summit in November 2014 in Myanmar. In these summits, Prime Minister Modi officially announced the upgrading of India's Look East Policy to the Act East Policy.[2] In December 2014, in the International Relations Conference on 'India's Look East – Act East Policy: A Bridge to the Asian Neighbourhood', held in Pune, India, the Secretary (East) of India's Ministry of External Affairs partly mentioned in his address the context, scope, objectives and deployment directions of the policy. This chapter will debate India's objectives in upgrading its Look East Policy (LEP) to the Act East Policy (AEP), and look into the larger geo-political and geo-economic objectives of AEP and the possible trajectory that it may take in future. The chapter will also highlight how Vietnam is placed in the narrative and possible plan of action towards enhancing ties with the country.

Elements of Indian foreign policy

Within India, there has always been a domestic element in deciding the direction of their foreign policy. As seen in the past, India's relations with its neighbours were influenced by their political parties, industrial conglomerates and merchant lobby groups. This includes Punjab's role in building ties with Pakistan. On the contrary, the role of regional parties in India–Sri Lanka relations during the Tamil movement in Sri Lanka was hostile. Similarly, West Bengal has influenced India's foreign policy direction towards Bangladesh, albeit to a very limited extent. Similarly, in the case of the Look East Policy, there have been two important aspects which have influenced ties. This included the trade and economic priorities, and connecting with the extended neighbourhood. To a certain extent, this was possible because of the political will and improved relations with Myanmar since the mid-1990s. Further, under A.B. Vajpayee's government, special emphasis was placed on building diaspora linkages, and Southeast Asia was considered a congenial region for reconnecting with the People of Indian Origin (PIOs).

34 *India's Act East Policy and Vietnam*

Domestic context

The legacy of the former government's (Congress) foreign policy acted as a foundation for Modi's government to enhance the LEP. The most suitable reason to affirm something new is to change its name, and as a result changing the LEP to the AEP was a way to prove the new government's policy of 'Acting', no longer only 'Looking'. Since 2011, India's de facto 'Act East' has been in operation, since it publicized its intention to interfere in the South China Sea dispute.[3] The policy measures undertaken by the Congress government were a precursor to this, driving Modi's government to follow and upgrade the policy.

In the fields of security and defence, India has been faced with challenges such as the emergence of Maoist insurgency, the danger of terrorism, and the issues with China over territorial disputes. According to a study released in 2013, Maoist insurgency was reported to have spread to over 40% of India.[4] In the past, India has been a victim of terrorist attacks, which were sponsored by Pakistani agencies.[5] India's security and stability have been influenced by the territorial dispute with Pakistan. India is now faced with threats posed by domestic and international terrorist groups, including the Islamic State.[6]

Most of India's challenges in terms of territorial security, however, come from China. India and China are now in the midst of territorial disputes over Aksai Chin and select pockets in Northeast. China is claiming sovereignty over India's state of Arunachal Pradesh. India has accused Chinese troops of entering India's land. These challenges have demanded that India consolidate its domestic security and defence on one hand, and, on the other hand, orient its cooperation with the countries and cooperative mechanisms in the East, and make use of strategic space in the East to solve those challenges.

Domestically, the weakness of the economy, corruption, poverty, high ratio of unemployment in the youth, impeded business environment, and development gap among regions and states are of high concern in India today. This is why, in election campaign speeches, Prime Minister Narendra Modi always highlighted these weak points under the Congress government.[7] Under the Congress-led UPA government, India's economic growth reached 10.3 per cent in 2010, decreasing to 5.6 per cent in 2012, but subsequently improving to 6.6 per cent in 2013.[8] However, inflation rates were too high throughout the four years before the 2014 general election (12 per cent in 2010, 8.9 per cent in 2011, 9.3 per cent in 2012, and 10.9 per cent in 2013 respectively).[9] The economic weaknesses under Congress made many Indians think about a new, different government.

Although India made achievements in the field of poverty reduction, the poverty rate was still high, at more than 21 per cent in 2011.[10] The unemployment rate was also high. According to the International Labour Organization (ILO), cited by the World Bank (WB), unemployment ratios at the age of 15–24 in India were at 10.3 per cent in 2011, 10.7 per cent in 2012, and 10.4 per cent in 2013.[11] The business environment in India was also not very conducive for many investors. Out of 180 economies listed by the World Bank in the Ease of Doing Business, India ranked lowly (139 in 2011, 132 in 2012 and 2013 respectively).[12] This changed in 2018, when India ranked at number 100 in global rankings, and was subsequently elevated to position 77 in the 2019 survey.[13]

Narendra Modi, being a pragmatic leader, saw that the economic benefits India could have from the Indo-Pacific region were very important. In terms of trade, economies in the Asia-Pacific have become important trading partners of India over the last decade. They have contributed a large portion of India's total trade. Their share in India's total trade has increased significantly, from 24.12 per cent in the fiscal year of 2002–03 to 27.45 per cent in the fiscal year of 2012–13. However, India's trade with its key trading partners, such as the European Union (EU) and North America, experienced a significant decrease. In India's total trade the share of EU and North America decreased from 21.75 per cent and 15.37 per cent in the fiscal year of 2002–03 to 13.71 per cent and 9.89 per cent respectively in the fiscal year of 2012–2013. Beside the Asia-Pacific region, only economies in Gulf Cooperation Council (GCC) had an increasing portion in India's total trade, from 6.2 per cent in the fiscal year of 2002–03 to 19.51 per cent of the fiscal year of 2012–13. However, the main commodities contributing to the increasing portion came from oil and oil products, gemstones and other jewelleries, and other valuable metals.[14] Increasing trade with economies in the Asia-Pacific region became more important to India when the trade portion of India's gross domestic product (GDP) increased from 26.4 per cent in 2000 to 44.9 per cent in 2007 and 55.8 per cent in 2012.[15]

Also in the field of trade, in the context of India's increasing economic integration in the international economy by joining free trade agreements (FTAs) in different forms, the Asia-Pacific has become a very important region. Among the FTAs India has signed, those with partners in the Asia-Pacific are the most important, including the ASEAN–India Comprehensive Economic Cooperation Agreement (CECA); the ASEAN–India Trade Agreement in Goods; the India–Singapore CECA; the India–Korea Comprehensive Economic Partnership Agreement (CEPA); the India–Japan CEPA, and the India–Malaysia CECA.

Besides that, developing the under-developed North East region (NER), partly due to the weakness in connectivity, is an urgent demand. Thanks to efforts made during the terms of two prime ministers under the Congress government, the NER made significant developments in the fields of economy, education and health care. For instance, in the economic field, GDP per capita in the NER in 1999–2000 was lower than the average level in India, but there was a significant improvement as states such as Arunachal Pradesh, Meghalaya, Sikkim, and Tripura reached more than US$ 1,000 GDP per capita in the fiscal year of 2009–10. GDP per capita in other states, however, in the NER such as Assam, Manipur, and Nagaland respectively, reached only 80 per cent, 84 per cent and 66 per cent of India's average,[16] although the NER has rich natural resources in comparison with many other regions in India. Due to the development gap, and other ethnic and political issues, the NER is one of the most unstable regions in India. The way to help the NER escape from poverty and unrest is by enhancing its integration into the Southeast Asian region. There are established cooperation frameworks and other cooperation projects planned, but the pace needs to intensify.

36 India's Act East Policy and Vietnam

Regional and international context

ASEAN was the centre of India's Look East Policy and the bloc continues to play a central role in the former's Act East Policy, when Indian Prime Minister Narendra Modi 'placed ASEAN at the core of India's Act East Policy and at the centre of India's dream of an Asian century'.[17] According to PM Modi, ASEAN has established its voice in global political and economic issues. PM Modi also appreciated ASEAN's centrality that India has also benefited from. Moreover, the ASEAN Community (AC) is like India's neighbourhood, having trade, religious, cultural, art and traditional relations since the ancient times with India, and the two sides have enriched each other through those relations.[18]

Southeast Asia, since the end of the Cold War, has brought opportunities for India to integrate itself deeply and engage in the Asia-Pacific region. India wanted to emerge as a regional player, rather than a South Asian hegemony, and, for that purpose, sought intense engagement with its eastern neighbourhood. India became the sectoral dialogue partner and full dialogue partner of ASEAN in 1992 and 1995 respectively, and joined the ASEAN Regional Forum (ARF) in 1996. India and ASEAN organized the first ASEAN–India Summit in 2002. In 2005, India was one of the founding members of the East Asia Summit (EAS), and, in 2010, the ASEAN Defence Ministers' Meeting Plus (ADMM+). India–ASEAN relations upgraded to a strategic partnership in 2012. Those moves helped India to participate more deeply in the Asia-Pacific region. Benefits gained from ASEAN, and ASEAN's centrality or driving force in fora and cooperation mechanisms in the Asia-Pacific, have encouraged India to use the Asia-Pacific as a springboard to playing a global role.

Besides security challenges posed by China over territorial issues (as mentioned above), Chinese ambitions in the Indian Ocean region (IOR) and seas in the West Pacific, especially in the South China Sea, encouraged India to 'Act East'. In the Indian Ocean, thanks to the String of Pearls strategy, China has significant influence in the region and this has threatened India's interests in the IOR.[19]

In the South China Sea, India challenged China when the Indian Navy transited through the South China Sea in 2000, and announced exercises in the area.[20] India, however, seems to have expressed its concerns related to freedom of navigation and maritime commerce in the South China Sea when China submitted a diplomatic note to the United Nations on May 7, 2009, including a nine-dashed line map officially for the first time.[21] Subsequently, in March 2010, China 'labeled the South China Sea a core interest, on par with Taiwan and Tibet'[22] and projected it as a core national interest. China started reclaiming islands and constructing new features in the Paracels and Spratlys, and, along with deploying civil and military personnel in those two island chains, China has been making efforts to complete its strategy of anti-access/access denial (A2/AD) in the whole South China Sea,[23] in order to totally control this region. In the context of India having important economic interests in the South China Sea, such as oil and gas exploration projects, and when 'nearly 50 per cent of Indian trade is east bound and transits through the Straits of Malacca',[24]

China's moves have created challenges for India. In other words, 'China's expanding presence in the Indian Ocean and assertiveness in maritime territorial disputes in East Asia has reinforced the relevance of an enhanced Indian role in East and Southeast Asia for India and its Asia-Pacific partners'.[25]

The US strategy of 'Pivot to Asia' encouraged India to expand its outlook towards the Asia-Pacific, especially since China's ambition, regardless of international laws, was a common threat to both India and the US. Besides the US, India's other strategic partners in the Asia-Pacific, such as Japan and Australia, marked China's illegal activities in the South China Sea as a threat and have acknowledged India as their important partner in the Asia-Pacific. Since China's activities (reclamation and construction) in the Paracels and Spratlys were highlighted in the media, the South China Sea has often been referenced in bilateral documents between India and the US. The first such reference found in the *U.S.–India Joint Statement*, released on Indian Prime Minister Narendra Modi's visit to the US on September 30, 2014.[26] Since then maritime security, freedom of navigation, and compliance with international laws in the South China Sea dispute are always mentioned in the India–US bilateral documents. Most noticeably, India and the US released *U.S.-India Joint Strategic Vision for the Asia-Pacific and Indian Ocean Region* in January 2015, in which the two countries 'affirm the importance of safeguarding maritime security and ensuring freedom of navigation and over flight throughout the region, especially in the South China Sea'.[27]

Along with enhancing strategic cooperation with the US in the Indo-Pacific region, India has promoted and deepened its strategic relations with US allies in the region, namely Japan and Australia. The South China Sea is a security issue mentioned in the *Joint Statement on India and Japan Vision 2025* (December 2015)[28] and many other bilateral documents between the two countries. At the multilateral level, concerns over the South China Sea situation made up part of the *Inaugural U.S.–India–Japan Trilateral Ministerial Dialogue*[29] held in Washington, DC on September 29, 2015, and part of the trilateral India–Australia–Japan dialogue[30] held in New Delhi in June 2015.

Economic interests benefiting India in the Asia-Pacific region were also an important factor. Beside the direct trade benefits gained by India, the market size and economic growth of economies in the region are factors which could help India maintain and enhance its economic growth. After the 2008–09 financial crisis, economic growth of the EU reached only 0.9 per cent in the period of 2010–2013, while that in the Asia-Pacific was 5.25 per cent.[31] The market in the Asia-Pacific is large, with a population of 2.25 billion persons in 2013 (excluding the Indian population), and this is predicted to reach 2.44 billion in 2025.[32] India assessed that the Asia-Pacific has truly emerged as the economic and geopolitical centre of gravity of the world in the 21st century.[33]

In contrast to the favourable conditions in the Asia-Pacific, the difficulties both in relations between Russia and Ukraine over the Crimea issue and in Europe over the migration issue, as well as political unrest in many countries in Northern Africa and Middle East, have made India pay more attention to making an effort to enhance their cooperation with the East.

38 India's Act East Policy and Vietnam

India in Vietnam's foreign policy discourse

While the LEP and AEP have made references to Vietnam as an important fulcrum of India's approach to the region, Vietnam policy documents have made much fewer references to India, and have preferred to address it in a regional context, such as South Asia. However, the visiting heads of state and heads of government from Vietnam, including the Party General Secretary and the President, have made it clear that India has been, and would remain, an important partner for Vietnam in the pursuit of peace and security in the larger Asia-Pacific and now Indo-Pacific region.

Even in the diplomatic blue book of Vietnam released in 2015,[34] India was referred to in terms of developing ties and increasing the volume and trade and investment from India. As discussed earlier, Vietnam has refrained from making any strong statements with regard to its strategic partnership with India. However, this has not been the case with defence cooperation and speeches made by various Vietnamese leaders during their visits to India.

Vietnamese President Tran Dai Quang,, in his public lecture at Delhi in 2018 said:

> ...our region in recent years has yielded a cornucopia of long-term ideas, initiatives, and strategies for cooperation. The Regional Comprehensive Economic Partnership Agreement between ASEAN and its six partners; India's "Act East" Policy; China's "Belt and Road Initiative"; Japan's "Free and Open Indo-Pacific Strategy"; the United States' "Free and Open Indo-Pacific Vision"; and, most recently, the establishment of the Comprehensive and Progressive Agreement for Trans-Pacific Partnership, joined by eleven economies on both sides of the Pacific.[35]

Referring to the Indo-Pacific as the Indo-Asia-Pacific, he said '[it] provides a solid foundation to further strengthen and foster friendship and cooperation between countries both within and outside of the region, thus enabling us to make greater contributions to mankind'.[36] In 2018, the President and Prime Minister of Vietnam visited India, showing the importance that is accorded to India in Vietnam's foreign policy approach. This cooperation is also manifesting in India's Act East policy.

Objectives of the Act East Policy

Political–strategic objectives

As a higher development and continuity of the LEP, the AEP aims to:

First, enhance cooperation, presence and engagement in the East to contain China's influence in South Asia and Indian Ocean region;

Second, protect India's political and strategic interests in the East in the context of China increasing assertiveness in sovereign disputes, especially in the South China Sea;

Third, enhance cooperation with collaborators which India did not pay much attention before, deepening and upgrading relations with other partners in the region;

Fourth, engage more deeply in strategic issues of the Asia-Pacific in order to play a more important role in the region, gradually extending its influence all over the world with a greater global position.[37]

Socio-Economic objectives

India is aiming at a new era of economic development, industrialisation and trade,[38] and the Asia-Pacific is regarded as the centre of this strategy. By upgrading the LEP to the AEP, the following socio-economic objectives will be achieved:

First, in the context of high economic growth which was slowing down while the inflation rate was high (as mentioned earlier), India wanted to promote trade, services and investment cooperation with economies in the Asia-Pacific to restore economic growth, and reduce the inflation rate to improve its macro economy in general, and better the lives of its people.

Second, as already mentioned, although India has been negotiating FTAs with economies from different parts of the world, FTAs in all forms with partners in the Asia-Pacific are more important. In other words, India's economic and trade interaction with the Asia-Pacific would open new markets and investment opportunities for the country.

Third, deeper trade and economic linkages would accelerate India's pursuit for a free-market economy on a par with many liberalised economies.

Fourth, in order to achieve the objective of 'Make in India', India has been making efforts to attract FDI to modernize infrastructure. The Indian government is scouting for FDI from Asia-Pacific institutional investors as well as private individuals.

Objectives of connectivity and regional integration

Among the regions of India, the NER is the least developed. Along with the low development of economy, health care and education, there is security unrest. Moreover, the state of Arunachal Pradesh, as claimed by China, is a disputed territory. To improve the situation, improvement of the NER's connections with China, Bangladesh and the Southeast Asian mainland is vital. However, beside sovereign issues, India's connectivity with China is difficult due to the uncomfortable terrain. Therefore, linking with Bangladesh and the Southeast Asian mainland is very important. That is the reason why in election campaigns, including one in Assam in February 2014, Narendra Modi accused the Congress government of not completing its role in improving the low development of NER.[39] When mentioning this objective, the Secretary (East) stated that:

40   *India's Act East Policy and Vietnam*

Enhancing connectivity with our Asian neighbourhood is one of our strategic priorities, making ASEAN our bridge to the wider Asia-Pacific region. This enhanced connectivity will undoubtedly bring multifarious benefits to all countries of the region. However, it holds, in particular, immense potential to bring about a significant positive developmental impact on our North-Eastern region.[40]

Deployment of Act East Policy

In order to achieve the above objectives, India has comprehensively deployed tools of modern diplomacy such as political, economic, defence and regional cooperation at different levels. In the political field, Narendra Modi's government placed India's neighbourhood as its top foreign-policy priority when the Prime Minister invited leaders of South Asian countries to his oath-taking ceremony.[41] PM Modi also chose Bhutan and Nepal as his two first foreign visits, in June and August 2014 respectively. In the beginning of September 2014, his first visit to a country outside South Asia was Japan. After Modi's visit to Japan, the then Indian President Pranab Mukherjee paid a visit to Vietnam in September. It is necessary to note that Japan and Vietnam are two of the five most important partners to India in the Asia-Pacific, including Japan, Australia, Vietnam, Indonesia and ASEAN.[42] The visits partly proved the importance of the AEP in India's foreign policy. During PM Nodi's official visit to Japan in September 2014, India and Japan released the *Tokyo Declaration for India–Japan Special Strategic and Global Partnership*.[43]

The upgrading of political and strategic cooperation with partners in the Asia-Pacific is also an important component of the AEP. India–Malaysia relations were upgraded from a strategic partnership (October 2010) to an enhanced strategic partnership (November 2015). The India–Republic of Korea strategic partnership (January 2010) was upgraded to a special strategic partnership (March 2015). The India–Japan strategic and global partnership (December 2006) was upgraded to a special strategic and global partnership (September 2014). The India–Singapore strategic partnership was established in November 2015, while India's strategic relations with Vietnam were upgraded to a comprehensive strategic partnership in September 2016. The India–Indonesia strategic relationship was also upgraded to a comprehensive strategic partnership in May 2018.

Those countries which India had paid relatively less attention to before, such as the Philippines, Brunei and Mongolia, have now become important. Among a few nation leaders with whom Indian PM Modi had a meeting with on the sidelines of the East Asia Summit in Myanmar in 2014 was the Philippine President B Aquino. The discussions between the two leaders, as reported in the media, included President Aquino's assurance of inking the ASEAN–India Free Trade Agreement on services and investments. The meeting took place in the context of the Philippines versus China argument over the South China Sea, and PM Modi made sure to mention the South China Sea issue at the ASEAN–India

Summit meeting and the EAS. Beside the Philippines, India paid more attention to Brunei Darussalam when Indian Vice President Hamid Ansari visited the Southeast Asian country in February 2016. This was the first official visit of an Indian leader to Brunei since the two countries established diplomatic relations in 1984.[44] India also upgraded its relations with Mongolia, a landlocked country located between China and Russia, to a strategic partnership in May 2015 under PM Modi,[45] although the bilateral trade between the two countries only reached its peak of US$ 60.2 million in 2012.[46]

At a multilateral level, Prime Minister Modi visited Myanmar and participated in ASEAN summit meetings in November 2014. At those meetings, PM Modi officially declared the upgrading of the LEP to the AEP, an affirmation of India's commitments to the Asia-Pacific and the importance of the region to India. India continues to appreciate the ASEAN-led mechanisms such as the EAS, ARF, ADMM+, and the Expanded ASEAN Maritime Forum.[47] India has been also making efforts to deepen and widen its integration in the Asia-Pacific since it applied for membership of the Asia-Pacific Economic Cooperation (APEC).[48]

At a higher level, India has engaged in some issues in the Asia-Pacific, including the South China Sea dispute. In fact, India officially raised its voice to 'support freedom of navigation in international waters, including in the South China Sea, and the right of passage in accordance with accepted principles of international law' and 'call all to respect these principles'[49] after the INS Airavat incident (June 2011). Since then, India has often raised its voice on the South China Sea issue, and even indicated that it would send its naval forces to protect its interests in South China Sea if those interests were violated.[50] In his keynote address at the IISS Shangri-La Dialogue (1 June 2018), Indian PM Modi mentioned the South China Sea as a global common that required 'freedom of navigation, unimpeded commerce and peaceful settlement of disputes in accordance with international law'.[51]

In a broader context, in the first trilateral dialogue between India, Japan and Australia that took place in June 2015, maritime security, was among the issues on the agenda, including freedom of navigation in the South China Sea and trilateral maritime cooperation in the Indian and Pacific Oceans.[52] Among the most important developments, India along with the US, Australia and Japan held the first Australia–India–Japan–US Consultations on the Indo-Pacific on 12 November 2017, on the sidelines of the East Asia Summit in the Philippines. The four countries also conducted the second Australia–India–Japan–US consultations in Singapore on 15 November 2018. They 'agreed to partner with other countries and forums in the region to promote a free, open, rules-based and inclusive order in the Indo-Pacific', and 'committed to strengthening connectivity and quality infrastructure based on sovereignty, equality and territorial integrity of all nations, as well as transparency, economic viability and financial responsibility'.[53]

In the field of defence, India has different levels of defence interactions, including defence exercises, liaison visits, and the nomination of its officers in high-level

42   India's Act East Policy and Vietnam

defence courses with its partners in the Asia-Pacific. India's bilateral defence cooperation with countries in the region has been enhanced in terms of establishing relations with new partners and upgrading relations with existing partners. The India–Philippines Joint Defense Cooperation Committee (JDCC) was established and held their first meeting in 2012. At the third India–Philippines Joint Commission on Bilateral Cooperation meeting, held in October 2015, India and the Philippines agreed to convene the second meeting of the India–Philippines JDCC in India. An MoU on Defence Cooperation between India and Brunei Darussalam[54] was signed in 2015. This could be seen as the realization of 'the need for cooperation in the defence sector', which resonated during the occasion of the State Visit of His Majesty Sultan Haji Hassanal Bolkiah Mu'izzaddin Waddaulah, the Sultan, and Yang Di-Pertuan of Brunei Darussalam to India in May 2008. India and Indonesia signed a Defence Cooperation Agreement (DCA) in May 2018 to 'further strengthen and renew the existing cooperation for the mutual benefit of the two countries and the region'.[55]

Since the situation in the South China Sea became complicated, India often sent warships on friendship visits to important ports in Southeast Asian countries, especially since China submitted a diplomatic note to the United Nation on May 7, 2009, including the nine-dashed line map. India's warship diplomacy has been stronger in recent years; this marks an affirmation of India's naval readiness to protect its economic and trade interests, as well as assuring the freedom of navigation in the region. During the visit of the then Indian President Pranab Mukherjee to China in May 2016, the Indian Navy deployed the ships of the Eastern Fleet, including indigenously built guided missile stealth frigates INS Satpura and INS Sahyadri; INS Shakti, a sophisticated fleet support ship; and INS Kirch, an indigenous guided missile corvette, to the West Pacific to participate in the Malabar exercise with the navies of Japan and the US. During the deployment, the ships made port calls at the Cam Ranh Bay (Vietnam), the Subic Bay (Philippines), Sasebo (Japan), Busan (South Korea), Vladivostok (Russia) and Port Klang (Malaysia).[56] It is necessary to note here that the Malabar exercise took place in Japan's Sasebo Sea and the Philippine Sea[57] that were both in close proximity to the South China Sea. The Chinese side expressed that the deployment was 'a matter of concern'.[58]

In the economic field, India has signed many important FTAs with its partners in the Asia-Pacific, such as the ASEAN–India CECA, the ASEAN–India Trade Agreement in Goods, the India–Singapore CECA, the India–Korea CEPA, the India–Japan CEPA, and the India–Malaysia CECA. Today, India is developing trade relations in the Asia-Pacific, by taking part in important bilateral and multilateral FTA negotiations, such as the Bay of Bengal Initiative for Multi-Sectorial Technical and Economic Cooperation (BIMSTEC) FTA, the India–Australia FTA, the India–New Zealand FTA, the India–Thailand FTA, and the India–Indonesia CECA. As mentioned above, India has applied for membership of the APEC.

In the field of connectivity, India has also been making efforts to galvanize existing sub-regional cooperation mechanisms and promote connectivity projects linking India and Southeast Asia. The sixth Mekong–Ganga Cooperation Ministerial Meeting was held in 2012 in New Delhi, five years after the fifth MGC Ministerial Meeting held in 2007 in the Philippines. The year of 2012 marked the 20th anniversary of the ASEAN–India dialogue partnership, the 10th anniversary of the ASEAN–India Summit-level partnership, and the establishment of the ASEAN–India strategic partnership. Therefore, the sixth MGC Ministerial Meeting that was held in India in 2012 should be seen as an occasion to celebrate the anniversary, rather than a step forward of the MGC. Four years later, thanks to the efforts of Modi's government, the seventh MGC Ministerial Meeting was held in July 2016 in Laos. At the meeting, a variety of cooperation issues were discussed, including consideration of the establishment of an MGC Joint Working Group to explore ways to enhance maritime cargo transportation and related issues amongst MGC countries, and the adoption of the Plan of Action to Implement Mekong–Ganga Cooperation (2016–2018).[59] Thanks to the efforts made, the MGC has made more positive steps, such as the holding of the first Joint Working Group (JWG) in the MSME Sector in September 2017, the first MGC Business Forum in January 2018, and the first MGC Policy Dialogue, a Track 1.5 event, on the theme of 'Stronger Connectivity, Enhancing Ties' on 8 April 2017 in New Delhi. Importantly, India was able to publicize its interest in becoming a partner of the Mekong River Commission (MRC) in the ninth MGC Ministerial Meeting in Singapore in August 2018.[60]

Another interesting point in the connectivity field is that India will 'Act', not 'Talk Only',[61] as PM Narendra Modi is considering, in coordination with the ASEAN member states, the establishment of a special facility or special purpose vehicle to facilitate the financing and quick implementation of projects.[62]

In this field, India has focused mostly on building inland connectivity between the NER and the Southeast Asian mainland. In the light of the AEP, besides the deployment of inland projects with Myanmar and Thailand, India is now 'simultaneously endeavouring to increase maritime and air connectivity between ASEAN and India so as to transform the corridors of connectivity into corridors of economic cooperation'.[63] The connectivity has been promoted, to reinforce Prime Minister Modi's idea of Information Highways, or 'I-ways'. Where road connectivity is poor, vast economic opportunities and employment could be created through I-ways.[64]

Other fields, such as cultural cooperation and people-to-people contact between India and the Asia-Pacific region, continue to be promoted under Modi's government.

Prospects

There will be positive conditions for India's AEP to be further enhanced. Domestically, Modi's government has the support of a large majority of Indian people, thanks to the progressive steps in economic development, corruption restraint and the improvement of social security. In the economic field,

44   India's Act East Policy and Vietnam

economic growth has improved and the corruption rate has decreased since Modi came to power. The Indian economy has continued its speed of growth since its lowest point in 2012 (since 2008), and reached 7.2 per cent in 2014 and 7.6 per cent in 2015.[65] Also during Modi's first few years as prime minister, inflation significantly decreased, from 10.9 per cent (under Congress) in 2013, to 6.4 per cent and 5.9 per cent in 2014 and 2015 respectively. In terms of the Ease of Doing Business, India has improved greatly, its rank upgrading from 130 in 2016 to 100 and 77 in 2017 and 2018 respectively.[66] This progress, over multiple areas, initially increased the Indian people's confidence in their new government. The government's anti-corruption has also achieved a positive response. Although the war against corruption has been said to have only cleared the surface of corruption, and an in-depth clean-up remains, the Rs. 36,000 crore (US$ 5.4bn) annual saving from stopping leakage and theft in various government schemes[67] has created a clearer face for the new government.

Social security schemes rolled out by Modi's government since 2015 have received a positive response from the Indian population. In a country with 80 per cent of population still outside the insurance coverage, the enrolment of 130 million people in the three new national social security schemes, including the Pradhan Mantri Jeevan Jyoti Bima Yojana, the Pradhan Mantri Suraksha Bima Yojana and the Atal Pension Yojana, has surely helped the new government gain more support just after more than a year of launching.[68] Particularly under the Congress, it seems that there were no large-scale social security schemes; small programmes were implemented, but they did not meet the demand of the population.

In the context of increasing security challenges posed by India's two neighbours, China and Pakistan, the Modi government approach to these challenges has gained support from the security and strategic wings in India. Narendra Modi was the first Indian Prime Minister to visit Pakistan in December 2015, 12 years after PM Vajpayee's visit in 2004, but a tougher approach towards Pakistan has been implemented. India cancelled scheduled foreign secretary level talks in August 2014 over a meeting between the Pakistani high commissioner to India and the Kashmiri separatist Hurriyat group. There was a distinct chill between Modi and Sharif at the SAARC summit in Kathmandu in November 2014.[69] Among their tough actions towards Pakistan, India launched 'surgical strikes' into Pakistan-controlled Kashmir after an insurgent attack on an Indian army camp left 19 soldiers dead in late 2014.[70] In 2016, Prime Minister Narendra Modi even talked about the possibility of re-considering the Indus Water treaty,[71] which could let India have more control over the Indus River, which was governed by Pakistan.

Despite seeing the rise of India and China as an unprecedented economic opportunity for both countries and the world,[72] Modi also considers China as a challenge in terms of security. In his election campaign in February 2014, Modi warned China to drop its mindset of expansionism.[73] Prime Minister Modi also raised serious concern over Chinese troops' incursions across the Line of Actual Control (LAC) during Chinese President Xi Jinping's visit to India in September 2014.[74] India's policy towards China of engagement and dialogue, while at the same time holding strong viewpoints on the South China Sea issue, shows the delicate balance in their relationship. In his remarks and statements at India–ASEAN summits and East Asia Summits in the years 2014, 2015 and 2016, Indian Prime Minister Narendra Modi called for a peaceful resolution for the East Sea/South China Sea issue. India stated that it was committed to supporting freedom of navigation, overflight, and unimpeded commerce, based on the principles of international law, as reflected notably in the 1982 United Nations Convention on the Law of the Sea. India also directly mentioned the Permanent Court of Arbitration's judgment on the Philippines–China case, and called for all parties to respect UNCLOS.

Favourable conditions in the East and difficulties in the West were seen as significant factors for India to boost its Act East Policy. Although Prime Minister Modi emphasised India's need for a policy that looked east as well as linked west,[75] in the context of its difficult relations with Pakistan, the unrest in the Middle East and Africa in the wake of the Arab spring; the instability in Central Asia caused by colour revolutions; challenges facing Russia related to Crimea issue, and the European Union's unpredictable security posed by mass immigration and Brexit phenomenon, the continuity of acting East is likely to be a policy compulsion.

In the Indo-Pacific, the continual assertiveness of China in territorial disputes, and its increasing presence in South Asia and the Indian Ocean, has made India engage more strongly with the East, especially since China announced its intentions to disobey the final ruling of the PCA on the Philippines' lawsuit on 12 July 2016. There is another reason for the Act East Policy to be further enhanced. With the exception of China and Malaysia, many ASEAN countries supported India's candidature in the EAS and Community-Building Process.[76] Further, India's success in enlarging and upgrading its relations with many countries (as mentioned above) was the most notable proof that those countries would support India's strategy. Beside the support of countries and territories in the region, India's increasing engagement in the Asia-Pacific has also been encouraged by the United States. Thanks to US exhortation, some multilateral mechanisms, such as India–Japan–Australia and India–Japan–US dialogues (now known as JAI), have been established that help India to have a significant presence in the region.

It seems that the most visible and favourable condition for the AEP to be further enhanced is the economic benefits that India has gained from the Asia-Pacific. Trading values between India and its partners in the region has continuously increased, from US$ 182.45 billion in FY 2010–11 to US$ 221.83 billion in FY 2012–13 and US$ 222.37 billion in FY 2014–15.[77] In the investment field, among the 30 countries and territories with the largest investment in India, many came from the Asia-Pacific, such as Singapore (15.90 per cent), Japan (7.27 per cent), Hong Kong (0.65 per cent), the Republic of Korea (0.62 per cent), PRC (0.47 per cent), Australia and Malaysia (0.28 per cent per each), and Indonesia (0.22 per cent). It is surprising that Mauritius accounted for 33.24 per cent of total FDI in India in the same period.[78]

46 *India's Act East Policy and Vietnam*

There are however challenges facing India's AEP in coming years. Indian people's expectations will put pressure on any policies deployed by Modi's government. Achievements gained and constraints left by the government in the years to come will be the factors that decide the momentum of the AEP. Besides that, as stated by Secretary (East) Shri Anil Wadhwa at the Inaugural Session of the International Relations Conference on 'India's Look East – Act East Policy: A Bridge to the Asian Neighbourhood' in Pune, 13 December 2014, India would be a solid and reliable partner to most countries in the region, instead of a 'No Action, Talk Only' country.[79] There will be three important constraints that India must overcome to promote its assistance to ASEAN, including (1) the democratic mechanism in consulting foreign policy could cause India to be slow or get stuck in rolling out its strategy towards the region; (2) India has a big economy, but it needs a huge source of finance to solve its own economic, social and security problems so there will be less financial assistance to ASEAN in particular and countries in the Asia-Pacific in general in compared to that of other key players such as China, the US, Japan and the Republic of Korea; and (3) there are worries about the slow progress of the financial disbursement for the projects sponsored by India.

There are challenges regarding the connectivity between North Eastern India and the Asia-Pacific. The unrest and insecurity of some states, plus their poor security and social infrastructure, continue to pose hurdles in India's plans for the region, especially the land links with countries in the Southeast Asian mainland. Moreover, there has been progress made, but the relations between India and Bangladesh continue to face challenges, especially in terms of water-sharing, energy cooperation, and transit and transshipment.[80]

India will also have to spend a significant amount of its resources on coping with challenges posed by Pakistan and China, especially in terms of security issues. China's increasing influence in South Asia and the Indian Ocean, along with its ambition of controlling the East Sea/South China Sea, is an opportunity for India to increase its engagement in the Indo-Pacific region, and also helps the country in making strategic partners. Particularly with regard to the South China Sea issue, if India does not have close cooperation with its partners, the key players in the region such as the US, Japan, Australia, Indonesia, Singapore and Vietnam, it will be difficult for India to secure its economic and strategic interests in the region, especially since the physical infrastructure of China's strategy of establishing the anti-access/access-denial (A2/AD) in the region seems to have been completed.

Another issue that that is raised by countries in the region is India's willingness and real commitment towards the region. India has been sometimes accused of being a 'No Action, Talk Only' country. In order to dispel this way of thinking, India needs to start acting.

Vietnam in India's Act East Policy

Vietnam has been an important factor in India's foreign policy since Indira Gandhi became Indian Prime Minister in 1966. When the Cold War ended in

1991, Vietnam became an important pillar in India's Look East Policy (LEP) launched in 1991, along with its economic reforms.[81] When the LEP officially upgraded to the AEP in 2014, Vietnam played an important role in the AEP as well. Vietnam was the first country in Southeast Asia to upgrade its strategic partnership to a comprehensive strategic partnership with India in September 2016. Vietnam was also the first nation in the east of India that Indian President Ram Nath Kovind paid a state visit to.[82]

The role of Vietnam in AEP has been affirmed in bilateral documents and Indian leaders' statements during their visits to or when receiving leaders of Vietnam. During his visit to Vietnam in September 2016, Prime Minister Narendra Modi reaffirmed that Vietnam is an important[83] and strong[84] pillar of India's Act East Policy. In his visit to Vietnam in November 2018, President Ram Nath Kovind underlined that Vietnam 'is pivotal to India's "Act East" policy'.[85]

India has paid more attention to strengthening its ties with Vietnam in the field of defence. The two countries adopted the Joint Vision Statement on Vietnan–India Defence Cooperation for the period of 2015–2020. India has cooperated with Vietnam in human resources training between the Armies, Air Forces, Naval and Coast Guards, as well as cooperating in cyber security and information sharing. Both sides have conducted cooperation in maritime domain including anti-piracy, the security of sea-lanes, the exchange of white shipping etc. Recently, the two sides agreed to hold the first Maritime Security Dialogue on issues related to maritime domain, and further encouraged port calls of each other's naval and coast guard ships, in the spirit of the proposal for an ASEAN–India Strategic Dialogue on maritime cooperation made at the commemorative summit held in New Delhi in January 2018.[86]

India has also promoted its relations with Vietnam in terms of trade and investment. In 2015, India became the eleventh largest trading partner of Vietnam.[87] Vietnam was the fourth largest trading partner of India in ASEAN, and replaced Thailand to become the ninth largest trading partner of India in the Asia-Pacific in FY 2016–17. Vietnam officially joined India's club of US$ 10 billion trading partners in the fiscal year 2016-17.[88] Notably, India agreed to continue its projects in coordination between the ONGC and the PVN (Vietnam) in oil and gas exploration on the continental shelf and the Exclusive Economic Zone (EEZ) of Vietnam in the South China Sea.[89]

In short, the AEP encompasses the region from Western boundary of Myanmar to the whole Asia-Pacific.[90] The 'act, not talk only' has been implemented in all fields of cooperation. India will make efforts to engage in sensitive issues in the region, such as maritime territorial disputes, and in developing understanding with its special strategic partners in the region or those who have interest in the region, namely the US, Japan, Australia, Vietnam, Indonesia and ASEAN. In India's LEP and AEP, Vietnam has been an important pillar, and India's increasing strategic engagement in the political, economic and defence fields is testimony to this. However, the distance between talking and acting is always far. Partners of India in the Asia-Pacific region are looking forward to seeing a real Act East Policy.

48 India's Act East Policy and Vietnam

Notes

1 This chapter has borrowed sections from the author's paper: Vo, Xuan Vinh. 2016. 'India's Act East Policy: A Perspective from Vietnam', *World Focus*, 443: 45–52

2 Modi, Narendra. 2014. Opening Statement at the 12th India-ASEAN Summit, Nay Pyi Taw, Myanmar, 12 November. http://mea.gov.in/Speeches-Statements.htm?dtl/24230/ (accessed 8 July 2016)

3 Vo, Xuan Vinh. 2016. 'India's Role in Ensuring Stability and Security in the South China Sea', *Journal of Indian Ocean Studies*, 24(1): 11–13

4 Ismi, Asad. 2013. 'Maoist Insurgency Spreads to Over 40% of India: Mass Poverty and Delhi's Embrace of Corporate Neoliberalism Fuels Social Uprising', *Global Research*, 20 December. http://www.globalresearch.ca/maoist-insurgency-spreads-to-over-40-of-india -mass-poverty-and-delhis-embrace-of-corporate-neoliberalism-fuels-social-uprising/5362 276 (accessed 8 July 2016)

5 Hussain, Wasbir. 2014. 'India accuses Pak agencies of backing terror groups', *Arab News*, 29 November. http://www.arabnews.com/world/news/667166 (accessed 8 July 2016)

6 'ISIS threatens attack on India; vows to wipe out Hindus', 2016. *DNA*, 14 April. http://www.dnaindia.com/india/report-isis-threatens-attack-on-india-vows-to-wipe-out-hindus-2202013 (accessed 8 July 2016)

7 '10 memorable speeches of Shri Narendra Modi from 2014 Lok Sabha elections campaign', 2014. *Narendramodi.in*, 14 May. http://www.narendramodi.in/10-mem orable-speeches-of-shri-narendra-modi-from-2014-lok-sabha-elections-campaign-3143 (accessed 11 July 2016)

8 The World Bank. 2014. 'Inflation, consumer prices (annual %)'. http://data.worldba nk.org/indicator/FP.CPI.TOTL.ZG?locations=IN (accessed 11 July 2016)

9 Loc. cit.

10 The World Bank. 2012. 'Poverty headcount ratio at national poverty lines (% of population)'. http://data.worldbank.org/indicator/SI.POV.NAHC?locations=IN (accessed 11 July 2016)

11 The World Bank. 2014. 'Unemployment, youth total (% of total labor force ages 15–24) (modeled ILO estimate)'. http://data.worldbank.org/indicator/SL.UEM.1524.ZS?locations=IN (accessed 11 July 2016)

12 The World Bank. *Doing Business 2012*; The World Bank. *Doing Business 2013*. The World Bank and the International Finance Corporation. Washington, DC.

13 Mishra, Asit Ranjan. 2018. 'India ease of doing business rank jumps 23 places to 77 in World Bank's Doing Business 2019 survey', *Livemint*, 1 November. https://www.livemint.com/Politics/GwXhAdltCo1TCbRTAm5z0H/India-up-23-places-in-ease-of-doing-business-rankings.html (accessed 21 January 2019)

14 Department of Commerce (Ministry of Commerce & Industry, Government of India). 'Export Import Data Bank Version 7.1 – TradeStat'. http://commerce.nic.in/eidb/default.asp (accessed 11 July 2016)

15 The World Bank. 2013. *World Development Indicators*, http://databank.worldbank.org/data/reports.aspx?source=2&series=NE.TRD.GNFS.ZS&country (accessed 11 July 2016)

16 Ministry of Development of North Eastern Region (Government of India). 2011. *Human Development Report of North East States*, December 7. New Delhi.

17 Wadhwa, Anil. 2014. 'Address at the Inaugural Session of the International Relations Conference on "India's Look East – Act East Policy: A Bridge to the Asian Neighbourhood"', Pune, 13 December. https://mea.gov.in/Speeches-Statements.htm?dtl/24531/ (accessed 12 July 2016)

18 Modi, 2014

19 Sokinda, Sanjive. 2015. 'India's Strategy for Countering China's Increased Influence in the Indian Ocean', *Indo-Pacific Strategic Papers*, October 1–2

20 Sakhuja, Vijay. 2011. 'India's Stakes in South China Sea'. Paper presented at the third international workshop on 'The South China Sea: Cooperation for Regional

Security and Development'. Hanoi, November 4–5. http://nghiencuubiendong.vn/en/conferences-and-seminars-/the-third-international-workshop-on-south-china-sea/633-indias-stakes-in-south-china-sea-by-vijay-sakhuja (accessed 12 July 2016)

21 Chubb, Andrew. 2016. 'Did China just clarify the nine-dash line?' *EastAsiaForum*, 14 July. http://www.eastasiaforum.org/2016/07/14/did-china-just-clarify-the-nine-dash-line/ (accessed 13 July 2016)

22 'Chinese Military Seeks to Extend Its Naval Power'. 2010. *The New York Times*, 23 April. http://www.nytimes.com/2010/04/24/world/asia/24navy.html?_r=0 (accessed 13 July 2016)

23 Vo, 2016: 95–96

24 Sakhuja, Vijay. 2012. 'Strategic Dimensions of India's Look East Policy', in Amar Nath Ram (ed.), *Two Decades of India's Look East Policy*. New Delhi: Manohar: 255

25 Rajendram, Danielle. 2014. 'India's new Asia-Pacific strategy: Modi acts East', The Lowy Institute Analysis, December: 1.

26 White House. 2014. 'U.S.–India Joint Statement', 30 September. https://www.white house.gov/the-press-office/2014/09/30/us-india-joint-statement (accessed 14 July 2016)

27 White House. 2015. 'U.S.–India Joint Strategic Vision for the Asia-Pacific and Indian Ocean Region', 25 January. https://www.whitehouse.gov/the-press-office/2015/01/25/us-in dia-joint-strategic-vision-asia-pacific-and-indian-ocean-region (accessed 11 July 2014)

28 Ministry of Foreign Affairs (Government of Japan). 2015. 'Joint Statement on India and Japan Vision 2025: Special Strategic and Global Partnership Working Together for Peace and Prosperity of the Indo-Pacific Region and the World', 12 December. http://www.mofa.go.jp/s_sa/sw/in/page3e_000432.html (accessed 15 July 2016)

29 US Department of State. 2015. 'Inaugural U.S.–India–Japan Trilateral Ministerial Dialogue in New York', 30 September. http://www.state.gov/r/pa/prs/ps/2015/09/247483.htm (accessed 15 July 2016)

30 Parameswaran, Prashanth. 2015. 'India, Australia, Japan Hold First Ever Trilateral Dialogue', *The Diplomat*, 9 June. http://thediplomat.com/2015/06/india-australia-japan-hold-first-ever-trilateral-dialogue/ (accessed 15 July 2016)

31 The World Bank. 2014. *World Development Indicators*. http://databank.worldbank.org/data/reports.aspx?Code=NY.GDP.MKTP.KD.ZG&id=af3ce82b&report_name=Popular_indicators&populartype=series&ispopular=y (accessed 18 July 2016)

32 ESCAP Online Statistical Database. http://www.unescap.org/stat/data/statdb/Data Explorer.aspx (accessed 18 July 2016)

33 Wadhwa, 2014

34 Diplomatic Bluebook. 2016. Ministry of Foreign Affairs, Socialist Republic of Viet Nam. Hanoi: National Political Publishing House: 21

35 Vietnam President Tran Dai Quang speech at Nehru Museum Library. 10 March 2018. http://economictimes.indiatimes.com/articleshow/63212961.cms?utm_source=contentofin terest&utm_medium=text&utm_campaign=cppst (accessed 11 February 2019)

36 Ibid.

37 Rajendram, 2014: 4

38 Modi, 2014

39 Modi, Narendra. 2014. 'Narendra Modi addresses rally in Assam, seeks support for BJP & attacks Congress for lack of development in Northeast', 8 February. http://www.na rendramodi.in/narendra-modi-addresses-rally-in-assam-seeks-support-for-bjp-attacks-congress-for-lack-of-development-in-northeast-5949 (accessed 18 July 2016)

40 Wadhwa, 2014

41 Chaudhury, Rahul Roy. 2015. 'Modi's Approach China and Pakistan', European Council on Foreign Relations. http://www.ecfr.eu/what_does_india_think/analysis/m odis_approach_to_india_and_pakistan (accessed 2 August 2017)

42 Rajendram, 2014: 4

43 Ministry of External Affairs (Government of India). 2014. 'Tokyo Declaration for India–Japan Special Strategic and Global Partnership', 1 September. http://www.mea.gov.in/bila

50 India's Act East Policy and Vietnam

teral-documents.htm?dtl/23965/Tokyo_Declaration_for_India__Japan_Special_Strategic_and_Global_Partnership (accessed 8 August 2016)

44 Parameswaran, Prashanth. 2016. 'India, Brunei Ink New Defense Pact', *The Diplomat*, 4 February. http://thediplomat.com/2016/02/india-brunei-ink-new-defense-pact/ (accessed 8 August 2016)

45 Ministry of External Affairs (Government of India). 2015. 'Joint Statement for India–Mongolia Strategic Partnership', 17 May. http://www.mea.gov.in/bilateral-docum ents.htm?dtl/25253/Joint_Statement_for_IndiaMongolia_Strategic_Partnership_May_17_2015 (accessed 8 August 2016)

46 Embassy of India in Ulaanbaatar (Mongolia). January 2015. 'Brief on India–Mongolia Relations'. http://www.eoi.gov.in/ulaanbaatar/?1051?000 (accessed 9 August 2016)

47 Wadhwa, 2014

48 Rajendram, 2014: 12

49 Ministry of External Affairs (Government of India). 2011. 'Incident involving INS Airavat in South China Sea', *Press Briefings*, 1 September. http://www.mea.gov.in/m edia-briefings.htm?dtl/3040/Incident+involving+INS+Airavat+in+South+China+Sea (accessed 9 August 2016)

50 'We'll send force to protect our interests in South China Sea, says Navy chief'. 2012. *The Hindu*, 3 December. http://www.thehindu.com/news/international/well-send-force-to-p rotect-our-interests-in-south-china-sea-says-navy-chief/article4160784.ece (accessed 9 August 2016)

51 Ministry of External Affairs (Government of India). 2018. 'Prime Minister's Keynote Address at Shangri La Dialogue', 1 June. https://www.mea.gov.in/Speeches-Statem ents.htm?dtl/29943/Prime+Ministers+Keynote+Address+at+Shangri+La+Dialogue+June+01+2018 (accessed 21 December 2018)

52 Parameswaran, 2015

53 Ministry of External Affairs (Government of India). 2018. 'India-Australia-Japan-U. S. Consultations', 15 November. https://www.mea.gov.in/press-releases.htm?dtl/30593/IndiaAustraliaJapanUS_Consultations (accessed 21 December 2018)

54 Parameswaran, 2015

55 Ministry of External Affairs (Government of India). 2018. 'India–Indonesia Joint Statement during visit of Prime Minister to Indonesia', 30 May. https://www.mea.gov.in/bila teral-documents.htm?dtl/29932/IndiaIndonesia+Joint+Statement+during+visit+of+Pri me+Minister+to+Indonesia+May+30+2018 (accessed 21 December 2018)

56 'Indian naval ships sail for operational deployment to South China Sea'. 2016. *The Financial Express*, 18 May. http://www.financialexpress.com/economy/indian-nava l-ships-sail-for-operational-deployment-to-scs/259084/ (accessed 15 August 2016)

57 'US, India and Japan kick off Malabar 2016'. 2016. *NavalToday.com*, 10 June. http:// navaltoday.com/2016/06/10/us-india-and-japan-kick-off-malabar-2016/ (accessed 15 August 2016)

58 Chaudhury, Dipanjan Roy. 2016. 'China objects to presence of Indian ships in South China Sea', *The Economic Times*, 21 May. http://economictimes.indiatimes.com/news/ defence/china-objects-to-presence-of-indian-ships-in-south-china-sea/articleshow/52369 749.cms (accessed 15 August 2016)

59 Ministry of External Affairs (Government of India). 2016. 'Joint Statement on the 7th Mekong-Ganga Cooperation Ministerial Meeting', 25 July. http://www.mea.gov. in/bilateral-documents.htm?dtl/27138/Joint_Statement_on_the_7th_MekongGanga_Cooperation_Ministerial_Meeting_Vientiane (accessed 22 August 2016)

60 Ministry of External Affairs (Government of India). 2018. 'Joint Ministerial Statement for the 9th Mekong-Ganga Cooperation Ministerial Meeting in Singapore', 4 August. https://www.mea.gov.in/Speeches-Statements.htm?dtl/30237/ Joint_Ministerial_Statement_for_the_9th_Mekong_Ganga_Cooperation_Minister ial_Meeting_in_Singapore (accessed 22 December 2018)

India's Act East Policy and Vietnam 51

61 Wadhwa, 2014
62 Modi, Narendra. 2014. 'Remarks at 12th India-ASEAN Summit', Nay Pyi Taw, 12 November. http://www.mea.gov.in/Speeches-Statements.htm?dtl/24236/Remarks+by+the+Prime+Minister+at+12th+IndiaASEAN+Summit+Nay+Pyi+Taw+Myanmar (accessed 15 August 2016)
63 Wadhwa, 2014
64 Modi, 2014. 'Remarks at 12th India-ASEAN Summit'
65 The World Bank. 2016. 'GDP growth (annual %)'. http://data.worldbank.org/indicator/NY.GDP.MKTP.KD.ZG?locations=IN (accessed 25 August 2016)
66 The World Bank. 2019. 'Rankings & Ease of Doing Business Score'. http://www.doingbusiness.org/en/rankings?region=south-asia (accessed 25 December 2018).
67 'Stopped "sweets of many": Narendra Modi on corruption'. 2016. *The Economic Times*, 5 June. http://economictimes.indiatimes.com/news/politics-and-nation/stopped-sweets-of-many-narendra-modi-on-corruption/articleshow/52608190.cms (accessed 25 August 2016)
68 Dhawan, Sunil. 2016. 'Social security schemes are more popular in urban than rural areas', *The Economic Times*, 12 October. http://economictimes.indiatimes.com/wealth/plan/social-security-schemes-are-more-popular-in-urban-than-rural-areas/articleshow/54806295.cms (accessed 17 October 2016)
69 Chaudhury, 2016
70 Marlow, Iain. 2016. 'Modi's set to get tougher on China and Pakistan', *Bloomberg*, 15 November. https://www.bloomberg.com/news/articles/2016-11-14/with-economic-box-ticked-modi-turns-assertive-on-foreign-policy (accessed 3 April 2017)
71 The Indian Express. 2016. 'Water that belongs to India cannot be allowed to go to Pakistan: PM Modi in Bathinda'. 25 November. http://indianexpress.com/article/india/india-news-india/water-that-belongs-to-india-cannot-be-allowed-to-go-to-pakistan-pm-modi-in-bathinda-4394371/ (accessed 3 April 2017)
72 'PM Modi slams Pakistan over terrorism, but reaches out to China'. 2017. *Hindustan Times*, 17 January. http://www.hindustantimes.com/india-news/pm-modi-at-raisina-dialogue-india-alone-can-t-walk-peace-path-pak-should-come-forward/story-ljH0uvav2gwAcKbgF9dSWO.html (accessed 17 April 2017)
73 Gottipati, Sruthi. 2014. 'Modi says China must drop "mindset of expansionism" over Arunachal Pradesh', *Reuters*, 22 February. http://in.reuters.com/article/india-modi-china-arunachal-idINDEEA1L03V20140222 (accessed 17 April 2017)
74 'Under Sangh pressure, Modi takes hard line on incursions'. 2014. *The Hindu*, 19 September. http://www.thehindu.com/news/national/narendra-modi-raises-issue-of-chinese-incursions-with-xi-jinping/article6422103.ece (accessed 17 April 2017)
75 'Philippines' Aquino assures Modi on FTA'. 2014. *Business Standard*, 13 November. http://www.business-standard.com/article/news-ians/philippines-aquino-assures-modi-on-fta-114111301300_1.html (accessed 18 April 2017)
76 Ghoshal, Baladas. 2013. 'China's Perception of India's "Look East Policy" and Its Implication', *IDSA Monograph Series*, No. 26, October: 39–43
77 Department of Commerce (Ministry of Commerce & Industry, Government of India). Export–Import Data Bank Version 7.1 – TradeStat. http://commerce.nic.in/eidb/default.asp (accessed 18 April 2017)
78 Department of Industrial Policy and Promotion (Ministry of Commerce and Industry, Government of India). 2016. *Quarterly Fact Sheet: Fact Sheet on Foreign Direct Investment (FDI) from April, 2000 to March, 2016*. https://dipp.gov.in/sites/default/files/FDI_FactSheet_JanuaryFebruaryMarch2016.pdf (accessed 20 April 2017)
79 Wadhwa, 2014
80 'Bangladesh–India relations: Progress made and the challenges ahead'. 2016. *The Daily Star*, 8 October. http://www.thedailystar.net/supplements/bangladesh-india-relations-progress-made-and-the-challenges-ahead-1295740 (accessed 19 April 2017)

52 India's Act East Policy and Vietnam

81 For more about Vietnam's position in India's Look East Policy, see Vo, XuanVinh. 2012. 'Vietnam–India Relations in the Light of India's Look East Policy', Sapru House Paper, No. 02, https://icwa.in/pdfs/SHP022012.pdf (accessed 21 December 2018)

82 Ministry of External Affairs (Government of India). 2018. 'Address by President at National Assembly of Vietnam', 20 November. https://www.mea.gov.in/Speeches-Sta tements.htm?dtl/30609/Address_by_President_at_National_Assembly_of_Vietnam (accessed 22 December 2018)

83 Ministry of External Affairs (Government of India). 2016. 'Joint Statement between India and Vietnam during the visit of Prime Minister to Vietnam', 3 September. https://www.mea.gov.in/bilateral-documents.htm?dtl/27362 (accessed 21 December 2018)

84 Ministry of External Affairs (Government of India). 2016. 'Banquet Speech by Prime Minister during his visit to Vietnam', 3 September. https://www.mea.gov.in/Speeches-Statem ents.htm?dtl/27364/Banquet_Speech_by_Prime_Minister_during_his_visit_to_Vietnam_Se ptember_03_2016 (accessed 22 December 2018)

85 Ministry of External Affairs (Government of India). 2018. 'Address by President at National Assembly of Vietnam', 20 November. https://www.mea.gov.in/Speeches-Sta tements.htm?dtl/30609/Address_by_President_at_National_Assembly_of_Vietnam (acc essed 22 December 2018)

86 Ministry of External Affairs (Government of India). 2018. 'India–Vietnam Joint Statement during State Visit of President to Vietnam', 21 November. https://www.mea.gov. in/bilateral-documents.htm?dtl/30615/IndiaVietnam_Joint_Statement_during_State_Vi sit_of_President_to_Vietnam (accessed 22 December 2018)

87 Calculated by the author from the data of the General Statistics Office of Vietnam at http://gso.gov.vn/default_en.aspx?tabid=780 (accessed 24 December 2018)

88 Calculated by the author from the data of the Department of Commerce (Ministry of Commerce & Industry, Government of India) at http://commerce.gov.in/EIDB.aspx (accessed 23 December 2018)

89 Ministry of External Affairs (Government of India). 2018. 'India–Vietnam Joint Statement during State Visit of President to Vietnam', 21 November. https://www.mea.gov. in/bilateral-documents.htm?dtl/30615/IndiaVietnam_Joint_Statement_during_State_Vi sit_of_President_to_Vietnam (accessed 22 December 2018)

90 Modi, Narendra. 2014. 'Opening Statement at the 12th India–ASEAN Summit', Nay Pyi Taw, Myanmar, 12 November. https://mea.gov.in/Speeches-Statements.htm?dtl/ 24230/Opening+Statement+by+Prime+Minister+at+the+12th+IndiaASEAN+Summ it+Nay+Pyi+Taw+Myanmar (accessed 22 December 2018)

4 Political convergence in the context of the Indo-Pacific

Vietnam and India have close political links in modern times. During their struggles for independence from the Western domination, the two countries conducted activities supporting each other, especially on the Indian side. The Vietnamese anti-French resistance received the support of the Indian government and Indian nationalists. In the context of the Cold War, the two countries supported each other in terms of regional and international issues. In the post-Cold War environment, the cooperation between Vietnam and India, especially in the political field, has been upgraded thanks to India's Look East/Act East Policy and Vietnam's reforms, and the changes in the evolving architecture in the Asia-Pacific. This chapter will highlight Vietnam–India relations in political dimensions in the regional and world order during the Cold War and post-Cold War landscapes.

From differences to shared common interests during the Cold War

As 'the key to the exploitation of the Asiatic and other non-European races of the Earth',[1] as described by Mahatma Gandhi, India was recognized as a supporter of the anti-imperialism nationalists in Asia and Africa, especially since the bi-polar world order with the East-West confrontation took shape after the Yalta and Potsdam Conferences in 1945. By deciding to stand for colonial countries in the world neither communist nor capitalist, India became the spirit leader of anti-imperialist resistance movements for national independence in those countries. The anti-France resistance struggle of the Vietnamese people also received the support of Indian nationalists and the National Congress even before India gained independence in 1947.

> Indian nationalists welcomed the establishment of republics by their Vietnamese and Indonesian counterparts, who had taken advantage of the time gap between the Japanese surrender and the arrival of the Western troops to proclaim their freedom.[2]

Acharya Kripalani, the President of the Indian National Congress, accused the French authorities of Hitlerism in the repressing of the nationalist struggle in

54 Political convergence in the Indo-Pacific

Vietnam after France rudely broke a *modus vivendi* signed by Ho Chi Minh and the French government at the Fontainebleau Conference in 1946, whereby both sides agreed to cease hostilities.[3] The Indian government extended support for the Democratic Republic of Vietnam (DRV) in 1947, in response to the call of the Ho Chi Minh government to condemn the French policy in Indochina, to block France in purchasing land for its mission in New Delhi, and to prevent the repair and refuelling of French ships in India. In February 1947, the then Indian government prohibited logistics or combat French aircrafts from flying across India, although permitting ambulances and other civilian planes to cross its territory.[4]

However, in this period, India pursued the policy of 'not at war with another country'[5] and was best encapsulated by the term 'non-alignment'.[6] Indian policy-makers were apprehensive in case 'the Communists overran the whole Indo-china'.[7] In the context of 'the Communist-dominated character of the Vietnam during its fight for independence against the French, and the cordial relations between New Delhi and Saigon during the second half of the 1950s',[8] India was reluctant to show any visible support for the DRV. In the Geneva Conference of 1954, Prime Minister J. Nehru presented his own peace plan for Indochina, in which he called for a ceasefire but not an immediate withdrawal of French troops from Indochina.[9] India, under Nehru, also refused the request of Sarat Chandra Bose (a member of Nehru's interim cabinet) for transport facilities and passports for the journey to Indochina for his volunteer force to fight against the French. India accepted the joint requests of the DRV and Indonesia at the Asian Relations Conference in 1947 in New Delhi. Both the countries requested:

> (1) placing the colonialism issue of Vietnam on the Security Council agenda; (2) immediately recognizing the Indonesia and the Vietnamese republics; (3) providing joint Asian action to force the withdrawal of foreign troops from all parts of "occupied" Asia; (4) providing joint Asian action to prevent Dutch and French reinforcements from going to Indonesia and Vietnam, and (5) sending Asian medical aid and volunteers to Asian battlefields.[10]

At the end of the 1950s and the beginning of the 1960s, the US' increasing support for the government of the South Vietnam and Pakistan; new approach of the Soviet Union post-Stalin; the India–China war, and the changing attitudes of both governments in Vietnam changed India's position towards the Southeast Asian region in general and Vietnam in particular. China's moves since 1950 surrounding India and Southeast Asia also prompted India to pay more attention to the region. In 1950, China annexed Tibet, bringing Chinese presence and power in direct contact with India on the latter's northern and north-eastern borders.[11] India felt uneasy with China at the first Afro-Asian Conference in 1955, when the Chinese Premier presented his conciliatory approach towards Western-aligned Pakistan.[12] The Indo-Chinese border war that broke out in 1962

Political convergence in the Indo-Pacific   55

provided India with a clear position towards China, since the latter said that the war was an instrument to teach the former a lesson.

> New Delhi's renewed preoccupation with China has, in turn, boosted the importance of Southeast Asia in the eyes of the Indian decision-making elite because of the region's close proximity to both India and China and the fact that it has been long considered a meeting ground of Chinese and Indian cultural and political influences. Just as the Indian obsession with the 'Pakistan' factor had enhanced the importance of West Asia in New Delhi's calculations in the 1950s and the 1960s, the increasing Indian concern with the 'China factor' in the late 1970s and in the 1980s has worked to enhance the strategic and political importance of Southeast Asia in the New Delhi's perceptions.[13]

Among Southeast Asian countries, India attached relatively high importance to Indonesia and Vietnam because of two factors: the impeccable anti-colonial credentials of the Indonesian and Vietnamese national movements, and their stature as pre-eminent regional powers interested in maintaining their position as autonomous decision-making centres in a world dominated by superpowers. This has led the Indian leaders to believe that Indonesia and Vietnam have not merely shared a common colonial past with India, but, more importantly, 'they share with [India] significant interests and aspiration with regard to the present and future workings of the international political system'.[14]

Beside the China factor, India also revised its general assessment of the Soviet Union's foreign policy, since Soviet in the post-Stalin period favoured conciliation and coexistence,[15] or 'groping towards peaceful coexistence'.[16] In addition, India relied, especially after 1954, on the Soviet Union for building up the public sector industries, which the US was reluctant to do,[17] though the latter gave great military aid to Pakistan in the mid-fifties. This led to 'the establishment of friendly relations between New Delhi and Moscow'.[18] In that context, the changes to the South Vietnam government's position towards the Geneva Agreements and the DRV government's 'India policy' had a significant impact on India's changing attitude towards both parts of Vietnam. '[The] United States and its protégé Ngo Dinh Diem who led the government in the South Vietnam determined from the outset to scuttle the Geneva Agreements',[19] and 'the great anxiety over the deterioration of law and order in the South Vietnam',[20] while the DRV subscribed to India's five principles, particularly to peaceful coexistence. The DRV also stood forth as a supporter of the Indian policy of increasing the area of peace and lessening tensions in Southeast Asia. As a result, the North Vietnam government assumed more respectability in India's eyes than ever before.[21] Although India, in this period, 'continued the *de facto* recognition to both regimes in Vietnam'[22] when Indian President Rajendra Prasad paid a state visit to both parts of Vietnam in 1959, India's renewal of the trade agreement with North Vietnam for three years beginning September 22, 1962,[23] was the best example for the shifting of India's policy towards the

56 Political convergence in the Indo-Pacific

DRV. In other words, thanks to the significant moves of strategic competition among major powers in the Asia-Pacific, and their consequences in the context of the bi-polar world, India and the DRV moved closer to each other.

From the Indo-Chinese border war in October-November 1962 to when Indira Gandhi became Indian Prime Minister in 1966, India–DRV relations were sometimes faced with challenges related to the International Control Commission reports on the situations in North and South Vietnam.[24] However, Indira Gandhi's 'commitment to Socialism was deep and firm',[25] as sincerely believed by the Soviet press and leaders, and in fact, 'the Soviet Union and India initiated in 1963 and signed in August 1964, August 1965 and November 1965, major armed deals by which the Soviet Union became the largest arms supplier to India and Indo-Soviet relations entered a qualitatively new phase',[26] Indira Gandhi started distancing herself from the US.[27] By supporting the anti-American resistance struggle of the Vietnamese people, Prime Minister Indira Gandhi, on behalf of Indian government and in coordination with the Russian government, jointly criticized the US actions in Vietnam.

> ...in July 1966, she issued a statement deploring US bombing in North Vietnam and its capital Hanoi. In the latter part of July, in Moscow, she signed a joint statement with the Soviet Union demanding an immediate and unconditional end to the US bombing and branding US action in Vietnam as 'imperialist aggression'.[28]

Mrs. Gandhi also enhanced the links with the founding countries of the Non-Aligned Movement (NAM), such as Egypt and Yugoslavia, and mobilized 'non-aligned countries to cooperate politically and economically in order to counter the danger of neo-colonialism emanating from the US and West European countries'.[29]

From 1971, in the context of 'the emergence of a Washington-Peking-Moscow triangle titled against the Soviet Union, Moscow decided to move closer to India',[30] because the 'Soviet Union saw in India a convenient counter-balance against China as well as a second front in its campaign to pressure Pakistan over Afghanistan'.[31]

New Delhi, for its part, also needed Soviet support on the Bangladesh issue since it perceived the collusion of China, Pakistan and the US, following the Sino-US rapprochement beginning in 1971, as a threat to India's vital interests,[32] especially when the US had warned India that it would not support the latter in the event of China helping Pakistan in such a war.[33] The establishment of a full diplomatic relationship between India and the DRV in 1972 could be seen as an obvious result of the strategic engagement between the two countries in the wake of the strategic competition posed by the US–Soviet–China triangle on Asian fronts.

The US–Soviet–China strategic competition triangle continued to dominate the direction of Vietnam–India political relations in the late 1970s and 1980s, especially in terms of the Cambodian issue and the Chinese invasion of Vietnam in 1979.

India defied China and the Western powers hegemony in Asia by recognizing the Heng Samrin regime in Cambodia and coming to the support of Vietnam. India's then foreign minister Atal Behari Vajpayee, in 1979, cut short his official visit to China in protest against inflicting a war of "punishment" on Vietnam on the question of Khmer Rouge in Cambodia.[34]

With the end of the Cold War (or the disappearance of the bi-polar world order), adjustments were made to the foreign policies of both Vietnam and India. The rise of China also created new dynamics within Vietnam–India political relations. In addition, their traditional ties and strategic engagement during the Cold War have been valued by the two countries to enhance their relations in the new phase.

Building a comprehensive strategic partnership

The end of the Cold War also marked the end of the bi-polar world order. The collapse of the Soviet Union led to a unipolar world in which the US became the dominant power. The end of the contradictory bi-polar world order was followed by a new development phase of the world, the era of regional and international integration. In the Asia-Pacific, especially in Southeast Asia, the Association of Southeast Asian Nations (ASEAN) established in 1967 became the driving force in ASEAN-led mechanisms, such as the ASEAN Regional Forum (ARF), ASEAN+1, ASEAN+3, East Asia Summit (EAS), and the ASEAN Defence Ministers' Meeting Plus (ADMM+). In short, as the driving force in the region, ASEAN has attracted the involvement and engagement of major powers in the world in dealing with challenges and maintaining good order in the region. In other words, ASEAN in particular, and Southeast Asia in general, has become the stage where major powers compete for influence.

China, after decades of reform since 1979, became the world's fastest-growing major economy with growth rates averaging 10 per cent over 30 years up until 2015. In 2011, China overcame Japan to become the second largest economy in the world. Thanks to its economic strength, China has been able to deploy strategies to enhance its influence in the world, beginning with the Asia-Pacific region, where the ocean has become an important domain in the eyes of Chinese strategists. China started to use the ocean as a means of reaching out to the world in 1978,[35] acknowledging the relationship between the ocean and their survival and development. In 1985, for the first time, The Chinese People's Liberation Army Navy (PLAN) sent ships overseas,[36] and very shortly after, in 1986, the first-ever sailing of PLAN to the Indian Ocean took place when a small Chinese flotilla docked in Chittagong port.[37] The ways in which China realizes its ambitions, especially by way of its aggressive and assertive activities in the South China Sea, where it claims over 80 per cent of the Sea, have created worries in the international community, especially with countries who had interests in Sea Lines of Communication (SLOC).

58 Political convergence in the Indo-Pacific

Anticipating China's rise and its strategic ambitions in the Asia-Pacific and beyond, the US, under the Obama administration, announced the Balancing/ Pivot to Asia Strategy as a commitment to contribute to Asia-Pacific security.[38] In order to implement this strategy, the US made efforts to strengthen alliances and global partnerships, including enhancing and deepening its relations with important countries in the region, such as Singapore, Indonesia, Malaysia and Vietnam.[39] 'Vietnam, Indonesia, Malaysia, and Singapore are growing security and economic partners of the United States'[40] in the US Indo-Pacific strategy under the Donald Trump administration.

In the wake of the collapse of the Cold War, India launched the Look East Policy (LEP) simultaneously with its economic reform in early 1990s. As stated by former Indian Prime Minister Manmohan Singh in a keynote address at the special leaders' dialogue of ASEAN Business Advisory Council in 2005, the LEP 'was not merely an external economic policy, but also a strategic shift in India's vision of the world and India's place in the evolving global economy'.[41] No clear objectives of the LEP have officially been publicised by the Indian government so far. However, the policy has been deployed, regularly adjusted in its two decades of development in conformity with the regional and international context, and the domestic political economic conditions of India. The objectives of the policy can be classified into two groups. The first group contains strategic and political dimensions such as: (1) building good relations with countries, regional cooperation institutions and fora in the Asia-Pacific in order to facilitate India's trade exchange and investment, and establish its influence and power in the region, and (2) enhancing India's economic and political influence in the region, especially Southeast Asia, to protect from a distance its own territorial integrity and interests in the South Asia region and Indian Ocean, and, directly, its economic interests in the Asia-Pacific. These strategic and political calculations partly originated from India's awareness of China's activities of increasing its influence in South Asia and on the Indian Ocean, as well as the latter's sovereign claims over the disputed territory of Aksai Chin and the Arunachal Pradesh state.[42] In the Look East Policy, Vietnam has been regarded as a trusted and privileged strategic partner and an important pillar of the policy.[43]

In the context of the growing assertiveness of China in the South China Sea, as well as China's ambitions in Aksai Chin and the Arunachal Pradesh state, India upgraded its LEP to the Act East Policy (AEP) under which India, among others, increased its engagement in the Asia-Pacific to protect its vital interests in the region, including freedom of navigation, over-flight and other economic interests in the South China Sea. Again, Vietnam is an important[44] and strong[45] pillar of and 'pivotal to India's "Act East" policy'.[46]

Vietnam, for its part, launched its *Doi Moi* (renovation) in 1986. From 1986 to 1991, its foreign policy was to resolve the Cambodian issue, normalise relations with China, and escape from the state of blockade and embargo. After the Cold War in 1991, Vietnam set its foreign policy's objective to be a friend of all countries in the international community and joined ASEAN. After joining ASEAN and normalising relations with the US in 1995, Vietnam from 1996

Political convergence in the Indo-Pacific 59

(after the eighth national party congress) wanted to become a friend and trustworthy partner to all countries in the international community, to promote peace, freedom and development of the world. In the context of an evolving Asia-Pacific architecture, there are 'intertwined interests among major powers such as the US, China, Japan and Russia. China's rise posed challenges for cooperation and security of the region'.[47] Since the beginning of the 21st century, Vietnam's foreign policy, from 2001 to 2006, was to actively integrate the international economy. After more than a decade of establishing relations with various partners in the world, as well as clearly identifying opportunities and challenges posed by the regional and international environment, Vietnam's foreign policy from 2006 (the 10th national party congress) to 2010 was to make its established international relations deeper, more stable, more sustainable, and to join the World Trade Organization.[48]

In order to make its foreign policy objectives come true, Vietnam has established and enhanced its relations with countries in the world in terms various forms of relationships, such as strategic and comprehensive partnerships. The changing landscape of the Asia-Pacific after the Cold War, especially since the beginning of 21st century, has created momentum for Vietnam and India to enhance their relations. The progress of political engagements between the two countries has encouraged Vietnam to forge strategic partnerships. Their political support for each other's initiatives at regional and international forums signify increasing convergence.

In 2001, Vietnam established its first strategic partnership with Russia. Vietnam's second strategic partner, Japan, was formalized in 2006. Although the Vietnam–India strategic partnership was built in 2007, even before that, in the Joint Declaration on the Framework of Comprehensive Cooperation between the Republic of India and the Socialist Republic of Vietnam as they enter the 21st Century released in 2003, the leaders of the two countries were 'aware of the strategic importance of their bilateral cooperation'.[49] Both sides expressed their desire to 'endeavour to develop a strategic dimension to their partnership for the mutual benefit of their people, and to contribute to peace, stability, cooperation and prosperity in the Asia-Pacific region and the world at large'.[50] The 2007 Vietnam–India Joint Declaration on Strategic Partnership stated that the new strategic partnership between the two countries would encompass bilateral relations in the political, economic, security, defence, cultural, scientific and technological dimensions, and steer their cooperation in regional and multilateral fora. The two countries also agreed to establish a strategic dialogue at the level of Vice Ministers. It is very important to note that building strategic ties with India had been a priority in Vietnam's foreign policy. As stated by Vietnamese Deputy Prime Minister and Foreign Minister Pham Binh Minh:

> The implementation of strategic and comprehensive partnerships has followed an active and positive roadmap with a particular focus on traditional friends Russia and India, neighbors in the region (China, Japan, the

60 Political convergence in the Indo-Pacific

Republic of Korea) and major European countries (Britain, Germany, France), and other important partners.[51]

In the Joint Statement issued in September 2016, the leaders of the two countries 'reviewed and expressed their satisfaction over the strong and comprehensive development of the relations of long-standing traditional friendship and Strategic Partnership between the two countries so far', and 'agreed to elevate the current Strategic Partnership to [a] Comprehensive Strategic Partnership'.[52] The leaders of Vietnam and India agreed to assign the two Ministries of Foreign Affairs as the focal point, in collaboration with other ministries and the agencies of both sides, in proposing the Plan of Action to implement the Comprehensive Strategic Partnership between the two countries. Notably, 'political relations, defence and security' were priority fields of the comprehensive strategic partnership mentioned in the 2016 Joint Statement. Since then, the relations between India and Vietnam have been enlarged comprehensively, including cooperation in the fields of defence and security, economic, trade and investment, development, science and technology, culture, tourism and people-to-people exchange, and other areas such as healthcare, and mutual judicial assistance in civic and commercial matters. The two countries also agreed to continue their regional and international cooperation.[53] With the development of these ties, the India–Vietnam strategic relationship was upgraded to a comprehensive strategic partnership. As a result, India–Vietnam relationship is seen at par with Vietnam's bilateral relations with Russia and China respectively.

However, unlike other strategic partners, even comprehensive strategic ones, India and Vietnam have enjoyed strong trust for decades. Although Vietnam and China established their comprehensive strategic partnership in 2008, the two countries still underlined the necessity of 'enhancing mutual comprehensive trust'[54] between them. In the Joint Statement by President Barack Obama of the United States of America and President Truong Tan Sang of the Socialist Republic of Vietnam in July 2013, the importance of 'deepening mutual trust'[55] between the two countries was also underlined. In contrast, the strategic partnership between Vietnam and India was based on 'traditional friendship, mutual understanding, *strong trust*, support and convergence of views on various regional and international issues'.[56] Indian President Pranab Mukherjee even noted that 'political relations between India and Vietnam have always been strong and cloudless'.[57] The 2007 Joint Declaration on Vietnam–India Strategic Partnership states that the two sides 'agreed to establish a Strategic Dialogue at the level of Vice Ministers in the Foreign Office'.[58] Vietnam is among a few countries in the Asia-Pacific, such as the US, China, Japan, Malaysia and Singapore, that have jointly organized a bilateral strategic dialogue with India in recent years. Beside political consultations and strategic dialogues, Vietnam and India agreed to hold defence dialogues between their defence ministries. India and Vietnam, in their Joint Statement during the State Visit of the Indian President to Vietnam in 21 November 2018, agreed to hold the first Maritime Security Dialogue on issues

Political convergence in the Indo-Pacific 61

related to maritime domain, and further encouraged port calls of each other's naval and coast guard ships in the spirit of the proposal for an ASEAN–India Strategic Dialogue on maritime cooperation made at the commemorative summit held in New Delhi in January 2018.[59]

At regional and international fora, Vietnam and India have been strongly supporting each other on political issues. Vietnam supports India's Look East/ Act East Policy, and welcomes India's engagement in the Asia-Pacific through regional cooperation mechanisms. Vietnam also supports India in becoming a permanent member of United Nations Security Council (UNSC) when this organ is reformed and enlarged. India, for its part, has supported the settlement of the South China Sea dispute in accordance with international law, including the 1982 United Nations Convention on the Law of the Sea (UNCLOS).

Vietnam has been a trusted friend of India in regional and international fora, and they considered India an important strategic partner. At a regional level, Vietnam bolsters India to engage in the Asia-Pacific region. Vietnam has raised voices in support of India's Look East/Act East Policy. Thanks to the support of Vietnam and India's other partners in the Asia-Pacific region, India has enjoyed an increasing presence in cooperation mechanisms in the region. In 2002, the first ASEAN–India Summit meeting, proposed by India in 1999, was held in Cambodia. Geographically, India is not a country located in East Asia. However, it was one of the first members of the first meeting of the East Asia Summit (EAS) held in Kuala Lumpur in 2005. India is also an official member of the ASEAN Defense Ministers Meeting Plus (ADMM+), which was held for the first time in Vietnam in 2010, and the Expanded ASEAN Maritime Forum. Before that, India became a member of the ASEAN Regional Forum (ARF) in 1996. India is now, along with other members of the EAS, in negotiations to conclude the Regional Comprehensive Economic Partnership (RCEP) which was formally launched in November 2012.

Since regarding Vietnam as a trusted and privileged strategic partner and an important pillar of its Look East Policy,[60] India has actively supported Vietnam in strategic political issues, including the South China Sea dispute. India accepted a much more multilateral approach[61] while China wanted to solve the South China Sea disputes bilaterally with other countries involved. After the Airavat incident in 2011, India officially raised its voice to support freedom of navigation in international waters, including in the South China Sea, and the rights of passage in accordance with accepted principles of international law, and called all parties to respect these principles.[62] India also rejected the legal aspect of China's nine-dash line when it rejected China's objections to the OVL's oil and gas exploration in Vietnam's EEZ, because the objections had 'no legal basis' as the blocks belonged to 'Vietnam.'[63]

In a very assertive way, Indian navy officials confirmed the navy's preparedness for deployment to protect its interests in the South China Sea, including the OVL's oil exploration blocks granted by Vietnam.[64] The Indian Prime Minister Manmohan Singh even used the term 'East Sea' to refer the South China Sea in his speech at the banquet hosted in honour of the General Secretary of the Communist Party

62   *Political convergence in the Indo-Pacific*

of Vietnam Nguyen Phu Trong in November 2013.[65] Notably, since 2011, the term East Sea/South China Sea has been used instead of the term South China Sea in some Vietnam–India bilateral documents.[66] In reality, India had been maintaining its exploration in blocks in the South China Sea offered by Vietnam. In the India–Vietnam Joint Statement made during the State Visit of the Indian President to Vietnam (21 November 2018), the two countries agreed to continue promoting bilateral investment, including cooperation projects between the PVN (Vietnam) and the ONGC (India) in terms of oil and gas exploration on the continental shelf and the Exclusive Economic Zone (EEZ) of Vietnam, and identify models for cooperation involving third countries.[67]

In short, after Vietnam gained independence in 1945, political interactions at the bilateral level were the precursor to better understanding between the two countries. Indian nationalists were among the first to support the DRV's struggle for independence. After a difficult period in the 1950s, due to India's perception of the DRV's struggle for the latter's independence, common challenges and shared interests brought Vietnam and India closer, particularly since the second half of 1960s. The rapid changes in the Asia-Pacific after the Cold War, especially at the beginning of the 21st century including, among others, the rise of China, the US's pivot to Asia and the emergence of the Indo-Pacific concept, have created momentum for Vietnam and India to upgrade their relations, from comprehensive cooperation in 2003 to a strategic partnership in 2007, and a comprehensive strategic partnership in 2016.

Notes

1 Nanda, Prakash. 2003. *Rediscovering Asia: Evolution of India's Look-east Policy.* New Delhi: Lancer and Publishers & Distributor: 74
2 SarDesai, D R. 1968. *Indian Foreign Policy in Cambodia, Laos, and Vietnam, 1947–1964.* Berkeley & Los Angeles: University of California Press: 9
3 Ibid.: 12
4 Ibid.: 18
5 Ibid.: 13
6 Ayoob, Mohammed. 1990. *India and Southeast Asia: Indian Perceptions and Policies.* London: Routledge: 3.
7 Ibid.: 38
8 Ibid.: 38.
9 Ibid.: 38
10 SarDesai, 1968: 13
11 Ayoob, 1990: 2
12 Ibid.: 9
13 Loc. cit.
14 Ayoob, 1990: 35–36
15 SarDesai, 1968: 76
16 Chandra et al. 2008. *India since Independence.* New Delhi: Penguin Books: 283
17 Ibid.: 192
18 SenBudhraj, Vijay. 1979. 'India and the Soviet Union', in Prasad Bimal (ed.), *India's Foreign Policy: Studies in Continuity and Change.* New Delhi: Vikas Publishing House: 361
19 SarDesai, 1968: 85

Political convergence in the Indo-Pacific   63

20 Ibid.: 202
21 Ibid.: 76
22 Ibid.: 194
23 Ibid.: 209
24 Ibid.: 201–209
25 SenBudhraj, 1979: 363
26 Chandra et al., 2008: 193
27 Ibid.: 282
28 Ibid.: 282–283
29 Ibid.: 283
30 SenBudhraj, 1968: 362
31 Gordon, Alexander. 1993. 'India's Security Policy: Desire and Necessity in a Changing World', in Chandran Jeshurun (ed.), *China, India, Japan and the Security of Southeast Asia*. Singapore: ISEAS: 44.
32 Ayoob, 1990: 5
33 SenBudhraj, 1979: 362
34 Muni, S D. 2016. 'How India is viewed as a regional actor', in Namrata Goswami (ed.), *India's Approach to Asia: Strategy, Geopolitics and Responsibility*. New Delhi: Pentagon Press: 78
35 Zhang, Wei. 2015. 'A General Review of the History of China's Sea-power Theory Development', *Naval War College Review*, Autumn, 68(4): 81–82
36 Zhang, 2015: 82
37 Singh, Swaran. 2003. *China–South Asia: Issues, Equations, Policies*. New Delhi: Lancer's Books: 115
38 Hagel, Chuck. 2014. *The United States' Contribution to Regional Security*. Singapore: The Shangri-La Dialogue
39 Ibid.
40 The White House. 2017. 'National Security Strategy of the United States of America'. Washington DC, December: 46
41 Singh, Manmohan. 2005. 'Make 21st Century truly an Asian Century', Keynote address at special leaders, dialogue of Asean Business Advisory Council, 12 December. http://pib.nic.in/newsite/erelcontent.aspx?relid=14102 (accessed 3 May 2017)
42 Vo, Xuan Vinh. 2012. 'Vietnam–India Relations in the Light of India's Look East Policy'. ICWA: Sapru House Paper, No. 2: 13–14
43 Ministry of External Affairs (Government of India). 2013. 'Indian Prime Minister's Statement to the media during state visit of General Secretary of the Communist Party of Vietnam', 20 November. http://mea.gov.in/Speeches-Statements.htm?dtl/22509/Prime_Ministers_Statement_to_the_Media_during_the_State_Visit_of_General_Secretary_of_the_Communist_Party_of_Vietnam (accessed 3 May 2017)
44 Ministry of External Affairs (Government of India). 2016. 'Joint Statement between India and Vietnam during the visit of Prime Minister to Vietnam', 3 September. https://www.mea.gov.in/bilateral-documents.htm?dtl/27362 (accessed 21 December 2018)
45 Ministry of External Affairs (Government of India). 2016. 'Banquet Speech by Prime Minister during his visit to Vietnam', 3 September. https://www.mea.gov.in/Speeches-Statements.htm?dtl/27364/Banquet_Speech_by_Prime_Minister_during_his_visit_to_Vietnam_September_03_2016 (accessed 22 December 2018).
46 Ministry of External Affairs (Government of India). 2018. 'Address by President at National Assembly of Vietnam', 20 November. https://www.mea.gov.in/Speeches-Statements.htm?dtl/30609/Address_by_President_at_National_Assembly_of_Vietnam (accessed 22 December 2018)
47 Pham, Quang Minh. 2010. *Vietnam's Foreign Policy in the Renovation Period 1986–2010*. Hanoi: World Publishing House: 106
48 Pham, 2010: 48–128

64 *Political convergence in the Indo-Pacific*

49 Ministry of External Affairs (Government of India). 2003. 'Joint Declaration on the Framework of Comprehensive Cooperation between the Republic of India and the Socialist Republic of Vietnam as they enter the 21st Century', 1 May. https://mea.gov.in/bilateral-documents.htm?dtl/7658/Joint+Declaration+on+the+Framework+of+Compr ehensive+Cooperation+between+the+Republic+of+India+and+the+Socialist+Repub lic+of+Vietnam+as+they+enter+the+21st+Century (accessed 3 May 2017)

50 Ibid.

51 Pham, Binh Minh. 2014. 'Building strategic, comprehensive partnerships – Viet Nam's soft power', *Communist Review*, 6 May. http://english.tapchicongsan.org.vn/Home/commentary/2014/800/Building-strategic-comprehensive-partnerships-Viet-Nams-soft-p ower.aspx (accessed 6 June 2019)

52 Ministry of External Affairs (Government of India). 2016. 'Joint Statement between India and Vietnam during the visit of Prime Minister to Vietnam', 3 September. https://www.mea.gov.in/bilateral-documents.htm?dtl/27362 (accessed 26 December 2018)

53 Ministry of External Affairs (Government of India). 2018. 'India–Vietnam Joint Statement during State Visit of President to Vietnam', 21 November. https://www.mea.gov.in/bilateral-documents.htm?dtl/30615/IndiaVietnam_Joint_Statement_during_State_Vis it_of_President_to_Vietnam (accessed 24 December 2018)

54 'Vietnam–China Joint Declaration' (in Vietnamese). 2008. Thanh Nien, 2 June. http://www.thanhnien.com.vn/chinh-tri-xa-hoi/tuyen-bo-chung-viet-nam-trung-quoc-198423. html (accessed 3 May 2017)

55 The White House. 2013. 'Joint Statement by President Barack Obama of the United States of America and President Truong Tan Sang of the Socialist Republic of Vietnam', 25 July. https://obamawhitehouse.archives.gov/the-press-office/2013/07/25/joint-statem ent-president-barack-obama-united-states-america-and-preside (accessed 3 May 2017)

56 Ministry of External Affairs (Government of India). 2014. 'Joint Statement on the State Visit of Prime Minister of the Socialist Republic of Vietnam to India', 27–28 October. http://www.mea.gov.in/bilateral-documents.htm?dtl/24142/Joint_Statement_on_the_Sta te_Visit_of_Prime_Minister_of_the_Socialist_Republic_of_Vietnam_to_India_October_ 2728_2014 (accessed 3 May 2017)

57 Ministry of External Affairs (Government of India). 2014. 'Statement to the Media by President on return from Vietnam', 17 September. https://www.mea.gov.in/Sp eeches-Statements.htm?dtl/24010/Statement_to_the_Media_by_President_on_return_ from_Vietnam_17th_September_2014 (accessed 5 May 2017)

58 Ministry of Foreign Affairs (Socialist Republic of Vietnam). 2007. 'Vietnam–India Joint Declaration on Strategic Partnership', 6 July. http://www.mofa.gov.vn/en/nr040807104143/ nr040807105001/ns070709164916#IhrFZb14XT4F (accessed 5 May 2017)

59 Ministry of External Affairs (Government of India). 2018. 'India–Vietnam Joint Statement during State Visit of President to Vietnam', 21 November. https://www.mea.gov.in/bilateral-documents.htm?dtl/30615/IndiaVietnam_Joint_Statement_ during_State_Visit_of_President_to_Vietnam (accessed 24 December 2018)

60 Ministry of External Affairs (Government of India). 2013. 'Indian Prime Minister's Statement to the media during state visit of General Secretary of the Communist Party of Vietnam', 20 November. http://mea.gov.in/Speeches-Statements.htm?dtl/ 22509/Prime_Ministers_Statement_to_the_Media_during_the_State_Visit_of_Genera l_Secretary_of_the_Communist_Party_of_Vietnam (accessed 5 May 2017); 'Joint Statement between India and Vietnam during the visit of Prime Minister to Viet-nam', 3 September 2016. http://www.mea.gov.in/bilateral-documents.htm?dtl/27362/ Joint_Statement_between_India_and_Vietnam_during_the_visit_of_Prime_Minister_ to_Vietnam (accessed 5 May 2017)

61 Bhasin, Avtar Singh. 2013. *India's Foreign Relations – 2012 Documents*, New Delhi: Geetika Publishers.

62 Ministry of External Affairs (Government of India). 2011. 'Incident involving INS Airavat in South China Sea', 1 September. http://www.mea.gov.in/media-briefings.

htm?dtl/3040/Incident+involving+INS+Airavat+in+South+China+Sea (accessed 8 May 2017)

63 'China objects to oil hunt, India says back off'. 2011. *Hindustan Times*, 15 September. https://www.hindustantimes.com/delhi-news/china-objects-to-oil-hunt-india-says-back-off/story-4B02pRQG4tzY1N3Px3fzUJ.html (accessed 26 December 2018)

64 Kumar, Vinay. 2012. 'We'll Send Force to Protect Our Interests in South China Sea, Says Navy Chief', *The Hindu*, 3 December. https://www.thehindu.com/news/international/We%E2%80%99ll-send-force-to-protect-our-interests-in-South-China-Sea-says-Navy-chief/article12433224.ece (accessed 8 May 2017)

65 Singh, Manmohan. 2013. 'Speech at the Banquet Hosted in the Honour of the General Secretary of the Communist Party of Vietnam', 20 November. http://pib.nic.in/newsite/PrintRelease.aspx?relid=100749 (accessed 8 May 2017)

66 Ministry of External Affairs (Government of India). 2011. 'Joint Statement on the Occasion of the Visit of the President of Vietnam', 12 October. https://www.mea.gov.in/bilateral-documents.htm?dtl/5341/Joint_Statement_ (accessed 10 May 2017)

67 Ministry of External Affairs (Government of India). 2018. 'India–Vietnam Joint Statement during State Visit of President to Vietnam', 21 November. https://www.mea.gov.in/bilateral-documents.htm?dtl/30615/IndiaVietnam_Joint_Statement_during_State_Visit_of_President_to_Vietnam (accessed 24 December 2018)

5 Enhancing strategic understanding and developing defence cooperation

One of the important aspects of India–Vietnam ties has been the fruitful development of their relationship in the defence domain. However, though many strategic thinkers have analysed this defence cooperation from the prism of anti-China cooperation, many have not noticed the fact that the two countries were overly dependent on Russian systems, and were even trained on erstwhile Soviet Union platforms. The mainstays of their armed forces have been erstwhile Soviet Union, and subsequently Russian military equipment and weapon systems. This was, to a large extent, facilitated because of the friendly prices offered to both countries, as well as the political understanding which developed between the major arms supplier – the former Soviet Union – and the two consumers of those weapon systems. Identical to the India–Vietnam relationship, the India–Malaysia defence relationship also developed because of the common Soviet/Russian systems.

The other aspect of this growing partnership with the erstwhile Soviet Union and now Russia was the communist regime, which was more in sync with the socialist welfare model adopted by Jawaharlal Nehru. The unification of North and South Vietnam under Ho Chi Minh was strongly endorsed by both the Soviet Union and China. However, differences of ideology and the Chinese aggression against Vietnam in 1979 subsequently dispelled the myth of communist unity. The mistrust between China and Vietnam grew, and the detente between the US and China between 1975 and 1979 showed that even adversaries can become friends because of geopolitical compulsions. These global changes became the foundation for developing a strategic understanding between India and Vietnam.

Building strategic understanding

As part of its Look East policy, India undertook the initiative in defence diplomacy to engage Southeast Asia, Oceania, and East Asian countries. During the period of 1991–2018, India has signed Memoranda of Understanding (MoU) on defence cooperation, or defence cooperation agreements, with more than ten countries across the region including Indonesia, Myanmar, Laos, Singapore, Australia, Japan, Vietnam, Malaysia, and Korea. During this period, under its defence diplomacy, India proactively engaged the countries of East and Southeast Asia in official high-level military interactions; liaison visits of naval ships; training of defence personnel; selective offering of courses in Higher Command courses; exchanges between officer training academies; and even limited non-lethal weapons exports at convenient prices or on a deferred payment schedule. In common parlance, defence exports (because of the commercial nature of the transactions) are not included as an element of defence diplomacy. However, defence equipment and weapons exports at 'friendly prices', 'Lines of Credit' or 'flexible payment' options make exports an important element of defence diplomacy.[1]

India has projected itself as a benign power in Asia, and explored complementarities with its extended neighbourhood nations. There has been a debate over whether India should expand its global role and act as an interventionist power in cases of localized conflict, where its interests are getting hampered. However, India's intervention in Sri Lanka under the Indian Peace Keeping Force (IPKF) had come under domestic criticism because of the loss of more than 1200 personnel in an asymmetric conflict. Therefore, during the Iraq war when the US asked for military deployment, the Parliament of India voted against the proposal. In light of this historical baggage, any military interventionist role by India is carefully scrutinized.

The military modernization of China and the possible role of India in future world order has been discussed. This needs to be evaluated in the context of changing dynamics and fluid responses to the rise of China. For a large number of nations in East and Southeast Asia, China is a challenge but none of the countries is willing to jeopardize its ties with the country, nor risk reducing its trade and investment relations. Further, Southeast Asian nations are keen on countering assertive China, but are not willing to evict China from a dialogue partnership status, nor are keen to accuse China of aggravating tensions, however strong the statements might be in ASEAN and its related forums. Statecraft takes precedence over rhetoric. There have been increasing references to India playing a bigger and active role.

Defence relations between India and Vietnam have become important against the backdrop of the Sanya submarine base and India's security concerns *vis-à-vis* China as the most likely area for the deployment of Chinese nuclear submarines would be the Indian Ocean as well as the East China Sea.[2] According to K Subramanyam, 'We have a large stake in ensuring that the pressure is contained. That has been our basic policy from the fifties. The only country that can do this is Vietnam, the most capable nation of the region. That is why where the strategic interests of India and Vietnam coincide.'[3] Defence diplomacy helps in forging 'sustained defence cooperative structures, in order to construct safe strategic spaces and bring about coordination and cooperation in a defence relationship which acts as a soft deterrent against possible aggressor or adversary.'[4]

The defence cooperation between the two countries pre-dates India's Look East policy. India's defence ties with Vietnam were a result of a similar policy

68   Strategic understanding and defence cooperation

of engagement with Southeast Asian nations. The bilateral understanding developed with bilateral training arrangements and visits. The great camaraderie between the political leaderships was an additional catalyst. The major turnaround in relations came due to the bitter experience of the two countries with regard to China in 1962 and 1979 respectively. In 1980, India inaugurated its military attaché office in Vietnam. Vietnam opened its military attaché office in Delhi in 1985. In April 1994, during a visit to Vietnam by the Minister for Power, N K P Salve, India was stated to have offered defence technology to Hanoi.[5] Vietnam acknowledged the offer, and thereafter, during the course of Prime Minister P V Narsimha Rao's visit to Vietnam in 1994, a protocol on defence cooperation was signed. This was one of the earliest protocols ever signed with a Southeast Asian nation. Consequently, Vietnam reached an agreement with Hindustan Aeronautics to overhaul the engines on the MiG-21 aircrafts operated by Vietnamese Air Force. In May 1995, deputy defence minister Lieutenant General Dao Dinh Luyen led a Vietnamese military delegation to India. The delegation toured military installations at Hyderabad, Chennai, Bangalore, Goa, Nasik and Pune.[6]

Indian defence personnel had been paying visits to Vietnam after the Cambodian crisis, so as to learn their military tactics and guerrilla warfare techniques. In the aftermath of the Cold War, there was cooperation with regard to the training of Vietnamese military officers in India, and also high-level military delegation visits between the two countries. In the year 2000, the Indian defence minister signed a Protocol on Defence Cooperation which encapsulated the areas of institutional set-up for dialogue between the two defence ministers; the sharing of strategic perceptions and intelligence sharing; naval exercises between the two countries and coordinated patrols by the Vietnamese Sea Police and Indian Coast Guard; repair programmes for Vietnamese Air Force fighter planes, and, finally, the training of Vietnamese Air Force pilots by the Indian Air Force.[7] New Delhi also agreed to help refurbish the Vietnamese air force, providing MiG-21s with new avionics and radar systems to integrate with onboard Russian missiles, including the R-77 AMRAAMSKI and the R-27 missiles used in dogfighting, and to help Vietnam set up a domestic arms industry to manufacture small and medium weapons and certain kinds of ordnance.[8]

In December 2007, the then Indian Defence Minister A K Anthony visited Hanoi and signed a Memorandum of Understanding (MoU) with his counterpart, General Phung Quang Thanh, in which cooperation in national defence, the army, the navy, the air force and training was included. The consultation mechanism in national defence has been organized annually at a deputy ministerial level, which is known as the 'Defence Security Dialogue'. With the passage of time the relationship has deepened and intensified in the defence and security domain. India agreed to transfer 5,000 naval parts belonging to the Petya class ships to Vietnam to make many of its ageing vessels operational. The Indian delegation also visited defence industries in Ho Chi Minh City. A Joint Working Group was also mooted for facilitating the realization of the MoU.[9] In June 2005, the Indian Navy provided 150 tons of warship machinery and other accessories worth US$ 10 million to the Vietnamese Navy. The Ordnance Factory Board also offered materials for turrets, and negotiations were initiated with regard to TNT explosives. The Indian and Vietnamese Navy have been working on setting up a satellite imagery station in Vietnam worth US$ 0.5 million, which is now in its final stages. The Vietnamese defence industry has signed a multimillion dollar contract with the Indian defence industry for the supply of small range missiles, large number of batteries, aerial photography films and aircraft tyres.[10] However, despite all these initiatives, the strategic dialogue was limited from both sides. The reasons were the low level of arms trade between the two countries and their defence objectives being of a different magnitude. For Vietnam, even though the border issues with China were resolved, the maritime borders in certain sections still needed to be agreed. Pakistan and China, the two nuclear powers in India's neighbourhood and India's large maritime border in the Indian Ocean, have been cited as reasons for the country's increasing defence expenditure. However, with both India and Vietnam keen on the modernisation of their respective navies and to address emerging maritime challenges, they have intensified interaction on maritime issues.

In the decade since Vietnam and India established their strategic partnership (2007), defence cooperation between the two countries has achieved relatively steady progress, and has been elevated to become a major component in Vietnam–India strategic relations. Meanwhile, the strategic environment and realities in the Indo-Pacific region changed dramatically. This has been seen from both a positive and a negative perspective. India's 'Enhanced Look East Policy' (now known as the Act East policy),[11] and Vietnam's growing perception of the Indian role in regional security, have resonated in policy circles. In the context of the strategic partnership, defence relations between the two countries have gained a thrusting momentum from the point of view of not only as a traditional good friendship, but also having an identical perspective on global challenges.

Vietnam's approach towards India

Vietnam defence white papers which have been released since the year 2000 have indicated the role and importance of India. This was not articulated in the defence white paper of 2009, but it was much more defined in the subsequent defence white papers. This can be explained by two major reasons: the rapid economic growth of Vietnam, which was complemented by the increasing role of India in the Southeast Asian theatre; and, secondly, the increasing Chinese assertiveness in its neighbourhood, which prompted Vietnam to look for strategic partners. In the first defence white paper released in 2004, Vietnam did not make any reference to India, and instead referred to 'cooperation and assistance of friendly countries as well as all likeminded countries striving for peace, independence and development in the region'.[12] However, in the 2009 defence white paper it stated:

70 Strategic understanding and defence cooperation

> Vietnam attaches importance to expanding defence dialogues with relevant countries, enabling all parties to grasp each other's viewpoints, creating the opportunity for solving issues relating to the interests of all parties. Vietnam has conducted frequent defence dialogues at various levels with other ASEAN member countries, and the other countries such as China, Russia, the United States, Japan, France, and India and so on.[13]

The Vietnam government focussed on increasing its investments in science and technology. This was meant to augment the scientific and technological acumen of the Vietnamese national defence forces, so that they could better prepare for high-tech warfare. Apart from the national defence academy, 'Vietnam has the institutes of military strategy, military science and technology, military history and the institute for defence international relations'.[14] In the defence domain, the number of visits that the Vietnamese delegation and Indian delegation undertook to the other's country was much higher than visits to and from other ASEAN countries. This emphasizes the fact that there was increasing defence and strategic convergence between the two countries.

Defence diplomacy and military cooperation

India and Vietnam had co-chaired the Expert Working Group on Humanitarian Mine Actions in the ADMM+ forum. Four Indian Naval ships, which included the indigenously built stealth frigate INS Satpura and fleet tanker INS Shakti, with a complement of around 1200 officers and sailors visited Da Nang on 6–10 June 2013. INS Shivalik, a stealth multi-role frigate, visited Hai Phong port on 5–8 August 2014, and the Indian Coast Guard vessel Samudra Pehredar visited Da Nang port on 14–16 October 2013.[15] Vietnam has conveyed it is interested in the purchase of Brahmos missiles. Some technical issues related to the possible exports of Brahmos to Vietnam still continue. India's successful entry into the elite Missile Technology Control Regime (MTCR) club[16] has facilitated India's missile export to third world countries, but end user agreements and the protection of technology need to be sorted between India, Vietnam and Russia. A US$ 100 million LoC agreement was signed in September 2014 for defence procurement. As part of a capacity-building exercise, India set up the Vietnam–India Centre for English Language Training in Danang.[17] The first Vietnam–India defence industry workshop was held in Hanoi on 8–10 July 2014. The Defence Industry Community from India and Vietnam attended and exchanged views, showed their capabilities and explored methods of cooperation. Colonel General Nguyen Chi Vinh, the Vietnamese Deputy Defence Minister, urged defence-related enterprises in Vietnam and India to make recommendations to the two ministries of defence. This was expected to support the two governments to build mechanisms for developing co-operation in the defence industry, helping businesses engage deeply and more effectively within the framework of Vietnam–India defence co-operation. In India, a new proposal for the defence industrial policy was tabled during the defence industry workshop. It raised hopes for both sides to realize their potential.

The Vietnamese Defence Minister General Phung Quang Thanh visited India on 23–26 May 2015, during which a five-year joint vision statement for the period of 2015–2020 on defence cooperation and an MoU on cooperation between the coast guards and sea police of the two countries were signed. The Indian Armed Forces were engaged with the capacity building of the Vietnamese Armed Forces, particularly the Navy. The areas of focus were training; repairs and maintenance support; exchanges between think tanks; study tours and ship visits.[18]

Vietnam embarked on military modernization with the induction of two smart frigates, six kilo class submarines, and one nearly full squadron of Sukhoi-30 MKV aircrafts. Considering these new acquisitions, India becomes the natural choice for training and maintenance assistance because of its experience in maintaining Russian aircraft and military equipment. India has been accorded the docking facility in Nha Trang and also in Cam Ranh Bay along with all other navies. India's Indo-Pacific approach might be reflected by liaison visits and docking rights in Vietnam ports. Moreover, Vietnam has been seeking technical expertise from India in e-governance and network centric warfare, to reduce its force strength and for better management of resources. However, it is an accepted fact that the two nations should work towards building a partnership not only in terms of defence, but also in search and rescue missions, as well as humanitarian assistance. There is still lot of potential in developing counter strategies against non-traditional security threats, like food security, water security, and pandemics. These affect the billions and therefore should be accorded priority in terms of mutual cooperation.

The Vietnamese Defence Minister General Ngo Xuan Lich visited India on 4–6 December 2015 to undertake wide ranging discussions with the then Indian Defence Minister Manohar Parrikar on issues related to the training of the Sukhoi pilots, technicians and maintenance assistance for Vietnamese Sukhoi-30 MKV fighter planes; aerospace cooperation, and, lastly, live-firing exercises for the Sukhoi pilots in Indian firing ranges. The last request, which was specifically made by the Vietnamese Defence Minister, was with regard to the training of Vietnamese pilots in short take offs and arrestor wire landing systems.

Training of Vietnamese pilots

The then Indian Defence Minister Manohar Parikkar had agreed on the permanent training facility for the Vietnamese pilots to train to operate Sukhoi-30 MKV aircraft. The configuration of a Vietnamese Sukhoi is slightly different to the Indian Sukhois, as the Indian Sukhois have been improvised to carry heavy weapons, and the Vietnamese Sukhois are slightly lighter as they were not configured for long-range weapon systems. However, the Indian air force would study the complexities of the Vietnamese Sukhois so that proper training could be imparted to the Vietnamese air force officers. The team would study the Vietnamese training facilities, as well as gain a general understanding of their systems. India needs to undertake an orientation programme for Vietnamese

72 Strategic understanding and defence cooperation

Air force officers, particularly Vietnamese trainers, to understand operational aspects. Meanwhile, Vietnam had already started English language training for its officers so that they could be sent to India. Subsequently, Vietnamese technicians could be given regular training in maintenance and operations at the Pune Airbase. They would also be given proper training about the standard operating procedures and learn to check mechanisms so as to keep the aircraft in operational readiness. Subsequently, with mutual consent, Vietnamese officers might be provided with live-firing exercises on Indian firing ranges.

Cooperation in aerospace

One of the important elements of cooperation is in aerospace. The benefit of aerospace cooperation is that it also has a civilian aspect, in terms of geospatial mapping and undertaking operations for the mapping of agricultural land and forest areas. The collaboration in geospatial mapping and hydrographic surveys was accepted by the Vietnamese side. This includes setting up an observation facility in one more coastal region in Vietnam, apart from the Danang, so as to monitor developments in the South China Sea as well as Hainan Island. This facility would utilize Nano satellites and atmospheric balloons to collect data related to the illegal and inimical activities in the region. The whole process would be coordinated and controlled by India, and Vietnamese officers would be given an operational, hands-on experience to help them understand the dynamics of the system . The network integration of the systems would be done by Indian professionals using the high-end Linux-based systems so as to reduce the possibility of any Chinese hacking.

Short take-off and landing operations

India has been operating short take-offs and arrester-wire landings in its naval airports in Kochi and Goa. Incidentally, the Kochi Naval air base is out of bounds for civilian aircraft, but in the Goa facility, particularly the use of the inclined airstrip, is open to both civilian and naval aircraft for training purposes. As a result of this, the facility in Goa, despite being very advanced, does not have a foolproof security system. India has been conducting short take-offs and landings on its MiG-29 K series aircrafts, simulating the aircraft carrier Vikramaditya. Vietnamese pilots can be trained for short take offs and landings in this facility.

Rear Admiral Pham Hoai Nam of the Vietnamese navy, during his visit to India (February 2016) for the International Maritime Fleet review, had met the Indian Naval Chief Robin Dhowan, and requested assistance in technical military training; maintenance of ordnance onboard ships and submarines; foreign language training for Vietnam's sailors, and naval ship reparation, with a particular emphasis on corrosion protection, onboard sonar systems, radar and electronic warfare training. India felt the need to cooperate with Vietnam in building operational logistics capacity, maintenance of onboard ordnance, and electronic warfare. The defence ministers' dialogue between the two countries addressed issues related to naval cooperation whereby India could assist in training the Vietnamese navy crew, both combat and technical personnel, and in training the Vietnamese support staff and maintenance engineers for warship repairs. Cooperation might also be explored in integrating modern weapons; small naval ship-building, particularly fast attack crafts; hovercraft, and interceptor boats.

It has been stated through joint statements and speeches of leaders that Vietnam has acknowledged India's defence capabilities, which includes weapon and systems integration; defence R&D; maintenance and support for weaponry of Russian origin; adaptation of Western defence technologies; integrated network modules, and developing advanced systems for both strategic and tactical deterrence. With expertise in using advance weapons from various sources, i.e. Russia, the US, the UK, and Israel, Indian defence establishments have been operating sophisticated machines and, under the Vietnam training policy adopted by India, Vietnam could access these invaluable capabilities to build a stronger force for itself. In the defence industry, Vietnam and India could focus on upgrading and integrating a life-cycle extension for equipment and combat systems; complementing old and new advanced combat assets, and technology transferring/acquisition of newly developed systems, such as Brahmos, Akash, Tejas, and AJT Hawk Trainers (particularly those fitted with indigenous engines).[19]

With the Vietnam Communist Party's multi-faceted diplomacy, the Vietnamese government has been proactively engaged in the international arena, making concrete contributions to world peace and security. As a country well-known for its expertise and contributions to peacekeeping operations (PKO), India has helped Vietnam in training personnel, and building their capabilities for their newly raised peacekeeping contingent, through exchanges of experience at both staff and field levels, and establishing English training institutes. Vietnam has requested India's help in the technical training of support staff; building capacities in aerial surveillance systems; integrating electronic warfare systems, and maintenance of on-board systems, including ordnance such as missiles and guns. 'Vietnam looks forward to sustained cooperation between the two countries under the rubric of Declaration on Vision for Indo-Vietnam Defence Relations 2015–2020.'[20]

During the visit of Prime Minster Modi to Vietnam the Lines of Credit has been enhanced, to the tune of US$ 500 million, and this is meant to promote the Indian defence industry, including those in the public sector as well as the private sector. Vietnam may consider procuring the following items and equipment from the Indian Defence Industry:

1 Pyrotechnic signalling devices and laser-guided munitions. These are being produced in the defence factory located near Pune. Pyrotechnic signalling devices would be a useful addition in the case of Vietnamese islands located in the South China Sea.

74   Strategic understanding and defence cooperation

2 Transporter, Erector and Launcher vehicles – India has been sourcing its requirements from both Tata and Ashok Leyland. These vehicles can be used for Brahmos.
3 Tata Motors high-mobility vehicles having 4×4 all-terrain vehicle for armed forces, Armoured Personnel Carriers, light armoured multi-purpose vehicles and light specialist vehicles
4 Import of Akash, ASTRA and Dhanush weapon systems.
5 Dhruv helicopters for both internal security and operational deployment. The advanced version of the Dhruv helicopter is already operational in the army.
6 Installation of the Battle Field Management system and subsequent training of the personnel.
7 Electronic warfare jammer systems. China is getting very active in electronic warfare and this needs serious thought from Vietnam.
8 USHUS-II Submarine sonar systems. This is a very advanced, widely appreciated sonar system developed by Naval Physical and the Oceanographic laboratory of DRDO, and India has installed it on Russian-made submarines.
9 Indian-made Kamov helicopters. The assembly line is already in its completion phase.
10 10 Surface-to-air missile Pichora, which can engage multiple targets with a maximum kill range of 25 kms.

While these are just a few of the items which Vietnam might like to import from India, the two countries can undertake joint ventures in communication, encryption and military grade ruggedized communication systems and Integrated Command and Control systems.

Possibilities for the future

The Joint Declaration on the elevation of the Strategic Partnership to Comprehensive Strategic Partnership between India and Vietnam has been endorsed by Prime Minister Modi during his visit in September 2016. The Line of Credit, which was announced to be US$ 100 million, has been enhanced to US$ 500 million, giving Vietnam the much-needed financial assistance to allow it to upgrade its weapons and the necessary infrastructure. In fact, Vietnam is one of the few nations which have received such generous financial support from India. The lines of credit need to roll over, so that the in case of non-utilization or less utilization, they can be carried over to next year. This will help Vietnam in planning its defence procurement (big ticket purchases) when the Lines of Credit corpus enlarges. Further, after a gap of two years, this line of credit could be reviewed.

The Defence Intelligence Cooperation Agreement has been agreed, and the different aspect of the cooperation has been looked into. The three wings of the Indian Defence forces have been asked to submit related proposals so that extensive discussions can be undertaken. This would provide the necessary platform for long term defence cooperation between the two countries. An MoU on Cooperation in UN Peacekeeping has been stressed by Vietnam, and India also felt it was a good initiative to have a regular arrangement as both countries in the future might have to cooperate under UN auspices in certain conflict zones. A lack of coordination has created a few unpleasant situations with select Southeast Asian countries, including Malaysia and the Philippines. PM Modi also discussed developments in the South China Sea and this would also form part of the Joint Declaration made between the two sides.

India and Vietnam have been working on a Long Term Spares Supply Agreement with Russia. This would help in generating demand so that sufficient orders can keep the supply line working. Indian technical experts would prepare a curriculum and develop the necessary expertise in maintenance. Terrestrial radar systems are another area for cooperation. Radar developed by DRDO, particularly vehicle-mounted Rajendra I radar systems, are good for coastal and island protection. This can be offered by India on a trial basis to determine their effectiveness and its response mechanism when integrated with missile systems.

Defence cooperation could be expanded to include more logistics support exercises. This would involve coordinated response and assistance. India and Vietnam should undertake regular Naval exercises and live-firing exercises. Between Vietnam and India, air force cooperation has been slightly undermined. This needs to be further enhanced. The two countries can work on a coordinated response mechanism in case of natural disasters and maritime emergencies like tsunamis. Vietnam, Japan and India can start a trilateral discussion forum which would involve the commercial, economic and defence aspects of trilateral cooperation. There have been proposals for increased interaction between the Vietnamese Sea Police and Indian Coastguard officials.

Shipbuilding can be one of the major areas for cooperation in defence, as well as the civilian sector. This can be explored under the Make in India initiative. The private shipyards in India, which are managed by the companies such as Reliance, L&T and Adani, can enter into a joint venture with the Vietnamese public and private companies to create ships for both civilian use and naval ships for the two countries. Already, L&T has received orders from Vietnam for the supply of four coastal patrol boats, while Garden Reach Shipbuilders (a public sector undertaking) has won the tender for supplying naval ships to the Philippines navy. The partnership between shipbuilding companies would help the two countries. However, to facilitate such a partnership, the Indian government would have to give tax concessions and other incentives to the private Indian and Vietnamese companies. The two countries could work in defence infrastructure development. India and Vietnam could explore joint enterprise in defence R&D, shipbuilding (LNG carriers) and the IT sector. In the IT sector, the hardware and software strengths of both countries can be combined. The fact that India now allows FDI of up to 75 per cent in the defence sector is a lucrative proposition to many defence contractors. Vietnam

76 Strategic understanding and defence cooperation

can sign an investment protection agreement with India to allow for more private sector investment. The two countries can engage private ship builders in developing ships, particularly frigates and corvettes, for the navies of both countries. Vietnam can offer to set up a small-arms manufacturing unit, including missiles, with assistance from India. The other areas of cooperation which could be proposed include manufacturing of military trucks and armoured personnel carriers.

Notes

1 Jha, Pankaj K. 2011. 'India's defence diplomacy in Southeast Asia', *Journal of Defence Studies*, 5(1): 47–48.
2 Reddy, C Ravindranatha. 2009. *India and Vietnam: Era of Friendship and Cooperation 1947–1991*. Chennai: Emerald Publishers: 36
3 Loc. cit.
4 Jha, 2011: 47
5 Storey, Ian and Thayer, Carlyle A. 2001. 'Cam Ranh Bay: Past Imperfect, Future Conditional', *Contemporary Southeast Asia*, 23(3): 467
6 Ibid.: 467
7 'The interference and support that China provided to Cambodia was not at the same level as cooperation between China and Pakistan'. Kapila, Subhash. 2007. India–Vietnam Strategic Partnership: The Convergence of Interests, Paper No. 177, South Asia Analysis Group. http://www.saag.org/papers2/paper177.htm (accessed 23 February 2017)
8 Storey and Thayer, 2001: 468
9 Jha, Pankaj K. 2008. 'India–Vietnam Relations: Need for Enhanced Cooperation', *Strategic Analysis*, 32(6): 1089–1090
10 Nguyen, Thang Anh. 2007. 'Enhancing Indo-Vietnam Defence Cooperation: Vietnamese Perspective', Paper Presentation at Joint USI–IDIR Seminar, Delhi, 4 October
11 Enhanced Look East Policy term was used by the UPA-II government just before the end of its term. This was also reflected in the Annual Report of the Ministry of External Affairs.
12 Defence White Paper. 2004. 'Vietnam's National Defense in the Early Years of the 21st Century', Ministry of National Defence, Socialist Republic of Vietnam, Hanoi: 14
13 Defence White Paper. 2009. 'Vietnam National Defence', Ministry of National Defence, Socialist Republic of Vietnam, Hanoi: 25
14 Dass, Nupur. 2018. Vietnamese Defence White Paper 2009, Unpublished Essay: 2
15 Eye on China: India and Vietnam Advance Their Strategic Partnership. http://econom ictimes.indiatimes.com/news/defence/eye-on-china-india-and-vietnam-advance-their-str ategic-partnership/articleshow/49002738.cms (accessed 25 May 2018)
16 Taking on China, India's Defence Ties With Vietnam Needs To Be Lauded. http:// www.firstpost.com/world/taking-on-china-indias-defence-ties-with-vietnam-needs-to-be-lauded-2264902.html (accessed 29 May 2018)
17 Eye on China: India and Vietnam Advance Their Strategic Partnership. http:// economictimes.indiatimes.com/news/defence/eye-on-china-india-and-vietnam-adva nce-their-strategic-partnership/articleshow/49002738.cms (accessed 25 May 2018)
18 Eye on China: India and Vietnam Advance Their Strategic Partnership. http://econom ictimes.indiatimes.com/news/defence/eye-on-china-india-and-vietnam-advance-their-str ategic-partnership/articleshow/49002738.cms (accessed 25 May 2018)
19 Author's interview with Defence Attaché of Vietnam to India on 24 September 2017.
20 India and Vietnam sign a Joint Vision Statement on defence cooperation, 11 July 2018. https://economictimes.indiatimes.com/news/defence/india-vietnam-sign-a-joint-vision-statement-on-defence-cooperation/articleshow/47427055.cms?from=mdr

6 Ensuring peace, stability and security in the South China Sea

The complicated situation in the South China Sea has been pushed to a new level since China undertook assertive naval activities and used fishermen militia to define its maritime zone in the SCS. Since 2013, China has been constructing artificial islands on the Spratly Islands and constructing military facilities on the Paracels. Recently, China has deployed long-range surface-to-air missile launchers and fighter jets on the Woody Island in the Paracels claimed by Vietnam. It is believed the Chinese have also installed radar facilities on artificial islands in the Spratly Islands. China has also recently constructed military infrastructures and hardware, and deployed defence systems, such as surface-to-air missiles and anti-diver rocket launchers,[1] to the artificial islands, regardless of the Permanent Court of Arbitration (PCA) rulings on 12 July 2016. The ruling clarified that China's claims in the South China Sea in the scope of nine-dash line map has no basis. China's recent moves confirm that it is making efforts to complete an anti-access/access denial (A2/AD) strategy to control the Sea Lines of Communication (SLOCs) which poses a threat to the freedom of navigation and over-flights in the South China Sea. Besides the challenges posed by China's activities of militarization, there are also threats of insecurity in the South China Sea, as the sea is one of the places where there has been a large amount of piracy, and armed robbery against ships has taken place for years. There is also the possibility of terrorist attacks in the South China Sea, after an attempt to attack Singapore in August 2016 and the current situation in Marawi of the Philippines. In July 2019, China conducted survey activities in Vietnamese waters (EEZ) which was condemned by the US and other major powers.

Vietnam and India depend heavily on seaborne trade and other economic activities in the South China Sea. In such context, the threats outlined above have posed great challenges to economies heavily dependent on SLOCs in the South China Sea. The chapter will highlight the situation regarding the South China Sea disputes, especially China's activities of militarization, the threats of piracy, armed robbery against ships and terrorism in the sea, and evaluate India–Vietnam cooperation in ensuring peace, stability, and security in the South China Sea.

78 *Peace and security in the South China Sea*

The South China Sea disputes

At present, there are two major types of disputes in the South China Sea: territorial disputes over the Paracels and Spratlys, and disputes over sea boundaries and overlapping continental shelves among countries having opposite or adjacent coasts. The Paracel Island dispute gained attention in 1974 when China captured many islands in the Paracels group of islands(belonging to South Vietnam) and tensions escalated in the Spratly Islands after the China–Vietnam naval conflict in 1988.[2] The territorial dispute over the Paracels involves Vietnam and China. Taiwan also claims sovereignty over the Paracels. Vietnam, China (including Taiwan), Brunei Darussalam, Malaysia and the Philippines are all in dispute with one another regarding the Spratlys.

Of the two kinds of disputes, the territorial disputes over the Paracels and Spratlys have been increasingly more complicated and dangerous due to China's assertive actions in the South China Sea, especially since 2009. On 7 May 2009, on the pretext of objecting to Vietnam's submission and the Vietnam–Malaysia Joint Submission on the Outer Limit of the Continental Shelf, China sent the United Nations Secretary General a diplomatic note attached to a map showing its 'cow-tongue line',[3] 'nine-dash line', or 'U-line', in which China declared that:

> China has indisputable sovereignty over the islands in the South China Sea and the adjacent waters, and enjoys sovereign rights and jurisdiction over the relevant water as well as the seabed and subsoil thereof . The above position is consistently held by Chinese Government, and is widely known by the international community.[4]

After China seized the Scarborough Shoal and denied the Filipino's activities of fishing at and within 12 miles of the shoal in and after 2012,[5] the Philippines brought China to the Permanent Court of Arbitration (PCA) in February 2013, under the Annex VII to the 1982 United Nations Convention on the Law of the Sea (UNCLOS). Since the beginning of 2014, the international press has widely reported that China has been conducting land reclamation and construction on six of its seven occupied features in the Spratlys in the South China Sea, transforming the submerged reefs and rocks into fully-fledged islands with airstrips, harbours, and other military and civilian structures.[6] In fact, China's reclamation work in the Spratly Islands appears to have begun as early as September 2013.[7] In 20 months, China has reclaimed 17 times more land than the other claimants combined over the past 40 years, accounting for approximately 95 per cent of all reclaimed land in the Spratly Islands.[8] Up until late 2015, China added over 3,200 acres of land to the seven features it occupies in the Spratlys.[9] In the beginning of 2016, China was also reported to have installed a high frequency radar on the Cuarteron reef in the Spratly islands.[10] CSIS' Asia Maritime Transparency Initiative (AMTI) on 13 December 2016 showed Chinese anti-aircraft guns and anti-missile point defence systems on the Gaven, Hughes,

Johnson, Cuarteron, Fiery Cross, Mischief and Subi reefs.[11] In the Paracels, in February 2016, China deployed surface-to-air missile systems and then sent Shenyang J-11 and Xian JH-7 fighter jets[12] to Woody Island in the Paracels, which China had captured in 1956 and 1974, taken from the control of the government of South Vietnam. Thanks to its military facilities in the Paracels and the Spratlys, it seems that China has completed its strategy of anti-access/access denial (A2/AD). In one of its most dangerous steps, in early July 2019, China test-fired at least one anti-ship missile in the area around the Spratly Islands in the South China Sea.[13] The launch was the first ever taken from one of the artificial structures built by China since the end of 2013.

The PCA's final ruling on the Philippines lawsuit against China was issued on 12 July 2016, but compliance to the ruling was never enforced.[14] China told the head of its navy that they would 'never stop' construction of illegal man-made islands in the South China Sea.[15] Importantly, China on one hand stated that it 'respect[s] and safeguards the freedom of navigation and over-flight in the South China Sea to which all countries are entitled under international law',[16] but it interprets the freedom of navigation under the UNCLOS[17] such that it should be the prerogative of the state which controls the maritime zone and territorial sea.[18] This means that the freedom of navigation (and over-flight) in the South China Sea would be forced to comply with rights and duties regulated by China, as well as respecting Chinese security interests and sovereign rights as stipulated in the Articles of 21 and 58 of the 1982 UNCLOS.[19] In this proposed situation, the actions of freedom of navigation in international waters and Exclusive Economic Zone (EEZ) of other countries in the South China Sea will be interfered with by China to some extent.

Threats of piracy and armed robbery against ships in the South China Sea

Piracy and armed robbery against ships, from the Indian Ocean through the Malacca Straits to the South China Sea, are obvious threats to both India and Vietnam:

> Over 97 per cent of India's trade by volume and 75 per cent by value is sea borne ... the 'direction of trade', nearly 50 per cent of Indian trade is east bound and transits through the Straits of Malacca through which over 60,000 vessels transit annually.[20]

India's trade-to-GDP ratio reached 43 per cent in 2012,[21] while economies in the Asia-Pacific region have increasingly accounted for a larger portion in the total trade of India, from 24 per cent in FY 2002–03 to more than 30 per cent in FY 2009–10.[22] Significantly, India is now interested in building the Mekong–India Economic Corridor, which connects its eastern ports with the Dawei port (Myanmar), through Thailand, Cambodia and Ho Chi Minh City of Vietnam and connects to the South China Sea.

80 *Peace and security in the South China Sea*

According to data given by the World Shipping Council, India and Vietnam have recently been among the top ten exporters-importers of containerized cargo of the world in 2010, 2013 and 2014.[23] Vietnam, for its part, has a long coastline of 3,260 kilometres, and one million square kilometres of exclusive economic zones in the South China Sea and its territorial waters that can be exploited are three times larger than the mainland, offering ideal conditions to develop sea shipping, aquaculture, oil and gas exploitation, and tourism. It is now considering a new strategy to develop a sea-borne economy to help foster economic growth, create more jobs and ensure territorial security.[24] The South China Sea, the Malacca Straits, Indian Ocean and East African Sea were the most affected areas by acts of piracy, attempted acts of piracy, and armed robbery against ships. The total incidents occurred in those seas accounted for 80.3 per cent (106/132), 81.58 per cent (217/266) and 78.2 per cent (237/303) of total incidents reported in the whole world in 1995, 2005 and 2015 respectively. Among those, the attacks reported to have taken place in the Straits of Malacca and the South China Sea were the highest number of incidents in 2015 (134) and 2013 (142).[25] It means that the passage of ships from any countries, including those of India and Vietnam, passing through SLOCs, including those in the South China Sea, could be threatened by the acts and attempted acts of piracy and armed robbery against ships.

Besides that, maritime terrorism is still a significant threat to both Vietnam and India, whose trade heavily depends on the safety and security of the SLOCs. The maritime terrorism actions have decreased in recent years, but the threat of sea-based terrorism aimed against targets on land requires collective efforts to deal with. The '26/11' Mumbai attacks in 2008 and the plot to fire rockets into Singapore's Marine Bay,[26] reported in August 2016, are a dramatic illustration of this threat.

Vietnam–India cooperation in SCS

India's official view on the South China Sea dispute has strategic significance to Vietnam–India political relations: 'India supports freedom of navigation in international waters, including in the South China Sea, and the rights of passage in accordance with accepted principles of international law' was the statement issued in September 2011 after the INS Airavat, which was warned off by the Chinese while it was sailing at a distance of 45 nautical miles from the Vietnamese coast in the South China Sea in July 2011. This was the message that the international community loving peace in general, and Vietnam in particular, needed. India's support to Vietnam in the South China Sea dispute was tested when the former Indian Prime Minister Manmohan Singh, in his speech at the banquet hosted in the honour of the General Secretary of the Communist Party of Vietnam, Nguyen Phu Trong, in November 2013, used the term 'East Sea' to refer to the South China Sea.[27] The two countries stressed the necessity of the early conclusion of a binding code of conduct during the visit of Indian President Ram Nath Kovind to Vietnam in November 2018.[28]

Vietnam–India security cooperation in the South China Sea has made significant achievements, including India's support to Vietnam in the maritime space in the South China Sea, Indian naval ship visits to strategic ports of Vietnam, and the former's assistance to the latter in maritime capacity building.

> Since 2010, there has been a concerted effort at augmenting maritime security cooperation in Southeast Asia. With regular forays by Indian naval ships to the Western Pacific and regular exercises with regional navies, India has displayed a clear commitment to the security of the Southeast Asian littorals.[29]

As a result, in every year since 2000, India's naval ships have paid friendship visits to some of the main ports of Vietnam, such as Dinh Vu (Northern province of Hai Phong), Tien Sa (Central province of Da Nang), Saigon (in Ho Chi Minh city), and Nha Trang (province of Khanh Hoa). The Indian navy was even reported to have been 'perhaps the only foreign navy in recent times to have been given this privilege by the Vietnamese at a port other than Halong Bay, near Hanoi'.[30] The Indian naval ships' frequent visits to Hai Phong port, near Hanoi (Vietnam) signifies mutual understanding. An Indian government official opined, 'the move will give India the key to a sustainable presence in the South China Sea'.[31]

Beside friendship visits, the navies of the two countries have also conducted joint exercises in the South China Sea. 'The Indian navy has been deploying through the South China Sea since 2000, generally twice a year, which has involved its own unilateral practicing, as well as bilateral port calls and exercises with local actors, particularly Vietnam'.[32] The Vietnam–India joint naval exercise took place in the South China Sea on 8 June 2013.[33] In May 2015, the Indian Naval Ships Satpura and Kirch arrived at Cam Ranh Bay in Vietnam on a four-day visit. The visiting ships conducted exercises with the Vietnam People's Navy, aimed at enhancing interoperability in communication, as well as search-and-rescue procedures, following their departure from Cam Ranh Bay.[34] India was likely to be Vietnam's only partner in terms of joint naval exercises until Vietnam and Japan conducted the first ever joint naval exercise in February 2016.[35] In the context of the increasing importance of the Cam Ranh Bay, the Indian navy has established a sustainable maritime presence as its warships have been granted permission to drop anchor and use the port,[36] which was inaugurated as an international port facility capable of receiving foreign warships in 2016.[37]

Besides this, India has been making efforts to support Vietnam in terms of their building naval capacity, including personnel training, upgrading of military equipment, and providing Vietnam with strategic weapons. Vietnam and India signed agreements in 2000 under which training cooperation, among others, was a very focal field, specifically training such as joint naval training; jungle warfare training; counter-insurgency training, and air force pilots training in India. India has also been helping the Vietnamese train submarine

82 *Peace and security in the South China Sea*

operators and pilots. Since the Vietnamese naval force owns modern submarines, including the Kilo-class, the Indian Navy has begun training a significant number of Vietnamese sailors operating submarines for underwater warfare. The 'comprehensive underwater combat operations' training for these Vietnamese sailors was conducted at the Indian Navy's INS Satavahana (Submarine School) in Visakhapatnam.[38]

Indian Defence Minister A K Antony announced in 2007 that India would transfer 5,000 items of naval ship spares belonging to the Petya class of ships to Vietnam. During the visit of the Indian Prime Minister Narendra Modi to Vietnam in September 2016, India and Vietnam signed 12 agreements, including one agreement signed with Larsen & Turbro (L&T), for the utilization of US$ 100 million of the US$ 500 million defence Line of Credit India offered to Vietnam to build patrol boats.[39] The implementation of the US$ 100 million Line of Credit for the building of high-speed patrol vessels for the Vietnamese Border Guards has gained significant progress, while the offer of the US$ 500 million Line of Credit to the defence industry is in the process of accelerating procedures for its approval.[40] Under the agreement, L&T will build high-speed patrol vessels designed in India to combat and protect sea security and sovereignty, and to control illegal activities such as smuggling, as well as engaging in search-and-rescue missions. Importantly, 'L&T will also provide transfer design and technology, as well as supplying equipment and material kits to construct follow-on vessels at a Vietnam shipyard'.[41] The move is very significant because India is the second country which has joint construction of military equipment with Vietnam.

Economically, oil and gas exploration is also an especially important field of cooperation between Vietnam and India.

> On May 19, 1988, ONGC Videsh Ltd (OVL) signed a petroleum sharing contract with Petro Vietnam for three blocks 06, 12E and 19 in Nam Con Son basin, about 370 km offshore of Vietnam ... The exploration efforts of OVL, along with British Petroleum and Petro Vietnam, in South China Sea in 1992 and 1993, led to the discovery of the Lan Do and Lan Tay gas fields. The project, which has reserves of around 58 billion cubic meters, will yield about three billion cubic meters of gas a year.[42]

OVL had acquired two offshore exploration blocks, 127 and 128, in Vietnam's Exclusive Economic Zone (EEZ) in the South China Sea in June 2006 as an operator with 100% stake. 'OVL had already relinquished the block 127 after it failed to find any hydrocarbons there'.[43] In July 2012, OVL 'accepted Vietnam's proposal to stay invested in Block 128 as Hanoi has offered additional data that can help to make future exploration economically feasible and discovering hydrocarbons commercially viable'.[44] In November 2018, India and Vietnam agreed to continue promoting bilateral investment in cooperation projects between the PVN and the ONGC in oil and gas exploration on the continental shelf and EEZ of Vietnam. The two countries also agreed to identify models for

Peace and security in the South China Sea   83

cooperation, including those involving third countries, in their joint projects in the South China Sea.[45] New steps in oil and gas exploration cooperation between the two countries were noted when PVN Vietnam and OVL India signed an agreement on cooperation in new blocks in Vietnam in 2014. In their Joint Statement in 2018, India and Vietnam for the first time identified models for cooperation involving third countries in their oil and gas cooperation projects.[46]

India's oil and gas exploration activities in the South China Sea have strategic implications for both countries and the rights of freedom of navigation (and over-flight) in the South China Sea. As a responsible nation, India is protecting international law by conducting economic activities in blocks granted by Vietnam in the latter's EEZ in conformity with international law, especially the UN Convention on the Law of the Sea. The projects could also be seen as solid evidence asserting that China's nine-dashed line map is not legal, hence China has no right to oppose India, or any other country, in its activities of oil and gas exploration and exploitation granted by Vietnam in its EEZ. India's oil and gas exploration activities in the South China Sea has now been supported by the award of the Permanent Court of Arbitration (PCA) on 12 July 2016 which officially rejected China's claim in the South China Sea.

The cooperation between the two countries in the South China Sea was further affirmed when, in their Joint Statement regarding upgrading the strategic partnership to a comprehensive strategic partnership in 2016, Vietnam and India:

> reiterated their desire and determination to work together to maintain peace, stability, growth and prosperity in Asia and beyond. Noting the Award issued on 12 July 2016 of the Arbitral Tribunal constituted under the Annex VII to the 1982 United Nations Convention on the Law of Sea (UNCLOS), both sides reiterated their support for peace, stability, security, safety and freedom of navigation and over flight, and unimpeded commerce, based on the principles of international law, as reflected notably in the UNCLOS. Both sides also called on all states to resolve disputes through peaceful means without threat or use of force and exercise self-restraint in the conduct of activities that could complicate or escalate disputes affecting peace and stability, respect the diplomatic and legal processes, fully observe the Declaration on the conduct of parties in the South China Sea (DOC) and soon finalize the Code of Conduct (COC). They also recognized that the sea lanes of communication passing through the South China Sea are critical for peace, stability, prosperity and development. Vietnam and India, as State Parties to the UNCLOS, urged all parties to show utmost respect for the UNCLOS, which establishes the international legal order of the seas and oceans.[47]

Obviously, the challenges posed by China's activities of militarization and from the threats of terrorism and acts and attempted acts of piracy and the armed

84 Peace and security in the South China Sea

robbery against ships in the South China Sea have had significant impacts on Vietnam and India, whose seaborne trade plays a very important role in the economic growth of each country. In recent years, Vietnam and India have had closed relations in maintaining and ensuring peace, stability and security in the South China Sea through, notably, the support from India. India has raised its voice to support and protect the solving of disputes through negotiation, in accordance with universally recognized principles of international law, including the 1982 UNCLOS, in the South China Sea. In practice, India has also conducted naval visits to Vietnamese ports, as well as the two countries holding joint activities, such as joint naval exercise. Vietnam and India have also been assertive in continuing their cooperation in oil and gas oil explorations in the Vietnam's EEZ, which is in line with the 1982 UNCLOS, especially after the PCA's rulings on 12 July 2017. The cooperation between India and Vietnam in the South China Sea will be enhanced since, during the visit of Indian President Ram Nath Kovind to Vietnam, India and Vietnam agreed to continue their projects in coordination between ONGC and PVN (Vietnam) in oil and gas exploration on the continental shelf and Exclusive Economic Zone (EEZ) of Vietnam in the South China Sea.[48]

India's approach towards the South China Sea is primarily to manage freedom of navigation, while at the same time to not be intimidated by China, which has been making gestures so as to challenge India's strategic interests in the region. Given the fact that India's exploration activities are in Vietnam's Exclusive Economic Zone, and India was present in Vietnamese waters for exploration activities in late 1980s, any withdrawal from the commercial exploration would be seen as subjugation to China. This act would have domestic repercussion, as well as cause a financial loss for the Indian company ONGC Videsh Limited.

Notes

1 Johnson, Jesse. 2017. 'China deploys anti-diver rocket launchers to man-made island in South China Sea: report', *The Japan Times*, 17 May. https://www.japantimes.co.jp/news/ 2017/05/17/asia-pacific/china-deploys-anti-diver-rocket-launchers-man-made-island-sou th-china-sea-report/#.XCTOGFUzbIV (accessed 4 July 2017)
2 Tran, Cong Truc. 2009. 'Measures for Maintenance of Peace, Stability and Enhancement of Cooperation on the South China Sea', *Proceedings of the International Workshop on The South China Sea: Cooperation for Regional Security and Development*, 26–27 November, Hanoi: 37
3 Diplomatic Academy of Vietnam. 2012. 'Cow-Tongueline – An Irrational Claim', Hanoi: Tri Thuc: 171
4 People's Republic of China. 2009. 'Letter to the Secretary-General of the United Nations', New York: The United Nations, 7 May. http://www.un.org/depts/los/clcs_new/subm issions_files/mysvnm33_09/chn_2009re_mys_vnm_e.pdf (accessed 4 July 2017)
5 Permanent Court of Arbitration. 2015. 'Hearing on Jurisdiction and Admissibility between the Republic of the Philippines and the People's Republic of China'. The Hague: Permanent Court of Arbitration, 13 July: 3
6 Tran, Truong Thuy. 2015. 'Vietnam's Maritime Security Challenges and Responses', *The National Institute for Defense Studies (Japan), Security Outlook of the Asia*

Peace and security in the South China Sea 85

Pacific Countries and Its Implications for the Defense Sector, NIDS Joint Research Series, No. 13: 87

7 Dolven, Ben et al. 2015. 'Chinese Land Reclamation in the South China Sea: Implications and Policy Options', *CRS Report*, 18 June: 13

8 The U.S. Department of Defense. 2015. 'Asia-Pacific Maritime Security Strategy'. Virginia: Department of Defense: 16

9 Office of the Secretary of Defense. 2016. 'Annual Report to Congress: Military and Security Developments Involving the People's Republic of China'. Virginia: Department of Defence, 26 April: 13

10 'China building radar on Spratly isles'. 2016. *The Star Online*, 24 February. https://www.thestar.com.my/news/regional/2016/02/24/china-building-radar-on-spratly-isles-installation-would-significantly-change-the-operational-landsc/ (accessed 4 July 2017)

11 Asia Maritime Transparency Initiative. 2016. 'China's New Spratly Island Defenses', 13 December. https://amti.csis.org/chinas-new-spratly-island-defenses/ (accessed 2 July 2017)

12 Thayer, C A. 2016. 'Background Briefing: South China Sea: China's Plans for Scarborough Shoal', *Thayer Consultancy*, 13 April

13 Lendon, Brad. 2019. 'China tests anti-ship missile in South China Sea, Pentagon says', CNN, 3 July. https://edition.cnn.com/2019/07/03/asia/south-china-sea-missile-test-intl-hnk/index.html (accessed 8 July 2019)

14 McGarry, B. 2016. 'Enforcing an Unenforceable Ruling in the South China Sea', *The Diplomat*, 16 July. https://thediplomat.com/2016/07/enforcing-an-unenforceable-ruling-in-the-south-china-sea/ (accessed 6 July 2017)

15 'China Tells Top US Admiral It Will Never Stop In South China Sea'. 2016. *Asia Maritime Reviews*, 27 July. http://asiamaritime.net/china-tells-top-us-admiral-it-will-never-stop-in-south-china-sea/ (accessed 6 July 2017)

16 Ministry of Foreign Affairs (The People's Republic of China). 2015. 'Vice Foreign Minister Zhang Yesui Makes Stern Representations to US over US Naval Vessel's Entry into Waters near Relevant Islands and Reefs of China's Nansha Islands', 27 October. http://www.fmprc.gov.cn/mfa_eng/wjbxw/t1310069.shtml (accessed 6 July 2017)

17 Permanent Court of Arbitration. 2016. 'PCA Case Nº 2013–19 in the Matter of the South China Sea Arbitration between the Republic of the Philippines and the People's Republic of China'. The Hague: Permanent Court of Arbitration, 12 July

18 Yang, Zewei. 2012. 'The Freedom of Navigation in the South China Sea: An Ideal or a Reality?' *Beijing Law Review*, 3(3): 40

19 Loc. cit.

20 Sakhuja, Vijay. 2012. 'Strategic Dimensions of India's Look East Policy', in Amar Nath (ed.), *Two Decades of India's Look East Policy*. New Delhi: Manohar: 225

21 The World Bank. 2013. 'Merchandise Trade (% of GDP)'. http://data.worldbank.org/indicator/TG.VAL.TOTL.GD.ZS (accessed 9 July 2017)

22 Department of Commerce (Ministry of Commerce and Industry, Government of India). India Export-Import Data Bank: Version 6.0 – Tradestat. http://commerce.nic.in/eidb/default.asp (accessed 9 July 2017)

23 World Shipping Council. 2018. *Trade Statistics*. http://www.worldshipping.org/about-the-industry/global-trade/trade-statistics (accessed 9 July 2017)

24 Arno, Maierbrugger. 2014. 'Vietnam To Expand Sea-Borne Economy', *Investvine*, 7 June. http://investvine.com/vietnam-to-expand-sea-borne-economy/ (accessed 9 July 2017)

25 Vo, Xuan Vinh. 2017. 'Vietnam–India Maritime Cooperation', *Maritime Affairs*, Issue 2. 69

26 Arshad, Arline. 2016. 'Batam terror suspects who planned attack on Singapore trained on public field to avoid suspicion', *The Straits Times*, 11 August. https://www.straitstimes.com/asia/se-asia/batam-terror-suspects-flown-to-jakarta-for-police-probe (accessed 11 July 2017)

27 Singh, Manmohan. 2013. 'Speech at the banquet hosted in honour of the General Secretary of the Communist Party of Vietnam', 20 November. https://www.mea.gov.

86 *Peace and security in the South China Sea*

in/Speeches-Statements.htm?dtl/22511/Prime_Ministers_speech_at_the_banquet_host ed_in_the_honour_of_the_General_Secretary_of_the_Communist_Party_of_Vietnam (accessed 11 July 2017)

28 Ministry of External Affairs (Government of India). 2018. 'India–Vietnam Joint Statement during State Visit of President to Vietnam', 21 November. https://www.mea.gov. in/bilateral-documents.htm?dtl/30615/IndiaVietnam_Joint_Statement_during_State_Vis it_of_President_to_Vietnam (accessed 8 July 2019)

29 Singh, Abhijit. 2016. 'The Indian Navy's Security Role in Littoral Asia', in Namrata Goswami (ed.), *India's Approach to Asia: Strategy, Geopolitics and Responsibility*, Delhi: Pentagon Press: 311–312

30 Ghoshal, Baladas. 2013. 'China's Perception of India's "Look East Policy" and Its Implication', *IDSA Monograph Series*, No. 26, October: 34

31 Balachandran, V. 2017. 'Presence in South China Sea will be a misadventure', *The Sunday Guardian*. http://www.sunday-guardian.com/analysis/presence-in-south-china -sea-will-be-a-misadventure (accessed 17 July 2017)

32 Scott, David. 2015. 'India's Incremental Balancing in the South China Sea', *E-International Relations*, 26 July. https://www.e-ir.info/2015/07/26/indias-incremental-bala ncing-in-the-south-china-sea/ (accessed 17 July 2017)

33 Mishra, Rahul. 2014. 'India–Vietnam: New Waves of Strategic Engagement', *ICWA Issue Brief*. New Delhi: Indian Council of World Affairs, 20 January: 4

34 'Indian Naval ships visit Vietnam and Philippines'. 2016. *Deccan Chronicle*, 31 May. http s://www.deccanchronicle.com/nation/current-affairs/310516/indian-naval-ships-visit-vie tnam-and-philippines.html (accessed 20 July 2017)

35 'Japan's maritime force conducts joint drills with Vietnam's navy in South China Sea base'. 2016. *South China Morning Post*, 18 February. http://www.scmp.com/news/asia/ east-asia/article/1913923/japans-maritime-force-conducts-joint-drills-vietnams-navy-sou th (accessed 25 July 2017)

36 Ghoshal, 2013: 69

37 Parameswara, Prashanth. 2016. 'Vietnam Unveils New Port Facility For Foreign Warships in Cam Ranh Bay', *The Diplomat*, 10 March. https://thediplomat.com/2016/03/ vietnam-unveils-new-port-facility-for-foreign-warships-in-cam-ranh-bay/ (accessed 6 June 2019)

38 Ghosh, P K. 2014. 'India's Strategic Vietnam Defense Relations', *The Diplomat*, 11 November. https://thediplomat.com/2014/11/indias-strategic-vietnam-defense-relations/ (accessed 25 July 2017)

39 'Construction of patrol boats among 12 India–Vietnam agreements signed'. 2016. *The Economic Times*, 4 September. http://economictimes.indiatimes.com/news/poli tics-and-nation/construction-of-patrol-boats-among-12-india-vietnam-agreements-sig ned/articleshow/53999981.cms (accessed 25 July 2017)

40 Ministry of External Affairs (Government of India). 2018. 'India–Vietnam Joint Statement during State Visit of President to Vietnam', 21 November. https://www.mea.gov. in/bilateral-documents.htm?dtl/30615/IndiaVietnam_Joint_Statement_during_State_Vis it_of_President_to_Vietnam (accessed 24 December 2018)

41 Chakraborthy, Srijanee. 2016. 'India's L&T wins contract to build high-speed patrol vessels for Vietnam', *Naval Technology*, 27 September. https://www.naval-technol ogy.com/news/newsindias-lt-wins-contract-to-build-high-speed-patrol-vessels-for-viet nam-5014725 (accessed 26 December 2018)

42 Subramanian, T S. 2003. 'The Vietnam Connection', *Frontline*, 20(1). https://frontline. thehindu.com/static/html/fl2001/stories/20030117003811200.htm (accessed 26 July 2017)

43 Pandey, Piyush. 2012. 'ONGC Videsh Limited pulls out of block in South China Sea', *The Times of India*, 16 May. https://timesofindia.indiatimes.com/business/india -business/ONGC-Videsh-Limited-pulls-out-of-block-in-South-China-Sea/articleshow/ 13159451.cms?referral=PM (accessed 26 July 2017)

44 Sharma, Rakesh. 2012. 'ONGC to Continue Exploration in South China Sea', *The Wall Street Journal*, 19 July. https://www.wsj.com/articles/SB10000872396390444464304577536182763155666 (accessed 5 August 2017)
45 Ministry of External Affairs (Government of India). 2018. 'India–Vietnam Joint Statement during State Visit of President to Vietnam', 21 November. https://www.mea.gov.in/bilateral-documents.htm?dtl/30615/IndiaVietnam_Joint_Statement_during_State_Visit_of_President_to_Vietnam (accessed 24 December 2018)
46 Ministry of External Affairs (Government of India). 2018. 'India–Vietnam Joint Statement during State Visit of President to Vietnam', 21 November. https://www.mea.gov.in/bilateral-documents.htm?dtl/30615/IndiaVietnam_Joint_Statement_during_State_Visit_of_President_to_Vietnam (accessed 24 December 2018)
47 Ministry of External Affairs (Government of India). 2016. 'Joint Statement between India and Vietnam during the visit of Prime Minister to Vietnam', 3 September. https://www.mea.gov.in/bilateral-documents.htm?dtl/27362/Joint_Statement_between_India_and_Vietnam_during_the_visit_of_Prime_Minister_to_Vietnam (accessed 5 August 2017)
48 Ministry of External Affairs (Government of India). 2018. Ibid.

7 Developing trade and economic ties

For any country, it is important that economic and commercial relations are developed to enhance trade so that manufacturing and production can be supported and further employment can be generated. For any developing country, the baseline is to promote exports and minimize imports. However, in order to facilitate trade, there is a need for both liberal tariff regimes and formal trade mechanisms to address issues related to trade, investment and customs. India and Vietnam have been facing challenges with regard to unemployment, and social issues such as poverty alleviation and food security.

The economic growth of any region has been propelled by intra-regional and inter-regional trade. With the emergence of new trading regimes and increasing support for services and investment, the trade might grow incrementally in future also. There are 17 bilateral FTAs (WTO notified) within different sub-regions of Asia. This excludes bilateral Free Trade Agreements among nations. In contrast to the lack of Bilateral Free Trade Agreements within the Gulf region and Central Asia nations, the East Asian nations have been instrumental in developing Regional Comprehensive Economic Partnership (RCEP) and are in the process of finalizing the feasibility study about the Free Trade Agreement of the Asia-Pacific (FTAAP). Asian countries would be facing challenges related to investment and building capital which would support their manufacturing sector. Given the fact that investment is dependent on returns and political stability in targeted countries, development based on peace and stability would be a major challenge. However, expansion of the Asian value chain is much foreseen with India, Indonesia, and Bangladesh, Vietnam, Cambodia and Myanmar emerging as low-cost production centres. The Gulf Sovereign fund is likely to emerge as a source of investment for Asian countries, because of the need for the Gulf countries to diversify their economic portfolio and reduce dependency on oil revenue. The anti-dumping litigation and unfair trade practices, including non-tariff barriers to market access, would emerge as a contentious issue among the Asian countries. The resource nationalism has resonated in countries such as Myanmar and Indonesia and would gain momentum in the near future, given income disparities and problems related to good governance. The lack of sanitation, health and education facilities in select Asian countries is likely to manifest in the form of protests and labour unrest.

Developing trade and economic ties   89

The Bilateral Investment Promotion and Protection Agreement (BIPPA) would remain a major source for investment across Asian countries. However, anomalies and differences between different BIPPA would need proper redressal and corrective measures. In the context of Asia, the emerging economies are India, Indonesia, Vietnam and Philippines with a 6–7 per cent rate of growth. In case of India and the Philippines, the services sector has been boosting growth while in the case of Indonesia and Vietnam, manufacturing and mining are emerging as the harbingers of growth. All the economies of East Asia and Southeast Asia have been integrated into various regional and sub-regional trade structures but the specific complementarities and the economies of scale and trade benefits still rest primarily on the bilateral trade agreements.

Trade and economic relations between any two countries increases with better political understanding between the countries. In the international economic discourse, there are three major platforms which have propagated international trade as well as regional trade. These include the membership of the World Trade Organization (WTO), regional trade organizations and bilateral free trade agreements. In the case of Vietnam, it became a member of the WTO in January 2007.[1] In contrast to Vietnam, India has been a signatory of GATT since 8 July 1948, and a member of the WTO since its inception on 1 January 1995.[2] India's relations with Vietnam have been marked by growing economic and commercial engagements. Both countries signed the Double Taxation Avoidance Agreement (DTAA) in 1994,[3] and the Bilateral Investment Promotion and Protection Agreement (BIPPA) in 1997,[4] which has helped to consolidate the economic relationship between the two countries.

India is now among the top ten trading partners of Vietnam. The total trade between the two countries during April–December 2016 stood at US$ 7.285 billion.[5] While trade reached US$ 12.8 billion in 2017, there is potential for growth in the investment. India has made investment in 182 projects, amounting to about US$ 816 million in Vietnam, while Vietnam's investments are relatively miniscule and amount to US$ 6 million investment in the country.[6] However, in order to achieve the mutually agreed target for bilateral trade of US$ 15 billion by 2020,[7] new trade and business opportunities need to be tapped. Some of the steps to realize the trade target include utilizing established mechanisms such as the Joint Sub-Commission on Trade; intensifying the exchanges among states of India and provinces of Vietnam; strengthening exchanges of delegation and business-to-business contacts; regular organization of trade fairs, and events such as the India–CLMV Business Conclave and the Vietnam–India Business Forum. The recognition of a standard system in 2016 between the Bureau of Indian Standards (BIS) and the Directorate for Standards, Metrology and Quality of Vietnam (STAMEQ) pointed to the possibility of furthering trade understanding between the two countries. Regarding investments, while there are 132 Indian projects, with total investments of about US$ 1.07 billion, India ranked at 25 in terms of total investments into Vietnam.[8]

90 *Developing trade and economic ties*

India lifted [its] import ban on six commodities including coffee beans from Vietnam after resolving phytosanitary issues with the latter. Vietnam removed [the] suspension on imports of five commodities (namely pods and seeds of peanuts, seeds of cassia, cocoa beans and tamarind) from India following the corrective action taken by India to improve pest management. Vietnam addresses phytosanitary concerns as a result of which India lifted temporary ban on import of six commodities (namely coffee beans, bamboo, black pepper, cinnamon, cassia and dragon fruit) from Vietnam in 2017.[9]

While there is potential for growth in trade and investment, structural constraints are hampering the momentum.

Exploring economic complementarities

India, after its independence, has always strived for controlling the commanding heights of the economy and promoting import substitution industrialization. This was meant to reduce import costs and provide employment to the large population. In the case of Vietnam, communist basics were applied, which meant more labour-intensive industrialization and the economy being highly regulated by the state. The prominence of state enterprises and the lack of any market liberalization have put both countries on the same pedestal. Indian economy has remained on a high growth path, with some moderation in the recent growth projections, especially in the wake of the recent global financial meltdown. However, the economy is characterized by strong macroeconomic fundamentals and an expanding domestic market. As per projections by Goldman Sachs, India's GDP growth will remain higher than 8 per cent until 2020 and it will become the world's second largest economy by 2050. Similarly, McKinsey & Company projections suggest that India will become the fifth largest consumer market by 2025 and India's aggregate consumption will quadruple in next 20 years. In the area of trade, sectors have emerged with significant cost competitiveness in diverse areas of both goods and services. India has also evolved as a preferred investment destination due to several locational and policy-induced factors. Much of these have happened due to a mix of policy reforms and private sector initiatives. Reforms in the areas of Trade Liberalisation, FDI liberalisation, Deregulated Exchange Rate Management, Banking and Financial Sector Reforms, Trade Finance etc. are noteworthy. India is also considered as a country with a demographic advantage, with a sizeable percentage of their young population entering into the workforce. This has contributed to the development of skills and human resource capacities. However, several developmental challenges relating to these issues remain in the areas of health and education, and regional cooperation can play an important role in this regard.[10]

With both India and Vietnam adopting market liberalization and divestment in 1991 and 1986 (*Doi Moi*) respectively, the trajectories of their economies were expected to be on nearly identical lines. In the case of Vietnam, this did

Developing trade and economic ties 91

not happen because the Communist Party regulated liberalization was slow in terms of capitalization and free market economy. Until 2010, the share of private equity in the market was barely 30 per cent. This has somewhat slowed the Foreign Direct Investment in Vietnam. On the other hand, India's attachment to the Public Sector Undertakings and their slow structural reforms did not entice foreign investors. Now the two countries have rectified institutional shortcomings to a large extent and are one of the most preferred destinations for Foreign Direct Investment. However, more structural adjustments and further liberalization are required. The two countries are also competitors in the case of select products such as cotton fabrics, yarn, electronics and manufactured goods. Both countries are also exploring possible forums for cooperation in the economic domain and the emerging regional and global trading systems have provided that platform.

From 2005 to 2017 the Southeast Asian region, including Thailand, Malaysia and Indonesia as well as Vietnam, has seen robust exports and investment. This has pulled a country like Vietnam ahead of its competitors given the fact that three countries in the region have experienced relatively slow growth. Vietnam also weathered the effects of the recession in the global economy and had sensed the vulnerabilities associated with integration with the global value chain and international political economy. The slow realization of the RCEP and the withdrawal of US from TPP has its own problems, as Vietnam has threatened to withdraw from the TPP as it is facing difficulties in exploring markets for its exports. The increasing protectionism witnessed in the markets of Europe and the US, as well as sanctions on Russia, have constrained markets for Vietnam. These developments have limited growth opportunities for Vietnam, which is trying hard to protect its economic and commercial interests between the US and China trade war. Some of the most vital exports of Vietnam, such as agricultural products, steel and electronics, have seen reduced demand because of trade war and protectionism.[11]

Vietnam's integration with the regional value chain and its disinvestment in equity markets has been slow. However, its economy has been doing better when compared to its regional competitors. Vietnam has been importing raw materials for its exports. This has reduced profits for manufacturers and, as a result, Vietnam reaps little dividends in terms of manufacturing exports. As a result, Vietnam needs a long term manufacturing plan and seamless logistical chain. In this regard, India's growing market and the complementarity that the two countries can explore in the manufacturing can yield dividends in the long term. Furthermore, debt servicing and limited disinvestment have led to a cumulative effect on the manufacturing and services sector. Vietnam also needs to work with regard to its financial system, legal issues and regulations and the lack of domestic investment due to less reforms in equity markets. This has amplified problems for Vietnam, because of the volatility of global commodity prices, increasing protectionism, sluggish growth in China, and limited inroads in global financial markets.[12] However, despite these limitations, both India and Vietnam have explored complementarities and, given the potential that the two

92 Developing trade and economic ties

countries have in exports and the development of the manufacturing sector, these possibilities need to be explored. The global and regional trading arrangements would provide more prospects for the two economies.

Global and regional trading arrangements

Within the Indo-Pacific region, different regional trading instruments have evolved over the years, and this includes the Asia-Pacific Economic Cooperation (APEC), Trans-Pacific partnership (TPP), Regional Comprehensive Economic Cooperation (RCEP), Asia-Pacific Trade Agreement (APTA) and, lastly, the Free Trade Agreement of the Asia-Pacific (FTAAP). These trading arrangements have different members drawn from both the Asian region and other regions. The Indo-Pacific region has defined new commercial and trade initiatives designed to be in sync with the changing geopolitical configurations. This includes the extended membership of existing institutions, while at the same time the germination of new institutions encapsulating the new regional construct. The major debate about the Indo-Pacific is whether it is a new geographically defined region, or a trans-regional area encompassing new strategic spaces. The inclusion of India into the Asia-Pacific is projected as the incubator for the Indo-Pacific. However, this is not the case as the fusion of the Indian and Pacific Oceans can been seen as a natural corollary to this initiative. For the strengthening of any new regional construct there are three basic premises which need to be met in the contemporary international relations. These are security, politics and economics. The fusion or interdisciplinary approach can be seen in any of the three basic fundamentals of regional multilateral grouping. This can be seen in the case of ASEAN supported groupings, the Asia-Pacific Economic Cooperation (APEC), the Trans-Pacific Partnership (TPP) and even the Pacific Islands Forum (PIF). Organizations which have been primarily formed to address security challenges, such as ASEAN, have transformed into more cohesive economic organizations. The expanse of ASEAN does include its dialogue partners, which are now engaged in the form of Regional Comprehensive Economic Partnership (RCEP). This includes ASEAN and six of its dialogue partners, excluding Russia and the US. Regarding economic cooperation, there are institutions which have supported à *la carte* formations, and, given time, have opted either for an inclusive membership with select invitations to a few emerging economic powers, or have kept their grouping as an exclusive club with a moratorium on new memberships.

Diplomacy as a tool for securing international peace and maintaining security has been the well-accepted norm. Similarly, protecting national interest through carefully calibrating statecraft is another dimension of diplomacy. In a regional setting, regional organizations such as ASEAN provide the platform for deliberating on regional issues and providing solutions. Over the years, ASEAN has been a multilateral institution, which has benefited the member countries as regular dialogue and economic integration lead to an incremental reduction in

Developing trade and economic ties 93

the threat perception and building of the ASEAN Community. However, many international critics and scholars have been disapproving of its non-interference in members' domestic affairs, and its consensus-building approach. India, Vietnam, and ASEAN have been discussing issues related to the three core areas of diplomatic cooperation, internal security, and regional security mechanisms, and there have been elements of mutual understanding but also phases of disagreement. The engagement has been at two different levels; with Vietnam, it precedes that of engagement with ASEAN and has been more nuanced and collaborative. With ASEAN, the apprehension related to it being an anti-communist initiative was contrary to India's Non-Aligned policy. Further, India's comprehensive approach, both at a bilateral level with ASEAN members and a structural level interaction with ASEAN, has provided a multifaceted dimension to the relationships spanning the defence, security, economic and cultural domains. ASEAN-linked institutions have been at work towards devising a common approach towards non-traditional security issues and have gained significant success in assimilating views and reaching a consensus on addressing these issues. This has led to multinational exercises addressing concerns related to non-traditional security issues. In terms of economic engagement, the ASEAN region has been alluded to as a 'noodle or spaghetti' bowl (multiple bilateral trade agreements existing within the ambit of ASEAN) by economists.[13] These two standards of non-traditional security cooperation and trade engagements have originated side by side but have somewhat evaded addressing the critical element of regional security which was the primary task of ASEAN. This might be construed as the necessary ignorance to build understanding. However, developments in the South China and East China Seas have raised the question of international obligations with regard to global commons and building compliance mechanisms. As a result, a few developments have taken shape, but the question is whether multilateralism is a necessary vehicle for negotiations and compliance with agreements effectiveness so far.

> The ADMM-Plus established in 2010 with eight extra-regional powers (ASEAN dialogue partners) in ADMM framework: Australia, China, India, New Zealand, Japan, Russia, South Korea and the U.S have the potential to address security issues. The ASEAN Maritime Forum was also enlarged to include the eight dialogue partners rechristen it as the Expanded ASEAN Maritime Forum.[14] The geographic expansion of institutions coincides with the Indo-Pacific geostrategic area. This meets ASEAN's objective to promote its centrality in the Indo-Pacific. ASEAN has always aspired for its centrality in an Indo-Pacific crisis management framework.[15]

India has calibrated its ties with the ASEAN institution and individual countries of Southeast Asia through regular exchange of ideas, ethos, perspectives, knowledge and practices. During the last five decades, since the formation of ASEAN, this connection has progressed to diverse areas. Since India's 'Look East' policy was launched in the early 1990s, the multi-layered partnership has

94 *Developing trade and economic ties*

gained momentum and the India–ASEAN relationship is the core component of this policy. Asia is slowly emerging as the epicentre of economic growth and strategic struggle and has assumed diverse responsibilities proportionate with its capacities. The shifting of the US pivot towards Asia has given a new dimension to the political and strategic discourse, shaping the regional security environment. Chinese military modernization, particularly its naval power capabilities, has triggered diverse reactions among its neighbours. The institutional structure built around ASEAN has provided forums for discussion and is now emerging as an annual dialogue process which promotes talks, but how ASEAN handles flashpoints and contentious issues assimilating varied opinion and interests needs to be seen. India and Vietnam need to discuss the future of ASEAN-related institutions and provide functional suggestions to make them effective.

The relevance of ASEAN as a regional multilateral institution for Vietnam evolves from the country's efforts to recalibrate its foreign, and trade policies in sync with the Asia-Pacific region. This was accelerated by the fact that with the disintegration of the erstwhile Soviet Union, Vietnam lost its foremost strategic partner and credible defence supplier. Vietnam, with the resolution of the Cambodian crisis, was seen as important player and its engagement was supported by many countries in ASEAN, including Singapore. Further, the evolution of regional economic cooperation agreements, such as APEC, expanded the horizons for Vietnam. Subsequently, expanded institutional mechanisms such as ASEAN plus Six, the East Asia Summit (EAS), the ASEAN Defence Ministers Meeting plus (ADMM+) and the Expanded ASEAN Maritime Forum created a new cooperative security architecture for Vietnam. For example, Southeast Asian states are for the most part well attached to ASEAN and APEC, Japan to APEC and EAS, and China to the EAS. These 'architectures are competing among themselves to become more relevant and important, which was potentially intensified by the Kevin Rudd proposal'.[16] Subsequently, Hatoyama proposed the East Asian Economic Community, which was an abridged version of the Kevin Rudd proposal with few exceptions and inclusions. Both these proposals were nearly identical to the Indo-Pacific concept.

The expanse of ASEAN as an institution is reinforced with the ASEAN Regional Forum (ARF) and ASEAN Free Trade Area (AFTA). The institutionalizing of the Regional Comprehensive Economic Partnership (RCEP), which includes the ten ASEAN members and six of its dialogue partners, is likely to create the largest regional trading bloc across the Indo-Pacific region as it might also include India.[17] RCEP is technically the East Asia Summit (EAS) area excluding US and Russia. With the increasing subscription to the Indo-Pacific construct, the US has proposed the Indo-Pacific Economic Corridor which entwines the South and Southeast Asia into one economic unit. The Trans-Pacific Partnership (TPP) was another such initiative which was meant to translate the geo-political construct into one supra-regional structure supported by the multilateral structures.

G20 and APEC

In the international discourse, the critical balance is between security and economics. Security alliances such as NATO are still judged as relevant in select regional theatres, but strategic and defence cooperation agreements, which include both traditional security concerns such as maritime security, are carefully designing new flexible cooperative structures. The security alliance has become, to a certain extent, a passé, but strategic partnerships and other flexible arrangements have become the preferred choice. This can be attributed to the increasing economic interdependence which has been experienced all across the globe. The economic organizations and forums are also being galvanized along the security lines, with the US support to the Trans-Pacific Partnership while China advocates for the Free Trade Agreement of the Asia-Pacific (FTAAP) with market and investment as the dividends of the trade and regional economic agreements. The Indo-Pacific as a construct still lacks the multilateral structure to support it and the closest structures are the East Asia Summit, APEC, and the G20. However, out of these, two (EAS and G20) are rather loose formations in which discussion and collaboration are more of a voluntary nature. For Vietnam and India, G20 is an important forum apart from ASEAN where both are members.

> The Group of Twenty (G20) evolved as an international forum of leading industrialized and emerging economies. The G20 represents more than four-fifths of global GDP and two-thirds of the world population.[18]

The core business is negotiated on the sidelines and in informal meetings. In the initial phases of its incorporation, finance ministers and central bank governors of member countries used to attend G20 summits. Since 1999, eighteen G20 meetings among finance ministers and central bank governors, and 10 summit-level meeting of G20 economies represented by heads of state/ government have taken place. The G20 was meant to address issues related to financial governance, management of fiscal deficit, uniform tax regulation, climate change finance, poverty alleviation, restructuring of the international financial institutions and the promotion of free trade. However, in the last five years, it has started addressing core social challenges such as terrorism, migration, poverty, climate change, and selective social issues. The leader's meetings have outlined a future plan of action and the group has made incremental progress. India and Vietnam are seen as emerging economies and have much to contribute to the forum because of the financial aspects of international economic and financial institutions, as well as to bring about uniformity in monetary, exchange and fiscal adjustments. While India is still in the development phase, Vietnam, in comparison, has reached satisfactory levels of manufacturing and tax regulation in conformity with the international regulations. The two countries can work together in the G20 to safeguard their interests. There are other organizations, such as APEC (of which Vietnam is a member), to which India is an aspirant

96 Developing trade and economic ties

for membership, but given the lack of consensus and support from the members, its entry to such organisations has not materialised.

In the contemporary discourse, the Washington system is being tested by the new nascent order being constructed around Beijing, posing new demands to post-Cold-War trans-regional institutions such as the Asia-Pacific Economic Cooperation forum (APEC). Identical to the Washington System, the APEC replicates a perspective that increasing economic interdependence would erode strains. Scholars, analysts, and thinkers who support APEC are confident that trade and commercial ties will bring about a peaceful new order. Although APEC promotes economic issues and has a relatively small budget, it lacks infrastructure, decision-making and dispute resolution measures. Beyond the classic liberal faith that trade encourages peace, there is anticipation that increased contact and communication among Asian and Pacific nations can serve to create a pan-Asian identity that will mitigate national and ethnic differences.[19] Unfortunately, at times, interdependence does not translate into peaceful relations; it may aggravate conflict. The best example has been US–Japan economic relations related to TPP negotiations, which have been marked by serious friction and contention, despite significant economic interdependence.[20] There have been contestations that APEC is intrinsically unable to act as the regional agenda-setter. This was reinforced when ASEAN and its affiliate institutions gained traction both in terms of political discussion and economic integration. APEC, the brainchild of small and medium Asian powers to forestall great-power domination, has lagged behind in terms of political dialogue. However, in terms of business interactions and facilitation, it has many success stories. Besides, economic prosperity does not ensure security. Liberal proponents of APEC have anticipated that power politics have ended and the American security guarantee for the region will remain for an indefinite period. In 1994, the same middle-sized powers structured the ASEAN Regional Forum (ARF) to deliberate on traditional security matters; however, the ARF was a loose and informal organization, and it failed to create a comprehensive understanding among regional players. In summary, an order built on APEC and ARF appears to be no less fragile than the Washington System.[21]

Since APEC's formation, India's entry as a member was impeded because of APEC's reservations regarding the expansion of membership. Going by the dialogue among academics and policymakers, it is important to look for the contours for the expansion of any regional organization. The formal guidelines for the acceptance of new members into regional institutions are important to the consideration of the processes of change and expansion, because they not only establish the rules but they are also important signals of the nature and parameters of the organization. The criteria an organization sets up for appraising the applications of new members conveys important messages about its rationale, its vision of the region and of regionalism, and its conception of its role in regional politics as well as more broadly.[22] As Robert Keohane perceives, regional organizations differ in goals and intent from universal membership organizations by the very fact of their restricted membership; the restrictions they place on

Developing trade and economic ties 97

membership are a crucial part of the goods and benefits they offer to their members.[23] The criteria establishing eligibility for membership are determined by and are crucial to selecting the combination of states thought best to deliver the desired objectives of the regional organization.[24]

The Trans-Pacific Partnership (TPP) now known as the Comprehensive and Progressive Agreement for Trans-Pacific Partnership (CPTPP),[25] is a projected regional free trade agreement (FTA) among twelve members, which include its four founder members New Zealand, Brunei, Chile, Singapore and eight new members – Australia, Canada, Malaysia, Japan, the United States (which has now withdrawn), Mexico, Peru, and Vietnam. The US negotiators and other analysts label and visualize the TPP as a 'comprehensive and high-standard' FTA that proposes to liberalize trade in most goods and services.[26] It includes rules-based commitments past those presently established in the World Trade Organization (WTO). It is also known as the WTO-plus forum. The contours of the agreement were announced on the sidelines of the Asia-Pacific Economic Cooperation (APEC) ministerial in November 2011, in Honolulu. The final negotiations for the TPP have concluded and if ratified, even though there is strong domestic resistance from a few member countries, the 'TPP potentially could eliminate tariff and non-tariff barriers to trade and investment among the parties and could serve as a template for a future trade pact among APEC members and potentially other countries'.[27] Faced with the predicament of security and economic supportive structures, the choices for India are rather limited. India does have trade and economic cooperation agreements with a majority of the nations in the Indo-Pacific region, but does not have security alliances with any. In the case of economic cooperation agreements, India was preparing to join the Regional Comprehensive Economic Partnership (RCEP) grouping by the end of 2019. In the case of the APEC, India is yet to be inducted as a member, whilst in the case of the FTAAP and the TPP, India is not even an observer. The Indo-Pacific as a geopolitical imagination is increasingly pertinent, but for India to engage in any counter-China strategy, this is still a very premeditated and calibrated move. In addition to the TPP and the RCEP, there are a number of ongoing large-scale trade negotiations that include Asia-Pacific economies, including the ASEAN Economic Community (AEC), the Transatlantic Trade and Investment Partnership (TTIP) between the US and the European Union, the Pacific Alliance which includes South American economies on the Pacific Rim, the China–Japan–Korea (CJK) agreement, and the WTO Doha Round. Of all of these agreements, regional opinion leaders were only positive about the likely conclusion of the AEC and the TPP by 2019.[28] However, the RCEP missed the deadline, while the withdrawal of the US meant the TPP was reduced to an 11-member organization. If India decides to join the TPP, it would have to measure the advantages and disadvantages of the trading bloc. The TPP in its current form is quite dissimilar from its previous version, when its members were New Zealand, Chile, Peru, Singapore, and Brunei. It has altered from a geoeconomic to a geopolitical construct. Further, one of the unspecified purposes of the TPP is to minimize growing economic dependence on China among the member countries. Since India has an identical objective, joining the TPP will serve

98 *Developing trade and economic ties*

India's interest in the long run. It will also help integrate its economy with a number of emerging and prosperous economies within APEC. However, TPP membership will have disadvantages for India. Firstly, the TPP is the advanced and comprehensive rules based version of the Free Trade Agreements so far signed, as is intends to eliminate all the tariffs on exports and imports to zero. Secondly, since the TPP ratifies very high standards for protecting the environment, labour and human rights worldwide, and production standards, India would have to prepare itself to meet these standards.[29] While the previous form of the TPP looked at harnessing the complementarities among the member countries, the present form of the TPP is looking at greater integration, not necessarily at the complementarities. It will help the advanced and manufacturing economies the most. India may gain in the service sectors, but in other sectors such as agriculture, it would have to make compromises. Further, on IPR and other related issues, there would be a conflict between domestic priorities and international obligations.

The TPP members concluded their negotiations in 2015. Therefore, one of the disadvantages to a new member joining the trading bloc would be to accept the rules already set by the existing members. It is yet to be seen whether India would be willing to subscribe the rules set by the 11 CPTPP members. Maybe it is time for the India to analyse the advantages and disadvantages of joining such a group. The case of Japan and other ASEAN members joining the TPP suggests that various domestic lobbies organized large-scale protests urging their governments to safeguard their interests. If India decides to join, it may face similar protests from the domestic constituencies, so it should also prepare itself to address and assuage domestic concerns.

Economic diplomacy and increasing convergences

The narrow outlook of economic diplomacy is seen as the behaviour of government officials/diplomats in the course of negotiations related to furthering economic ties between nations. In other words, negotiations provide a sense of benefit for all:

> In a broader perspective, economic diplomacy thrives on the management of international relations through negotiations by the government officials/diplomats; the skills required for such management; adroitness in personal relations; tact and engagement with private sector and civil society, etc.[30]

In other words:

> economic diplomacy deals with the articulation of foreign policy in the real world of economic relations between nations to flesh out and implement the principles and objectives set out in the policy. It involves the application of skills and tact in the conduct of official relations, particularly trade and investment, and in engaging the private sector and civil society constructively by governments of sovereign states.[31]

Developing trade and economic ties 99

Economics has always been a vital component of India's foreign policy. However, in the post-Cold war period only that economic interests have become the primary agent of international relations. India's economic diplomacy, in order to promote and protect trade, investment and commercial interests has increasingly started posting commercial counsellors in its embassies/missions abroad and instituted high powered economic groups. Greater interaction at official level and integration with the extended neighbourhood, and bilateral Free Trade Agreements have accelerated economic engagement. The success of European Union, NAFTA, and ASEAN have been testimony to free trade bringing greater prosperity.[32]

In order to achieve primary objectives to catapult India as a key economic power, multilateral trade and investment negotiations, comprehensive regional and expanded bilateral trade agreements (including services sector), easier access to foreign resources, promotion of exports and Indian businesses abroad through institutions such as India Brand Equity Foundation (IBEF) and India Investment Centre, simplifying ease of doing business, and promotion of foreign investments in India through tax holidays and increasing equity participation. To impart greater knowledge and information about government's large term objectives, different ministries have already started orienting and training existing bureaucrats and diplomats.[33]

India has adopted an import-substitution policy since its independence until the early 1990s. Since 1991, India has introduced wide-ranging economic policy reforms and is moving towards a market-driven economy. This has resulted in consistent high economic growth over the last one and a half decades, making India the tenth-largest economy in the world. At present, India is the second-fastest-growing economy in the world. Both India and Vietnam have been getting integrated into the world economy, and the enhancement of their role in the future international economic order is expected.[34] Further, India initiated playing the economic aid card – either by way of assuring billions of dollars as aid assistance to underdeveloped nations, or as soft loans through concerned divisions in the foreign affairs ministry. Further, it entered into trade agreements – to assist the twin purposes of market entry and the fulfilment of strategic commercial interests. Most of these enterprises were meant to bolster, or safeguard, the country's interests in economically important European, African, and ASEAN regions. In fact, India has negotiated a Free Trade Agreement in Services and Investment with ASEAN; a CECA with Malaysia; a CECA with Australia is in final stages; a review of its CECA with Singapore and Korea; an FTA with Thailand is under review; and an FTA with the EU has reached a deadlock, but there are possibilities of new phase of negotiations with EU. Given the plethora of new trade agreements that both India and Vietnam have embarked upon, the services sector of both countries needs complementary concessions offsetting the negative balance in merchandise trade. Therefore, an FTA in merchandise trade needs to be complemented by an FTA in Services and Investment.

100 Developing trade and economic ties

India has effectively tried to engage itself in larger institutional mechanisms supporting economic integration and the creation of value addition chain. This in a way supports South-South cooperation and complements economic processes. Under RCEP, India has been slowly adhering to the general philosophies of high economic ambitions. With ASEAN FTA+1 procedure has been approved in which 11,500 tariff lines are under dialogue. With ASEAN, India is ready for an 80 percent drop in its tariffs and as per the MFN agreement under the India–ASEAN FTA, the aim is to reduce tariffs to zero. India has adopted a structured approach so as to cater to differential and individual strengths. With ASEAN countries, the arrangement would be the having maximum elasticity because of the existing trading arrangement.[35]

However, with regard to Japan and Korea, India has offered a 62.5 per cent reduction while the two countries asked for the 80 per cent tariff reduction. With Australia, New Zealand, and China, 80 per cent tariff lines are under negotiation, but India would adopt a differential approach. China has offered a 40–42 per cent reduction in tariffs while Australia has proposed a 55–60 per cent decrease and New Zealand has envisaged a 55 per cent lessening of tariffs. India had offered a staggered 42.5 per cent reduction in products from China, and 52.2 per cent to Japan. During the discussion with Japan, the country had offered to reduce tariffs up to 72 per cent.[36] There has been a discussion to raise the threshold levels. In terms of Non-Tariff Barriers (NTB), there are still lingering issues with the ASEAN countries on services, investment, and MFN. Under RCEP, e-commerce is one area which India has been keenly looking forward to. India desperately wants investments and for that, it needs to ease its procedures, which it is doing incrementally.

For India, the biggest issues are the rules of origin and it has increased the percentage value addition to 35–40 per cent in the manufacturing country to overcome Chinese rerouting. With regard to the Sanitary and Phytosanitary issues, customs and other ministries need to take into account combined and simplified checking so that countries like Australia and New Zealand can find a market within India, but it would need a better approach among the ministries. While India is preparing itself for the RCEP, it is already missing in the frame with regard to FTAAP and TPP.[37]

In 2006, APEC economies approved a long-term vision for a Free Trade Area of the Asia-Pacific (FTAAP). APEC Leaders discussed and distributed a 'Pathways to FTAAP' document and suggested the APEC take tangible steps toward the realization of the FTAAP, which could be developed as a comprehensive free trade agreement catering to the ASEAN members and its six dialogue partners, along with the members of the Trans-Pacific Partnership. This overarching regional economic integration initiative could be steered by the APEC, which could motivate the members and possible partners in

Developing trade and economic ties   101

pursuing the FTAAP vision.[38] On the other hand, TPP negotiations concluded in October 2015. This was seen as the 'WTO-plus trade regulations within the grouping, which would benefit only the members'.[39] India fulfils five fundamentals to buttress its candidature for the APEC: firstly, the applicant member needs to be located in the Asia-Pacific region; secondly, it is mandatory to have greater economic ties with the members of the APEC, and the APEC's share in its total trade should be quite large; thirdly, it must adopt economic liberalization measures and relatively free trade policy; fourthly, it should agree to the various objectives enunciated in the APEC statements; and lastly, it should outline an individual plan of action for accomplishing these objectives and start taking part in collective plans of action through the APEC's programmes of work. 'New Delhi also promised to remove all trade barriers by 2010, in order to meet APEC's membership criteria'.[40] India has already propelled several liberalization initiatives, for example in the services sector, particularly in telecom, air and rail transport, insurance, media and construction services. Another possible area of collaboration between India and the APEC is government procurement and competition, where India's improvement is quite comparable to those of the APEC's developing countries. India has also started reforms in customs procedures, whereby procedures have been cut down and the transparency standards are comparable to numerous APEC economies. Other benefits of an official engagement between India and the APEC would include a lessening in transaction costs of undertaking business, as well as greater harmonization and mutual recognition of standards, specialized qualifications, and soft infrastructure. Indian entrepreneurs would undoubtedly benefit from the APEC travel card which permits virtually visa-free travel among member economies. India might infuse vigour and strengthen economic integration in the region.

The Indo-Pacific Economic Corridor (IPEC)

India, in order to support sub-regional economic integration, started promoting the Mekong–India Economic Corridor. The US commissioned a feasibility study about the Indo-Pacific Economic Corridor (IPEC), which begins in South Asia, extending to Southeast Asia and beyond. This economic corridor is meant to promote industrialization in parts of Southern Asia and also better integrate the US economy with this growing region.

> The IPEC vision includes physical infrastructure, energy, trade integration, and increased people-to-people ties. This activity will focus solely on economic integration through trade, investment, and private sector engagement. Through a coordinated analysis with other U.S. government departments – such as the Department of State, U.S. Agency for International Development (USAID), the Office of the United States Trade Representative (USTR), and the Department of Commerce.[41]

102   *Developing trade and economic ties*

It aims to support the United States' vision of an Indo-Pacific Economic Corridor that bridges South and Southeast Asia to promote regional stability and economic prosperity. This particular study focuses exclusively on trade integration and considers various ways that the U.S. government can play a more influential role in fostering regional trade integration in South and Southeast Asia.[42]

The IPEC would act a bridge between the two economies as it intends to bring south Asia and Southeast Asia closer.

Promoting trade and investment

Trade between the two countries can be enhanced through the take-offs of regular flights and easy business visas. The two countries have extended the visa-on-arrival and e-visa provision schemes for the nationals of each other's country on a reciprocal basis. However, organizing direct flights between the cities of the two countries would help in facilitating greater business and civil society interactions. In terms of costs, Vietnamese steel is slightly costlier than Chinese steel, but the quality is better. Vietnam has been slowly progressing towards market equity, and the share of government and private-sector participation is in the ratio of 3:2. Nearly 40 per cent of the Vietnamese equity market is disinvested.[43] However, the state enterprises need more disinvestment from the government, and Vietnam would like to learn from Indian experience.

The trade between the two countries is slated to meet the target of US$ 15 billion by 2020, which will be hard to meet if the trade basket is not expanded. Regarding a select negative list of items, including pepper and coffee, there needs to be more dialogue because the two countries can form pepper and coffee boards to keep the international prices within a certain specific range. The setting up of a pepper exchange board is a politically sensitive subject, given the domestic pepper producers located in Kerala would not like any such initiative, but as the BJP doesn't have any political presence in Kerala, it would not mind establishing the exchange board. However, it would be primarily to regulate and cooperate regarding the pepper prices in the international market.

The Protocol on Double Taxation Avoidance Agreement would promote investment between the two sides. However, India wants the Double Taxation Avoidance Agreement to comply with new revised agreements negotiated with Singapore and Mauritius, so that money laundering can be weeded out. PM Modi stressed cooperation in the field of medicine and health because of the huge market that Vietnam offers to India. Further, the possibility of cooperation in telemedicine and the development of low-cost generic drugs can be explored. Traditional medicine would give employment and provide cheap drugs to people living with low income in both countries. The two countries also require collaboration in developing and exploring the medicinal properties of seaweeds, and marine and other sea-based plants.

Agriculture and cooperation in the field of animal husbandry, sericulture and floriculture has been stressed form India. Further, India wants to develop rice varieties which require less water during cultivation and have a high nutrition value, as this would help in catering to food security initiatives from both sides.

The MoU between BIS and STAMEQ is one area where there are a number of problems and in a way this has hampered the cooperation between the two sides. A dispute settlement between the exporters and importers, as well as the development of an India–Vietnam trade and investment board, would help in creating synergies.

The MoU between the CDSCO of India and the Drug Administration of Vietnam has been signed for quite some time and it was felt that in order to develop better understanding and cooperation an institutional arrangement was a must. However, the MEA and especially the Ministry of Health in India has listed that the Vietnamese response to the initiatives have been lukewarm. Traditional systems of medicine and homeopathy are a normal process of engaging ASEAN nations, India has signed a similar agreement with Malaysia and Singapore. The MoU on cooperation in the field of medicinal plants has been promoted by the Department of Ayush. It is felt that unexplored territories and research in this field would give India a unique opportunity to explore ancient medicinal plants which have been extinct in India but have a high possibility of being found in Vietnamese high lands.

In the services sector Asian countries, particularly India, the Philippines, Indonesia, China and Vietnam, are likely sources of services both in Business Process Outsourcing (BPO) and Knowledge Process Outsourcing (KPO) sectors. With increasing literacy levels, the services sector is likely to grow in the near future. The market for the Asian services sector would predominantly remain European nations and the US. The strong reservations in select countries in Europe and the US about outsourcing the services sector without data security and privacy protocols would be detrimental to both India and Vietnam. Providing strong data security infrastructure and adopting European norms for e-commerce security would be two other challenges. The Mutual Recognition Agreement (MRA) related to educational and professional degrees would be a debatable issue amongst the Asian nations, as it would hamper skilled labour mobility and also create problems in services agreements.

Given the fact that India and Vietnam have developing economies and are likely to benefit from liberalized trade and tariffs, the two countries might complement each other in sectors such as pharmaceuticals and steel, while at the same time competing in sectors such as automobile spares, cement and a few other sectors. However, the challenge is to compete against Chinese subsidized exports (Chinese dumping), as well as countering cheap Chinese raw materials in global markets. However, in the future, the complementarities between two nations are going to increase in industrial production, energy, services sectors and telemedicine.

104 *Developing trade and economic ties*

Notes

1 Viet Nam and the WTO. https://www.wto.org/english/thewto_e/countries_e/viet nam_e.htm (accessed 18 June 2017)
2 India and the WTO. https://www.wto.org/english/thewto_e/countries_e/india_e.htm (accessed 19 June 2017)
3 Section 90 of the Income-Tax Act, 1961 – Double Taxation Agreement – Agreement For Avoidance Of Double Taxation And Prevention Of Fiscal Evasion With Foreign Countries – Vietnam. https://www.incometaxindia.gov.in/DTAA/Comprehensive%20Agreements/1086900000000001011.htm (accessed 11 February 2019)
4 Dhar, Biswajit, Reji, Joseph and James, T C 2012. 'India's Bilateral Investment Agreements: Time to Review', *Economic and Political Weekly*, 47(52): 113–122
5 Consulate General of India, 'India–Vietnam Relations', Ho Chi Minh City, April 2017. http://www.india-consulate.org.vn/en/commerce/india-vietnam-relations-0 (accessed 28 April 2017)
6 'Vietnam and India agree to boost trade, defense cooperation'. 2018. Associated Press, November 19. https://www.seattletimes.com/business/vietnam-and-india-aim-to-boost-trade-defense-cooperation/ (accessed 12 February 2019)
7 Ibid.
8 Chaudhary, Dipanjan Roy. 2017. 'India–Vietnam: 45 years, partners in peace', *The Economic Times*, 18 January. http://economictimes.indiatimes.com/news/poli tics-and-nation/india-vietnam-45-years-partners-in-peace/articleshow/56637016.cms (accessed 26 April 2017)
9 'India lifts import ban on six commodities from Vietnam'. 2017. Financial Express, March 22. https://www.financialexpress.com/economy/indian-lifts-import-ban-on-six-commodities-from-vietnam/598276/ (accessed 28 April 2017)
10 Ministry of Commerce. 2009. 'Report of the Joint Study Group on the Feasibility of India–Indonesia Comprehensive Economic Cooperation Agreement (CECA)', Delhi, September 15: 6
11 'Against China, Vietnam Stands Alone'. 2016. Stratfor Assessment, December 22. https://worldview.stratfor.com/analysis/against-china-vietnam-stands-alone (accessed 25 December 2016)
12 Ibid.
13 Bhagwati, Jagdish. 1995. 'U.S. Trade Policy: The Infatuation with Free Trade Agreements', in Jagdish Bhagwati and Anne O. Krueger, eds *The Dangerous Drift to Preferential Trade Agreements*. Washington DC: AEI Press
14 Koh, Swee, Lean, Collin and Darshana, M Baruah. 2014. 'Managing Indo-Pacific Crises', *The Diplomat*, November 19. http://thediplomat.com (accessed 1 November 2016)
15 Ibid.
16 Ministry of Commerce. Report of the Joint Study Group on the Feasibility of India–Indonesia Comprehensive Economic Cooperation Agreement (CECA), Delhi, 15 September 2009: 71
17 Ravenhill, John. 1998. 'Adjusting to the ASEAN way: Thirty years of Australia's relations with ASEAN', *The Pacific Review*, 11(2): 270
18 'G20 countries account for 85 percent of global GDP, 75 percent of world trade', *The Times of India*, 15 June 2015. http://timesofindia.indiatimes.com (accessed 31 July 2016)
19 Pyle, Kenneth B. 2003. 'Regionalism in Asia: Past and Future', *Cambridge Review of International Affairs*, 16(1): 24
20 Loc. cit.
21 Ibid: 25
22 Wesley, Michael ed. 2003. *The Regional Organizations of the Asia–Pacific: Exploring Institutional Change*. New York: Palgrave Macmillan: 94

Developing trade and economic ties 105

23 Keohane, Robert O. 1990. 'Multilateralism: An Agenda for Research', *International Journal*, 45(4), Multilateralism: Old & New (autumn): 731–764
24 Wesley, Michael ed., 2003: 98
25 'What is the CPTPP?' https://international.gc.ca/trade-commerce/trade-agreements-accords-commerciaux/agr-acc/cptpp-ptpgp/index.aspx?lang=eng (accessed 12 February 2019)
26 Fergusson, Ian F, McMinimy, Mark A and Williams, Brock R. 2015. *The Trans-Pacific Partnership (TPP) Negotiations and Issues for Congress*. Washington DC: Congressional Research Service. March 20: 15
27 Fergusson, McMinimy, Williams, 2015: 15
28 Ibid.: 16–19
29 Ibid.: 16–19
30 Moitra, Kasturi. 2013. 'Theoretically Reassessing India's Economic Diplomacy: From the "New" to the "Neoliberal" International Economic Order'. http://fgsisc.files.wordpress.com/ (accessed 7 July 2016)
31 Mehta, Pradeep. 2016. Preface. Available at http://www.cuts-international.org/ (accessed 11 November 2016)
32 Sahoo, Pravakar, Durgesh, Kumar Rai and Rajiv, Kumar. 2009. 'India–Korea Trade and Investment Relations'. Working Paper No. 242, Indian Council for Research On International Economic Relations, December: 1
33 Loc. cit.
34 Loc. cit.
35 Jha, Pankaj K, Rahul, Mishra and Samshad, Khan. 2016. 'India in the APEC: Building the Case'. Special Report. http://www.icwa.in (accessed 12 September 2017)
36 Interview with Ministry of Commerce Official, 25 June 2016. Jha, Pankaj K, Rahul, Mishra and Samshad, Khan, 2016.
37 Ibid.
38 Annex A – Beijing Roadmap for APEC's Contribution to the Realization of the FTAAP. 2014. http://www.apec.org (accessed 21 July 2016)
39 Jha, Rahul and Samshad, 2016
40 Ibid.
41 Indo-Pacific Economic Corridor (IPEC) Phase I: Coordinated Regional Trade Analysis, Assessment Report Asia and the Middle East Economic Growth Best Practices (AMEG) Project Chemonics International, Inc. Task Order No. AID-OAA—12–00008, April 2015. http://pdf.usaid.gov/pdf_docs/PA00KZQ1.pdf (accessed 12 September 2017)
42 Ibid.
43 Vietnam, 2019 Article IV Consultation – Press Release; Staff Report; And Statement by The Executive Director for Vietnam, IMF Country Report No. 19/235, July 2019: 5–9

8 India, Vietnam and ASEAN regionalism

India and Vietnam have been involved in ASEAN regionalism as a dialogue partner or a member respectively. The two countries have been actively involved in the political, economic and social processes under the multilateral structure. With the signing of the India-ASEAN Free Trade Agreement, implemented since January 2010, the possibilities are increasing. The full ratification of the ASEAN–India Agreement in Trade and Services by all ASEAN members would integrate the two regions in services and investment network. The easy visa facilities and greater interaction during the ASEAN Summit level talks between ASEAN and India on a regular basis have built the political understanding, while at the same time facilitated interactions at multiple levels. As discussed earlier, India on its part has also rechristened its 'Look East Policy' as the 'Act East Policy', further amplifying the action-oriented approach towards this region. In areas such as diplomacy, public security and national defence, the institutional engagement has been relatively productive and futuristic. India and Vietnam have been interacting at different levels regularly to discuss public security and national defence under structured dialogue processes. Likewise, India's interaction with ASEAN, particularly in diplomacy, has been good, but has been relatively subdued in terms of public security and regional defence. India's participation in ADMM+ processes has built understanding on the non-traditional security, maritime issues, and military medicine, but the core regional security concerns have been left unaddressed. The primary bottleneck in addressing core security concerns is the ASEAN structural mechanism, which stresses consensus and non-interference in the internal affairs of any member nation. This chapter addresses areas like diplomacy, public security on a bilateral basis between India and Vietnam, and how under the ASEAN process it can be expanded.

In a regional setting, regional organizations such as ASEAN provide the platform for deliberating on regional issues and providing solutions to them. India, Vietnam, and ASEAN have been discussing issues related to the three core areas of diplomatic cooperation, internal security and regional cooperative mechanisms and there have been elements of mutual understanding, but also phases of disagreement. The engagement has been at two different levels; with Vietnam, it precedes the engagement with ASEAN and has been more nuanced and collaborative. Within ASEAN, the members adopted consensus-building as part of

India, Vietnam and ASEAN regionalism   107

ASEAN's way to emerge as a potent regional bloc. Further, India's comprehensive approach, both at a bilateral level with individual ASEAN members and at a structural level with ASEAN, has provided a multifaceted dimension to the relationships spanning, defence, security, economic and cultural domains.

Building understanding under multilateral framework

India and Vietnam's bilateral understanding of the issues of diplomacy, public security and regional security has been incremental but substantive. Diplomatic engagement between the two countries started in 1972; however, the consular relations had been established since the early 1950s. India has supported Vietnam against the colonial powers such as France (1954) and the US (1975) and this has formed the foundation of the long lasting relationship between the two countries. Further, the political understanding between the two countries was enhanced because of positive personal equations between the political leaderships. The personal chemistry between Jawaharlal Nehru and Ho Chi Minh was testimony to this. The relationship transcended the Cold War phase, and the momentum was preserved even after the Cold War.

India's ties with Vietnam go back a long time in history, and more often than not it has been embedded in terms of ancient civilisation links, particularly the Cham civilisation and the Khmer empire, cultural ties as well as personal equations between the leaders of the two countries. The civilisation remnants can be seen in the Buddhist temples in Southern Vietnam, as well as temples constructed during the Cham civilisation. The narrative with regard to Buddhism has taken a different course, with Vietnam becoming more influenced by Mahayana Buddhism. However, the major converging point has been the rise of China and the legacy of the war with China in 1962 and 1979 with India and Vietnam respectively. Even in the face of the perceived threat presented by China, the India–Vietnam relationship remained essentially one of mutual political and diplomatic support. Although India provided limited economic aid to Vietnam in the late 1970s and early 1980s, bilateral trade remained marginal until well after the Cold War. The diplomatic establishment desisted from developing a security relationship, although there were influential calls within India to create an India–Vietnam axis to contain China, in the nature of the relationship between China and Pakistan (which the Indians saw as aimed at containing them).[1] However, there was reluctance in India to sign a strategic partnership agreement or friendship treaty, like the Soviet Union with Vietnam, because the Chinese and Vietnamese Communist parties had a very close connection. The Vietnamese did make at least one attempt to add a security element to the relationship with India. In 1978, Vietnamese General Giap, *en route* to Moscow to negotiate Vietnam's Friendship Treaty with the Soviet Union, made an unpublicized stop in New Delhi to seek Indian assistance in the establishment of local arms manufacturing capability to reduce their increasing reliance on the Soviets. The Indians politely shelved the request. It is uncertain whether the Indian response reflected caution about the Soviet relationship or

108 *India, Vietnam and ASEAN regionalism*

their traditional reticence about security ties with other countries outside of South Asia. Whether or not an India–Vietnam security relationship may have been possible during the 1970s and 1980s, India did not pursue the opportunity and security relations were limited to information sharing arrangements. Indian support for Vietnam remained firmly at a political-diplomatic level even after the Chinese invasion of Vietnam in February 1979. There had been political understanding on a number of global issues before the unification of Vietnam, but defence cooperation started much later.[2]

India's relationship with Vietnam also had a major impact on its relations with Southeast Asia. From the early 1970s, the burgeoning relationship between New Delhi and Hanoi was viewed with a significant degree of suspicion by Southeast Asian states, in light of Hanoi's open hostility to ASEAN and its apparent strategic designs on the remainder of Indochina. This came to a head with India's recognition of the Vietnamese-installed Phnom Penh government in July 1980, an episode which would set back India's relations with ASEAN nearly a decade. India had at that time been seeking recognition as an official dialogue partner of ASEAN. In June 1980, in a major diplomatic oversight, the Indira Gandhi government cancelled scheduled discussions with ASEAN and officially recognized the Vietnam-backed Heng Samrin government, becoming the first non-communist state to recognize the regime. The ASEAN states interpreted India's action as proof of it toeing the Moscow–Hanoi line, not only placing India in opposition to the more hawkish ASEAN states such as Singapore and Thailand, but also as sabotaging attempts by Malaysia and Indonesia to work out a compromise settlement in Cambodia. Indian leadership saw ASEAN's concerns as merely reflecting Sino-US demands.

> … India's extended support to Vietnam over Cambodia (along with its failure to condemn the Soviet occupation of Afghanistan) which adversely impacted India's relations with Southeast Asian countries throughout the 1980s. India's unsuccessful attempts over the next decade to work with Hanoi to facilitate Vietnam's withdrawal from Cambodia … continued to place it at odds with the ASEAN states. ASEAN nations feared Vietnam as a Soviet ally more than China. It was only with the collapse of the Soviet Union that India's relationship with Vietnam has become a potential asset in its Eastern periphery.[3]

The resolution of the Cambodian conflict in early 1990s led to the strengthening of the concept of regional security and the enmeshment of Vietnam in the regional security structures.

The biggest transition, which marked a shift from the Cold War mindset, was India's engagement with Israel, and the economic liberalization compelled because of the Balance of Payment (BoP) crisis. At the same time, India tried to match alternative models of development and in this context, the Southeast Asian 'tiger economies' provided a successful economic model. However, it was based on export-based industrial growth. India started looking for markets and understood the need for economic liberalization for fast-paced economic growth. The Look East Policy (LEP) was acclaimed as a visionary policy having political, economic and strategic objectives ingrained into it. The LEP, now better known as the Act East Policy (AEP), had been expanding in the Northeast Asian region since 2005, and South Korea and Japan were the expanded horizons of the policy; this approach also reverberated in the Oceania region. With major powers paying more attention to the Asia-Pacific region, particularly the US, China, and now Russia and Japan, it is likely that India will amplify its pragmatic and proactive stance to catapult itself as a major stakeholder. Meanwhile, Australia is reconfiguring its strategic thinking towards the Indian Ocean, leading to convergence. Korea has also started looking for enhanced connectivity with its western region and Southeast Asia. India has taken into account the concerns of the regional powers, namely Australia, Japan and Indonesia, while at the same time courting the leading power, the US. This has disturbed, albeit to a partial extent, the precarious balance between India and China. This was reflected during the 2007 Malabar series exercises which saw the participation of Japan, US, Australia and Singapore, but was protested by China. However, China's concerns were addressed at proper forums and also at the bilateral level. With the changing strategic compulsions, the Malabar series of exercises permanently included Japan, and was conducted in the south of Japan near the Philippines in 2016. The deployment of Indian ships showcased the outreach to the Northeast Asian region.

India and Vietnam's entry into ASEAN as a dialogue partner and a member respectively was also a test for the organization's adaptation to a changing geopolitical scenario. The disintegration of Soviet Union and the need for ASEAN to project itself as a more inclusive organization facilitated the entry of the two countries into the regional multilateral structure. From a diplomatic point of view, Vietnam gains immense importance for its increasing clout in international bodies like ASEAN, the ARF and even the UN, and India is likely to gain from its support, especially when it is again building up momentum for its UN Security Council membership along with three other nations. Geopolitically, Vietnam has been harping on the Code of Conduct with regard to the South China Sea issue, so that there is freedom of navigation as well as exploration of oil and gas from the EEZ of the claimant countries, propelling the growth of the respective economies. In fact, India's stance on the South China Sea has always been that of Freedom of Navigation and peaceful resolution of dispute through a multilateral route. India's support for freedom of navigation in the SCS strengthened its ties with Vietnam. More so, Vietnam's international stature has been growing, with economic writers advocating for a second tier of multilateral forums like VISTA, which includes Vietnam, Indonesia, South Africa, Turkey and Argentina.[4] It was also proposed that BIMSTEC should be expanded to include Vietnam. While Vietnam and India do not want their strategic partnership to be seen through the Chinese prism, it is still not prudent to say that China doesn't figure as a factor in their relationship. The bilateral cooperation between the two countries in public security and defence has been a success story.

110 *India, Vietnam and ASEAN regionalism*

Public security

Among the Southeast Asia nations, public security is one aspect in which there are varying degrees of engagement. India has signed a Mutual Legal Assistance Treaty with the maximum number of countries in the region. However, in terms of internal security and other related aspects, only two countries have been engaged in a more comprehensive manner. Singapore and Vietnam stand out in terms of engagement in public security areas. Singapore has been one of the nations with which India's home ministry has institutional arrangements, while at the same time India and Vietnam hold regular high-level talks on internal security issues. The liaison between the two countries also projected itself in the form of guerrilla warfare training of the Indian armed forces by their Vietnamese counterparts in 2003. In May 2003, India signed a Joint Declaration on a Framework of Comprehensive Cooperation with Vietnam. The areas of cooperation included:

- the conduct of regular high-level meetings;
- close cooperation in the United Nations and other international forums;
- assistance with regard to the safeguarding of mutual interests;
- gradual steps to expand cooperation in the security and defence fields.[5]

Vietnamese personnel have attended jungle warfare school in Vairengte, Mizoram, while the Indian armed and paramilitary forces have been trained in counter-guerrilla techniques in Vietnam. The Joint Commission Meeting at the Foreign Ministers' level and the Foreign Office Consultations (FOCs) and the strategic dialogues at secretary level provide the larger framework for bilateral cooperation in various areas. There is an Annual Security Dialogue at the defence secretary level, and a Joint Committee on Science and Technology that meets periodically.[6] Though public security is one aspect of cooperation, the defence cooperation between the two sides has also gained momentum. Under the ASEAN rubric, the two countries have cooperated and also coordinated their stance on issues related to regional security and counter-terrorism.

Developing a security framework under ASEAN

India signed a Strategic Partnership Agreement with ASEAN in 2012 and, sensing it as the bedrock of the relationship between the two sides, PM Modi has endorsed the plan of action for 2016–2020, outlining the objectives for future relations. India and Japan, as well as India and Australia, have entered into a security agreement; a similar arrangement can be explored with ASEAN. Article 1.1.5 of the Plan of Action to Implement the ASEAN–India Partnership for Peace, Progress and Shared Prosperity (2016–2020) calls for the need to 'further promote and substantiate comprehensively the ASEAN–India Strategic Partnership',[7] and a more focused approach to the regional security. This would highlight India's intentions and commitment to the regional security.

The objective is to defeat terrorism and extremism, intercept and counter weapons of mass destruction, and help in deterring any rogue states from carrying out any such activity which jeopardizes human life, national security and economic activity. India and Vietnam, under the ASEAN framework, can work on building a comprehensive understanding on rules-based order, protecting the free flow of commerce and freedom of navigation.

The India and ASEAN security relationships need to develop into an important element of the India–ASEAN Strategic Partnership. India, Vietnam, and ASEAN share common security interests and have developed synergies in terms of human resource management; the training of security and defence forces; liaison visits of high level intelligence and police officials, and cooperation in matters pertaining to legal assistance, extradition issues, and apprehending transnational criminals. There is a need to develop synergies between the governments, security and intelligence communities and highlight the importance of research and development in satellite, space and other sophisticated technology to counter threats to security from both state and non-state actors.

The framework agreement between the two sides, as per the ASEAN–India Joint Declaration for Cooperation to Combat International Terrorism signed in Bali, Indonesia on 8 October 2003, expresses a more comprehensive approach and regional legislation in relation to counter-terrorism and related security issues. It highlights that the framework agreement should build on the defence and strategic dialogue between multiple nations at a bilateral and multilateral level.

Any cooperative security agreement between ASEAN and India should focus on the conduct of regular official interactions, joint and integrated exercises and exchanges, and collaboration in multination and multilevel operations as and when the need arises. Enhanced cooperation between not only the security agencies but also among the paramilitary, coast agencies, and armed forces would help in seamless cooperation not only at times of disasters, but also in meeting any contingency. There is a need for cooperation in military training, security sector reforms, and collaboration between defence universities and identified defence and strategic studies centres of both sides. India and ASEAN could contribute forces for the purpose of maritime surveillance and security, as well as develop expertise and manage resources so that the resources could be managed to the required and desired levels. India and Vietnam, under the ASEAN framework, might explore the possibility of instituting a high-level security policy and discussion group to highlight important challenges and focus areas. The high-level security and policy group would decide the format and framework of discussions. It would institute various subgroups which might contribute to the better sharing of information and exchanges which are important to address regional security challenges. This includes both traditional security and non-traditional security challenges.

In 2019, within ASEAN, there have been discussions with regard to utility of the concept of Indo-Pacific, and how it fits into the larger objective of the regional organization. The next section would discuss this aspect.

112 *India, Vietnam and ASEAN regionalism*

ASEAN and Vietnam's stance on a Free and Open Indo-Pacific

At the 34th ASEAN Summit on 23 June 2019 held in Thailand, ASEAN adopted the ASEAN Outlook on the Indo-Pacific.[8] The first and very important point that ASEAN wanted to clarify was that ASEAN centrality should be preserved, the role that the Quad (comprising the US, Japan, Australia, and India) had advocated in their recent consultations.[9] The Free and Open Indo-Pacific (FOIP) has been largely explained as an anti-China initiative,[10] and supporting the FOIP has been always a sensitive issue for ASEAN countries. Luckily, maintaining ASEAN centrality has been supported by China,[11] so it was easy for ASEAN to reaffirm the role in its outlook. Importantly, ASEAN countries did not want to see FOIP as a mechanism that could replace ASEAN centrality in the evolving regional architecture. That was the reason that the Outlook 'involve[d] the further strengthening and optimization of ASEAN-led mechanisms, including the East Asia Summit (EAS), the ASEAN Regional Forum (ARF), the ASEAN Defence Ministers Meeting Plus (ADMM-Plus), the Expanded ASEAN Maritime Forum (EAMF) and others such as the relevant ASEAN Plus One mechanisms'.[12]

Established in 1967, ASEAN history has been attached to the evolution of Asia-Pacific, especially the rivalry among major powers in the region. In other words, ASEAN is not a factor that has created mainstreams in the region. Instead, it is a product of the developments created by major power rivalry. For example, the US-imposed trade and tariff restrictions against China indirectly affected key economies in ASEAN.[13] Countries in the bloc do not want to see a large scale rivalry between the US and China. While China has deployed the One Belt One Road (OBOR) initiative to materialise its world leading ambition, the US and like-minded countries in the Quad initiated the FOIP, which has been seen as 'a tool for the US and its allies to counteract China's rise and its expanding influence in the Indo-Pacific region'.[14] Besides, ASEAN countries have been in the process of negotiating a Code of Conduct (COC) in the South China Sea with China. Therefore, avoiding confrontation and pursuing dialogue has been a method that ASEAN has consistently upheld since its establishment.

In the Outlook, ASEAN also envisaged maritime cooperation as the most important area of cooperation among ASEAN countries and between ASEAN and its partners. Besides maritime cooperation, connectivity and sustainable development are among other important areas of cooperation. Notably, sustainable development and maritime security were also two out of three fields that the Quad, affirmed their intent to continue close coordination and collaboration in, in their consultations in May 2019,[15] as well as good governance, which is another of the principles that ASEAN is pursuing in the Outlook.

ASEAN countries have continued to share the Quad's vision in maritime security cooperation. On the other hand, ASEAN countries and China have shared 'their mutual respect for each other's independence, sovereignty and territorial integrity in accordance with international law' and 'respect for and commitment to (i) freedom of navigation in and over-flight above the South China Sea' ... 'in accordance with universally-recognised principles of international law including the 1982 United Nations Convention on the Law of the Sea (UNCLOS)' as indicated in the ASEAN–China Strategic Partnership Vision 2030.[16] However, China's rejection of the Permanent Court of Arbitration's ruling on 12 July 2016 has raised concerns over Chinese tactics in COC negotiations. China's non-cooperative attitude towards resolving the SCS dispute compelled the Quad's FOIP and ASEAN Indo-Pacific Outlook, as they saw the enlistment of maritime cooperation as the most important element for cooperation. In other words, in the field of security, ASEAN considers the FOIP a counter to security challenges posed by China in the South China Sea.

Although the ASEAN Outlook on the Indo-Pacific was argued as the same old wine in a new bottle,[17] it reflects the timely response of the grouping to the newly established mechanism which was not initiated or led by ASEAN. Buttressing its centrality in underlying principles for promoting cooperation in the Indo-Pacific region, ASEAN looks to consolidate its prime to any cooperative mechanisms in the region. Australian leaders' ideas of building a Asia-Pacific forum in 1973 and am Asia-Pacific Community in 2008 respectively received objections from some ASEAN key members, as the ideas denied ASEAN's role in the region.[18]

Vietnam's position

The US Free and Open Indo-Pacific strategy was defined by the US Deputy Assistant Secretary of State Alex N. Wong in early April 2018,[19] and restated in the US Department of Defense's Indo-Pacific Strategy Report,[20] released in early June 2019. As per the report, 'Free Indo-Pacific' means 'to be free from coercion' on the international plane, and 'free in terms of good governance, in terms of fundamental rights, in terms of transparency and anti-corruption'[21] at the national level. An 'Open Indo-Pacific' means open Sea Lines of Communication and open airways, more open logistics infrastructure, more open investment, and more open trade. The FOIP strategy is largely compatible with Vietnam's national interests.[22] In the field of security, China's claims and its assertiveness, especially its activities of militarisation in the South China Sea in recent years, is one of the biggest security challenges to Vietnam. Therefore, the FOIP's principle of non-coercion by any country (including China) if operational will benefit Vietnam. Freedom of navigation and over-flight as advocated and conducted by the Quad's navies in the South China Sea in recent years has ensured that the international law, including UNCLOS (adopted in 1982), is being implemented in the sea. In terms of economics, the principles of more open logistics infrastructure, more open investment, and more open trade create momentum for Vietnam's economic reforms, especially since it signed a free trade agreement (FTA) with the European Union in June 2019, and is now undergoing negotiations regarding the Comprehensive and Progressive Agreement for Trans-Pacific Partnership (CPTPP) and the

114 *India, Vietnam and ASEAN regionalism*

Regional Comprehensive Economic Partnership (RCEP). In the context that Vietnam has been in the process of diversifying its international trade to decrease its economic dependence on China, good political relations with the Quad help Vietnam achieve its goals. On the political front, Vietnam and Japan upgraded their relations to an extensive strategic partnership in 2014. Vietnam and India enhanced their relationship to a comprehensive strategic partnership in 2016. The Vietnam–Australia strategic partnership was established in 2018. Before that, during the visit of General Secretary of the Central Committee of the Communist Party of Vietnam (CPV) Nguyen Phu Trong to the US in 2015, the US and Vietnam expressed their respect for each other's political systems.[23] In other words, there are now no major concerns between Vietnam and the Quad over political issues.

However, there have been differences between diplomatic statements and the maritime operational measures implemented by Vietnam in response to the FOIP. Diplomatically, Vietnam has not officially responded directly to the strategy to date. During the visit of President Tran Dai Quang to India in March 2018, the Vietnam–India Joint Statement reflected Vietnam's viewpoint for the first time regarding the Indo-Pacific, when the two countries 'reiterated the importance of achieving a peaceful and prosperous Indo-Pacific region where sovereignty and international law, freedom of navigation and over-flight, sustainable development and a free, fair and open trade and investment system are respected'.[24]

In the same visit to India, President Tran Dai Quang did not use the term 'Indo-Pacific' in his speech. Instead, in his speech at the Nehru Museum Library, he used 'Indo-Asia-Pacific' to mention the geographical scope stretching from the Indian Ocean to the Asia-Pacific.[25] President Quang clarified the Vietnamese approach towards the Indo-Pacific, which was to support (1) an open and rules-based region, and a common interest in the maintenance of peace, stability, and inclusive prosperity; (2) the promotion of the freedom of navigation, and facilitating unimpeded trade, and to prevent the Indo-Asia-Pacific from being balkanized into spheres of influence; (3) a common space for co-existence and development, in the belief that the Indo-Asia-Pacific is vast enough for every country to flourish and prosper; and (4) the development of effective mechanisms to maintain peace, stability, and the rule of law, so as to ensure the common security, prevent conflict and war, and effectively address security challenges.

It is obvious that Vietnam's vision for the FOIP is no different from that of the ASEAN Outlook towards the Indo-Pacific. President Quang's aspiration of establishing effective mechanisms to maintain peace, stability, and the rule of law in the region was materialised by the ASEAN Outlook, in which ASEAN plays a central role in the Indo-Pacific region.

There has been reluctance to use the term Indo-Pacific in exercises or other humanitarian efforts conducted by ASEAN countries. However, it is logical that while the Quad members are competing with each other, especially the US and Japan, and the US and India, in terms of trade, and India and Japan have not attached values such as human rights and democracy to their diplomatic activities in the region, security has become a common point in the Quad's engagement in the Indo-Pacific. In this context, maritime security, including freedom of navigation, has become a priority field. In the last few years, there have been Freedom of Navigation Operations (FONOPs) conducted by the Quad's navies in the South China Sea. Besides the Quad, the navies of France and Britain have also deployed FONOPs in the Sea. Lying at the centre of Indo-Pacific and owning the most strategic port Cam Ranh, and other important ports in the region, Vietnam has been a natural destination for the Quad's naval ships' friendship visits in the last few years.

In short, anti-China connotations attached to FOIP prevent countries from expressing their positions on the Indo-Pacific strategy. However, the benefits that FOIP could provide, especially in the security field, have been approached cautiously by countries in the region. An Indo-Pacific region of cooperation, instead of rivalry, is an aspiration of most countries in the vast Southeast Asia.

Conclusion

While much narrative exists with regard to the bilateral relations between India and Vietnam, the utility of ASEAN multilateral meetings to enhance understanding about the Indo-Pacific is another dimension of engagement. The issues of regional security, maritime security, and economic cooperation have gained more attention between India and Vietnam. Issues such as internal security, cooperation among security institutions are likely to be more focused by the two countries.

The National Security Council of India and the Ministry of Public Security of Vietnam have long been of the view that an MoU between the two could be undertaken. This would provide the required arrangement to discuss issues related to the training of Indian personnel in counter-insurgency and guerrilla warfare. Further, Vietnamese personnel could visit the Jungle Warfare School established by the Indian army in Mizoram. The sustained engagement would build necessary cooperation. India is keen to implement regular intelligence cooperation to stop Fake Indian Currency Notes (FICN) reaching India. In the past, in a few instances, a few Vietnamese travelling to India were apprehended with large quantities of FICN. India also wants to have a regular dialogue with the Internal Security division of Vietnam on a yearly basis. This has been strongly promoted by the NSA. The NSA would also be accompanying the Prime Minister during his visit to Vietnam. Cyber security is one area where India is very keen to work with Vietnam, as well as with ASEAN. This would include working on industrial cyber security instruments and data protection, and the same might be replicated in the defence domain. Moreover, India and Vietnam would like to work together on Linux-based systems to make their programmes less vulnerable and more secure. This cooperation would be primarily in the defence domain. In this regard, IIT Bombay has been doing pioneering work.

116 India, Vietnam and ASEAN regionalism

Information technology is another area where both Vietnam and India are keen to cooperate. India has planned internships for Vietnamese students so that they could be trained by Indian software professionals and thereby develop software programming skills. However, this internship would include mandatory work in Vietnam on their return. India is keen to engage Indian private companies to secure employment after internships for Vietnamese software professionals.

The setting up of a satellite tracking centre and data reception has been already agreed and the work has been underway in this regard. However, the location needs more secure facilities, so that there is no intrusion or unwarranted snooping by any outside agency. In this regard, both the Cabinet Secretariat and the National Technical Research organisation, along with DRDO, should work together. The skill training and the software development would create a pool of skilled professionals which would contribute to the development of Vietnam as a software sufficient country. This would also help Vietnam in developing its e-commerce and e-governance architecture.

White shipping information has been shared between India and Singapore, as well as India and the US, under agreements and joint declarations that have been signed in the past. With Vietnam being one of the strategically important countries, it would be advantageous to get a similar agreement signed.

Notes

1 Brewster, David. 2009. 'India's Strategic Partnership with Vietnam: The Search for a Diamond on the South China Sea?' *Asian Security*, 5(1): 26
2 Loc. cit. For recent debates on strategic issues see Pant, Harsh V. 2008. *Contemporary Debates in Indian Foreign and Security Policy: India Negotiates its Rise in the International System*. Palgrave McMillan: New York
3 Brewster, 2009: 27. See also Sridharan, Kripa. 1996. *The ASEAN region in India as foreign policy*. Dartmouth: Singapore
4 Dutram, Eric. 2011. 'Forget BRIC ETFs: Look to VISTA Nations For Better Opportunities', October 24. https://etfdb.com/2011/forget-bric-etfs-look-to-vista-nations-for-better-opportunities/ (accessed 25 February 2020)
5 Jha, Pankaj K. 2008. 'India–Vietnam Relations: Need for Enhanced Cooperation', *Strategic Analysis*, 32(6): 1089
6 India–Vietnam Relations at http://www.mea.gov.in/Portal/ForeignRelation/Vietnam_Dec_2013.pdf (accessed 21 September 2015)
7 2016–2020 Plan of Action to Implement the ASEAN–India Partnership For Peace, Progress And Shared Prosperity, adopted in Vientiane, Lao PDR on 30 November 2004. https://cil.nus.edu.sg/wp-content/uploads/formidable/18/2016-2020-PoA-to-Implement-the-ASEAN-India-Partnership.pdf (accessed 25 February 2020)
8 'ASEAN Outlook on the Indo-Pacific'. https://asean.org/storage/2019/06/ASEAN-Outlook-on-the-Indo-Pacific_FINAL_22062019.pdf (accessed 9 July 2019)
9 See Department of Foreign Affairs and Trade (Government of Australia). 2018. 'Australia-India-Japan-United States Consultations', 15 November. https://dfat.gov.au/news/media/Pages/australia-india-japan-united-states-consultations-2018.aspx; and US Department of State. 2019. 'Australia-India-Japan United States Consultations ("The Quad")', 31 May. https://www.state.gov/u-s-australia-india-japan-consultations-the-quad/ (accessed 11 July 2019)

India, Vietnam and ASEAN regionalism   117

10 Hiep, Hong Le. 2018. 'America's Free and Open Indo-Pacific Strategy: A Vietnamese Perspective', *Perspective*, ISEAS Yusof Ishak Institute, 7 August: 3
11 'ASEAN–China Strategic Partnership Vision 2030'. https://asean.org/storage/2018/11/ASEAN-China-Strategic-Partnership-Vision-2030.pdf (accessed 11 July 2019)
12 'ASEAN Outlook on the Indo-Pacific'. https://asean.org/storage/2019/06/ASEAN-Outlook-on-the-Indo-Pacific_FINAL_22062019.pdf (accessed 9 July 2019)
13 Kusaka, Kiyoshi. 2019. 'US–China trade war will hit ASEAN economy harder', *Nikkei Asian Review*, 9 July. https://asia.nikkei.com/Economy/US-China-trade-war-will-hit-ASEAN-economy-harder (accessed 11 July 2019)
14 Hiep, 2018: 3
15 Ministry of Foreign Affairs of Japan. 2019. 'Japan-Australia-India-U.S. Consultations', May 31. https://www.mofa.go.jp/press/release/press4e_002464.html (accessed 11 July 2019)
16 'ASEAN–China Strategic Partnership Vision 2030'. https://asean.org/storage/2018/11/ASEAN-China-Strategic-Partnership-Vision-2030.pdf (accessed 11 July 2019)
17 Hoang, Thi Ha. 2019. 'ASEAN Outlook on the Indo-Pacific: Old Wine in New Bottle?' *Perspective*, ISEAS Yusof Ishak Institute, 25 June: 2
18 Frost, Frank. 2016. *Engaging the neighbours: Australia and ASEAN since 1974.* Canberra: Australian National University Press. 150–153
19 Wong, Alex N. 2018. Briefing on The Indo-Pacific Strategy, US Department of State Special Briefing, 2 April. https://www.state.gov/briefing-on-the-indo-pacific-strategy/ (accessed 11 July 2019)
20 US Department of Defense. 2019. 'Indo-Pacific Strategy Report', 1 June: 4.
21 Ibid.: 4–6
22 Hiep, 2018: 4
23 The White House. 2015. 'United States–Vietnam Joint Vision Statement', 7 July. https://obamawhitehouse.archives.gov/the-press-office/2015/07/07/united-states-%E2%80%93-vietnam-joint-vision-statement (accessed 11 July 2019)
24 Ministry of External Affairs (Government of India). 2018. 'India–Vietnam Joint Statement during State visit of President of Vietnam to India', 3 March. https://www.mea.gov.in/bilateral-documents.htm?dtl/29535/IndiaVietnam_Joint_Statement_during_State_visit_of_President_of_Vietnam_to_India_March_03_2018 (accessed 11 July 2019)
25 'Full speech of Vietnam President Tran Dai Quang at Nehru Museum Library'. 2018. *The Economic Times*, 10 March. https://economictimes.indiatimes.com/news/politics-and-nation/full-speech-of-vietnam-president-tran-dai-quang-at-nehru-museum-library/articleshow/63212961.cms (accessed 12 July 2019)

9 The China factor in India–Vietnam relations

The rise of China has been the most important development in the post-Cold War phase which has defined strategic and political relations. Further, it has given a new dimension to regional politics and security. The Beijing consensus is challenging the Washington consensus, leading to new permutations and combinations in the geopolitical matrix. Questions have invariably been asked within the East Asia politics about whether India–Vietnam relations have a 'China shadow' which forces China's neighbours to cooperate closely. The two narratives that have emerged in the recent past have been primarily related to the increasing economic and political clout of China, which has fuelled its defence and strategic ambitions across Asia, particularly in East and Southeast Asia.

Inevitably the narratives which germinate from India and China are at contrast with regard to the view that India–Vietnam relations have a China factor embedded into the partnership. The clear-cut analogies which have been drawn is that while China is the bigger neighbour for both countries, it has also fought wars with both, and the two countries have water sharing problems with China, which is the upper riparian state. There are three basic areas where China remains a dominant factor in the bilateral ties between the two countries. Firstly, the increasing assertiveness of China at the India–China border. Secondly, China, being the upper riparian states, uses its geographic advantage to divert water from both the Brahmaputra and Mekong rivers and make hydroelectric dams on the Mekong. The third aspect is the exploration of oil and gas in the legitimate EEZ of Vietnam which has been protested by China. The issue connects indirectly with China's claims over the Spratly and the Paracel Islands. The South China Sea is critical for regional maritime trade. China is facing competition from Vietnamese and Indonesian fishermen in the SCS, which is the third-largest fishing ground in the world, and therefore intimidating the two countries.

Primarily from these issues, there are two issues which put China at the centre for the two countries: the Sino-Indian territorial dispute, and Vietnam's maritime border dispute with China.

China as a neighbour – an opportunity as well as a threat

While China has been one of the major trading partners with India and Vietnam, looking at China as an opportunity has two dimensions. Low-cost production has led to low cost inputs for more advanced production facilities in the cases of iron and steel, while, on the other hand, low-cost production and government financial support has led to many domestic industries losing the production advantage because of cheap Chinese imports (facilitated by China's state subsidies in production). China has been supporting both the development of infrastructure and the building of ancillary industries which have supported its manufacturing capacity. However, the increased dumping of goods in the Asian markets has hampered the growth of domestic industries and, at times, caused the closure of select industries which could not withstand the cheap Chinese imports. However, for India and Vietnam, the issue is the need to look for cooperation in different domains and this includes water security. The building of dams on the Mekong and Brahmaputra is a matter of concern for both countries.

Water-sharing and Chinese dams – Mekong and Brahmaputra

The riparian states of the Mekong have established the Mekong River Commission to discuss the issue of water scarcity in the downstream countries, and how the water issues and resource management need to addressed by the riparian countries of the Mekong. The Mekong River Commission, to which both China and Myanmar have been observer countries, has been seeking a possible solution to the crisis. During the summer seasons, owing to the shortfall in rain, the river is dried out in many stretches, and this has seriously affected low-lying areas which have been dependent on fisheries and river tourism for their livelihood. Communities living near the Mekong river are dependent on rice cultivation, which is a water-intensive crop. Any depletion in water availability also affects rice crops. Lower riparian countries have raised the issue of China obstructing the natural flow of Mekong river. Cambodia had accused China of contaminating the Mekong river water, which has been used by tanneries and other polluting industries in southern China. The Mekong River Commission has been meeting regularly to address the issues of water security, fisheries, riverine transport and tourism, and the issue of dams, but compliance among member states and observers is voluntary. Many groups in Southeast Asia have been accusing China of both the depleting water flow, and of constructing multiple dams on the Mekong river. China has already built many dams and has plans for building about half a dozen dams on the river in its territory. China has been defying all these accusations by saying that dams had been constructed to regulate the flow of water, and also to curb any flash floods which would occur during the rainy season. The looming issue is whether the lower riparian states of the Mekong can address their grievances and seek concessions from China, the upper riparian country.

120   *The China factor in India–Vietnam relations*

The issue has become serious because of the fact that this has been one of the severest droughts in the region in the last five decades. The Mekong also supports the livelihood of more than 60 million people who are dependent on cargo transfer through river, fisheries and irrigation. The Mekong has one of the most diversified fishing cultures, and has been one of the world's largest inland fisheries resources. For years, non-governmental organizations (NGOs) have blamed Chinese dams for shrinking the Mekong River, known in China as the Lancang River, which originates in the Tibetan Plateau and runs through Yunnan. Now the river – a lifeline not just for people living in those parts of China, but also for the tens of millions living downriver in the nations of Cambodia, Laos, Myanmar, Thailand and Vietnam – is at its lowest level in two decades, disrupting cargo traffic.

The Mekong is the eighth-largest river in the world, with a basin covering more than 800,000 square kilometres of mainland East Asia. Rising in the Tibetan plateau, it flows through the Yunnan province in southwest China, forms parts of the boundaries at the 'Golden Triangle' between Laos, Thailand, Myanmar and China, and then runs through Laos, demarcating a large part of the Thai–Laotian border, before flowing into Vietnamese and Cambodian territory, and eventually emptying into the South China Sea via the delta south of Ho Chi Minh City in Vietnam. The Mekong basin is populated largely by agrarian communities; in all, more than 80 million people depend on the river for resources ranging from drinking and irrigation water to fish and transport. Apart from being a natural lifeline, the Mekong has, over the last decade, become a major hub of the economic development plans of many of its riparian states. The river itself offers significant development resources in terms of hydropower and water for large-scale irrigation projects, and is also a major potential regional shipping route.

As the uppermost riparian country, China enjoys significant geographical advantages over the lower riparian states, particularly Cambodia and Vietnam. Control of the river basin may also be measured in terms of each state's proportion of river discharge, basin area and basin population. Laos contributes the largest amount of water flow, and accounts for a larger basin area than any other state. Thailand dominates in terms of basin population, and has the second-largest flow contribution and land area. Cambodia and Vietnam make significant flow and population contributions, but are fundamentally disadvantaged by their downstream position, which subjects them to floods, droughts and the effects of development upstream.[1]

The levels of co-operation among the various states of Mekong are quite limited, but there have been scholars that sit on both sides of the fence. Blake Ratner, in one of his articles, speculates that there are limitations to the joint management and cooperation. He opines that the opportunities for the six states that share the Mekong River to benefit directly from its joint management are more limited, and the risks to the livelihoods of downstream communities from development schemes are more important than the historic rhetoric of Mekong development has implied. Changes in the broader political

The China factor in India–Vietnam relations 121

and economic context have sidelined the Mekong River Commission, the one institution charged with regional cooperation to manage the river. Improved regional governance in the decades to come depends upon the efforts made by many actors to raise the incentives for intergovernmental cooperation, expand civil society engagement, and strengthen the mechanisms for cross-border accountability.[2] The Indochinese states are approaching Mekong development with a mix of national, bilateral and multilateral ventures. At the regional level, Mekong-wide cooperation structures are welcomed particularly as a means of improving access to international project aid and funding.

Politically, Laos and Cambodia especially see regionalism as advancing their shared aim of cultivating more trading partners and donors. Vietnam, Laos and Cambodia have also tried to develop better cooperation amongst themselves, ranging from cross-border trade agreements to coordinated infrastructure development in their border provinces, targeting agriculture, education, environmental conservation, tourism, and trade. Overall, the political and economic picture in the Mekong basin is one of significant imbalance. Myanmar is very weak on all counts, except that it has no pressing national need for the Mekong's resources. China is autonomous enough, and Thailand probably economically strong enough, to unilaterally develop or dominate their sections of the basin. Their activities will compete with and adversely affect the interests of communities living near the Mekong river in Laos, Cambodia and Vietnam, which are more dependent upon the Mekong's resources and, as such, are the most vulnerable. The upstream–downstream conflict element is very strong, especially because of the correlation between a downstream position and dependence on the common resource. On the other hand, all riparian states share an extremely strong developmental imperative and greatly value regionalism as a means of furthering economic development and regional security. The question is, to what extent can the predilection for regional cooperation overcome the competitive, and sometimes zero-sum, elements of national development goals? Moreover, in a situation where physical, political and economic geography dictate such a strong asymmetry of power, to what extent will the benefits of regional integration reflect the interests of the weaker downstream states, rather than the needs of the strongest upstream state?[3]

In Asia, India and China share a complicated relationship, with elements of both cooperation and competition in their engagement. Although the cooperation between the two emerging powers is significant, there is also rising competition in the geostrategic space, especially in the Asian region. Some open questions deepen mistrust: the unresolved dispute on the India–China border; China's recent claim to the northeast Indian province of Arunachal Pradesh; China's issue of stapled visas for people from Jammu and Kashmir, and rumours of plans to build dams on the Chinese side of the Brahmaputra are all areas of serious Indian concern. These irritants have been further amplified during the past two decades by China's ties and aid to Pakistan. Conversely, China is not pleased with India giving refuge to Dalai Lama and has raised concerns over India's tacit support to Tibet's freedom initiatives.[4] The media

122 *The China factor in India–Vietnam relations*

and strategic hawks from both sides have been exploiting these issues to the hilt. One of the main contentions between India and China has been in the area of water scarcity, the issue being for both countries to provide water both for drinking and for agricultural purposes. With the increase in the industrial production and the shift of the rural pollution to the urban centre in the industrial hubs of the southern China, it has become imperative for China to provide water to both its industrial units and the increasing migrant population working as labour in those units. This issue has gained so much concern in Chinese discourse that it has initiated projects to divert waters both in southern China and also now, increasingly, on the Tibetan plateau. Diversion of the water in Tsangpo (also known as Yarlung Tsangpo) has also been discussed by Chinese decision-makers for quite some time. The plan to divert the Tsangpo river water started in 2000, with two proposed Chinese projects on the river that are likely to affect India. One is the proposed Great South–North Water Transfer project diverting Tibetan waters, and the first phase proposed to build 300 kilometres of tunnels; the other plan was to build channels to draw waters from the Jingsha, Yalong, and Dadu rivers on the eastern rim of the Tibetan plateau.[5] The Chinese need for water, and their need to create irrigation systems for its water-parched southern region, has also led to the building of dams on the Brahmaputra.

According to media reports in 2010, China initiated construction work along the Brahmaputra river at Medog in lower Tibet, which is only '30 kilometres north of the Indian border. There have been reports that China has planned to divert 200 billion cubic metres of the waters of the Brahmaputra from south to north to feed the Yellow River since 600 to 800 cities in north China have been experiencing water shortage, particularly Shaanxi, Hebel, Beijing and Tianjin. There are also reports that China has been using the manpower earlier involved in the Lhasa-Beijing railway for the construction of a US\$ 1.2 billion hydropower/diversion project on the Brahmaputra. Estimates are that the project would generate 40,000 megawatts of power and would be completed in a five to seven year time period'.[6] While Beijing declared in 2011 that it would go ahead with the construction of a US\$ 1.2 billion hydroelectric power station on the Brahmaputra (known as Yarlung Tsangpo in China), it maintains that this project will not impact the flow of water to downstream countries like India and Bangladesh. While the run of the river Zangmu dam is meant to deal with shortages of power in Tibet, China is said to be also considering diverting the waters in the upper reaches towards Xinjiang.[7] India has started survey work to divert the Brahmaputra through a gravity link canal, taking off from Jogighopa and joining the Ganges just above Farakka to meet water shortages in the western and southern parts of the country in its ambitious inter-state river linking project. The river linking plan of India envisages the construction of a dam on the Manas river and a 457 km link canal. Further, a dam and barrage on the river Sankosh (the two tributaries of the Brahmaputra that originate from Bhutan) has been proposed.[8] India is working on a plan of action for the interlinking of rivers and taking contingency measures to resolve the water

The China factor in India–Vietnam relations   123

crisis in the water-scarce parts of India. Chinese plans for diverting the Brahmaputra is a concern for India and therefore it has to garner support from lower riparian countries of Mekong, so that a joint stance can be adopted against China (the upper riparian country) and Tibet, being the source of the two rivers – the Brahmaputra and the Mekong.

China's island building in South China Sea

One important element which impacts both India and Vietnam is the development with regard to island building in South China Sea. China's island building and assertive position on the South China Sea islands forced the Philippines to file a case in the Permanent Court of Arbitration (PCA), an intergovernmental organisation, against China's artificial islands in the South China Sea. The PCA gave its judgment in favour of the Philippines, outright rejecting China's claim of a 200-nautical-mile Exclusive Economic Zone (EEZ) around its reclaimed islands. Instead of complying with the ruling, China rejected the verdict. The issue highlighted the concern among Spratly-Islands claimant countries about whether powerful nations can redefine geographical boundaries, and undermine global institutions. The recent spurt of island building and reclamation, as well as the building of air strips and subsequent positioning of missiles by China, has aggravated problems. The naval patrols and group sorties undertaken by the US have increased tensions in the SCS. The SCS has emerged as a global hot spot because of the US and China tensions. In the past, the EP-3 event, which happened in the early 2000s, had aggravated tensions in SCS. The US has been, to a large extent, ambivalent, both politically and strategically on the SCS issue, but has been conducting regular naval patrols and maritime surveillance sorties. ASEAN as an institution failed to bring China on board, and failed in cajoling the country into signing the Code of Conduct on the South China Sea. The South China Sea as a region was dependent on the Declaration of the Code of Conduct promulgated in 2002, which was more of a voluntary declaration with no compliance or implementation provision.

In the case of Southeast Asia, and particularly the South China Sea, the competing narratives have dominated the discourse, while the ad hoc statements and compliance mechanisms have compromised regional security or deferred decision making and even discussion regarding prickly issues. In the post-Global War on Terror phase (post-2001), there were five major things which have happened in the case of Southeast Asia, which in a way influenced the dynamism that now exists in contemporary times. Firstly, estranged partners of the US became engaged again, for example Indonesia and Thailand. Secondly, the role of India in the larger geopolitical set-up was seen as indispensable. Thirdly, the smaller powers, such as Vietnam and the Philippines, were seen as necessary outposts to monitor developments in both Southeast Asia and the South China Sea. This was also amplified by the fact that these two economies started showing signs of reinvigoration, with a better-than-average rate of growth. Manufacturing also started to emerge in Indonesia, Vietnam and the

124 *The China factor in India–Vietnam relations*

Philippines, posing competition to China's state-subsidized production and manufacturing. Fourthly, military modernization across Southeast Asia was spurred on by an increasingly assertive stance from not only China, but many other players, including the US, India and Japan. Lastly, the US pivot to Asia policy was a stark reminder that US was and would remain an indispensable player in the region. This was further accentuated by informal dialogue mechanisms, such as the East Asia Summit, which included the US and Russia as members. The primacy of China in Southeast Asia was becoming increasingly challenged. This was apparent with the increasing references to Southeast Asian security, and the importance of extra regional powers to maintain peace, clearly indicating the negative role played by China. Further, there has been increasing pressure on select Southeast Asian countries to deport Uighur refugees and enforce effective border control measures with neighbouring countries of Southeast Asia, such as Myanmar and Vietnam. At times, the Chinese border guards have violated the borders of Myanmar and Vietnam in pursuit of Uighurs, leading to tension between the countries.

The ineffectiveness of ASEAN in checking Chinese aggression in the SCS was raised by India, Japan, and Australia, but the three countries have accepted ASEAN as a vital institution to address regional security issues. The institutionalization of ADMM+ and the ASEAN Maritime Forum have anchored multilateralism to the defence and maritime domain, leading to a power struggle within the Southeast Asian region. ASEAN's communiqués have also made frequent references since 2011 to the South China Sea, which was not liked by China. China has made it clear that the SCS is one of its core areas of national interest and is non-negotiable. Among the other claimant countries, two countries – Vietnam and the Philippines – have defied China's dominance in ASEAN-led forums, particularly on the issue of the South China Sea.

It is not that there has never been any possibility of cooperation between China, Vietnam and the Philippines in the past. Way back in the late 1990s, China, Vietnam and the Philippines discussed the possibility of trilateral cooperation in the region, both with regard to disasters and joint exploration of oil and gas in the South China Sea. Vietnam has the largest group of islands under its control, followed by China, Malaysia, the Philippines (which lost one of its islands – the Scarborough Shoal), Chinese Taipei (Taiwan), and Brunei. The Philippines, with its Visiting Forces Agreement (VFA) with the US, was perceived by China as a threat to its dominance in Southeast Asia. There were larger nations, such as Singapore and Malaysia, which had been more accommodative to Chinese charm.

From the perspective of the Philippines, the developments have been supported because of ASEAN's inaction. China pressured Cambodia during the ASEAN Summit in Phnom Penh in 2012, insisting that the communiqué must not make any reference to SCS issues, showing China's diplomatic clout with select countries of Southeast Asia. The result was that ASEAN failed to release a communiqué for the first time in its history. It also reinforced the belief that ASEAN has still been divided into three major camps – pro-China, anti-China, and neutral players. The ASEAN chairmanship now will be increasingly scrutinized accordingly. However, there are still many examples which were perceived to be pro-China but have adhered to the ASEAN consensus. In the current context, there are three measures which need to be undertaken by ASEAN. Firstly, it should strengthen its dialogue with its dialogue partners on specific issues of security. Secondly, ASEAN have to address core security issues and seek the indulgence of dialogue partners in developing a peaceful region. Thirdly, ASEAN nations should recognize the status quo to be maintained by the claimants, and finalise the draft agreement for adopting the Code of Conduct in the South China Sea.

India, Vietnam and China

The dynamics evolving in Southeast Asia, as well as the South China Sea, impact India and Vietnam from a political, strategic and economic perspective. Southeast Asia have witnessed tensions between great powers in South China Sea in the past. The serious incident in April 2001, between the United States and the People's Republic of China (PRC), involved a collision over the South China Sea between a US Navy EP-3 reconnaissance plane and a People's Liberation Army (PLA) naval F-8 fighter. After surviving the near-fatal accident, the US crew made an emergency landing onto the PLA's Lingshui airfield on Hainan Island, and the PRC detained the 24 crew members for 11 days.[9] While ASEAN has chosen to remain non-committal since 2008 when it comes to pushing the code of conduct, China has been claiming that it has abided by the Declaration of the Code of Conduct on the South China Sea that was signed in 2002. This voluntary declaration has, in a way, stymied any binding agreement on the South China Sea. The Chinese charm had really worked on non-suspecting ASEAN nations.

Following the Global War on Terror phase (post-2001), many Southeast Asian nations showed their allegiance to the US. For example, Indonesia and Thailand, two major beneficiaries of the US foreign military assistance programme, returned to the US fold. Indonesia was excused of its human rights abuses and military excesses during East Timor crisis, and a partial embargo on the US arms supply to Indonesia was lifted. Vietnam has been compelled to get closer to the US because of bullying by China in the SCS. The Philippines, on the other hand, has been contemplating the return of US presence to its country.

India also started taking a rather proactive role, and made statements referring to growing tensions in the South China Sea during PM Modi's visits to Japan and the US. India's stance has been projected as a stakeholder in the SCS. The issue of India being an assertive player has been debated within India, but then India's 'ambition' to be a major power was defined in two different narratives emerging from the strategic and foreign policy debating communities.

Between the years 2010 and 2019, the military modernization across Southeast Asia was spurred on by the increasingly assertive stance of China and the intimidating manoeuvres made by the Chinese navy and fishermen militia.

126 *The China factor in India–Vietnam relations*

The US Indo-Pacific strategy projected that the US was and would remain a stakeholder in the region. US involvement in the region has always been a need for many countries. However, for many countries, such as Malaysia, Singapore, Thailand, and Indonesia, Chinese diaspora were still an economically dominant community, and therefore they have to balance domestic priorities and security compulsions.

The most significant trend has been a distinct shift in Manila's national security planning, from a focus on neutralizing domestic insurgencies and coping with natural disasters toward a more external orientation, directed at securing its maritime environment and cultivating a regional balance of power in response to growing Chinese influence. The US-led security network in this region is largely based on the San Francisco System of bilateral security alliances.[10] However, the hub-and-spokes model has its flaws, as the US has not started prioritising its spokes according to its strategic utility, economic strength and international clout. As a result, the Philippines has been left, to a certain extent, ignored. However, with the Philippines posting a healthy economic growth average of 6.5 per cent in 2018, and slowly building its military particularly naval capability, albeit with second-hand naval vessels imported from the US.

The Philippines has persevered in its insistence that the South China Sea disputes are a regional and international issue. Its prior efforts in engaging ASEAN to produce statements and documents about the dispute are indicative of this approach. Moreover, the Philippines' arbitration case with the PCA under the guidelines of the United Nations Convention on the Law of the Sea (UNCLOS) is another sign of how it involves multilateral bodies in building new foundations in the region, which are based on international law and over-all stability in the region.[11] Mischief Reef in 1995 and Scarborough Shoal in 2012 projected the Philippines' resolve to internationalize the South China Sea territorial disputes. The 1995 Mischief Reef incident was the first time that a confrontation between China and the Philippines was reported, and the Philippines was the second country apart from Vietnam which faced Chinese wrath in the high seas.[12] The Scarborough standoff was resolved because of US intervention, but the Philippines lost its territory as the Chinese returned to reclaim it.

The Philippines has repeatedly raised the issue of the South China Sea in ASEAN meetings. The December 1998 ASEAN Summit in Hanoi, dealt the Philippines' efforts a blow, as the organization avoided dealing with the disputes in public. The conflict de-escalated in the early 2000s, although not because of significant progress in conflict management and resolution.[13] ASEAN wariness to raise security issues in a multilateral setting emboldened China. Again, despite pressure from Vietnam and the Philippines, the ASEAN communiqué was not released during the Phnom Penh Summit in 2012. The reluctance of ASEAN to work together as a unit was exposed, and the fissures were apparent. However, consequently, a reference to the South China Sea was made in the subsequent ASEAN communiqués but it was only a soft indication.

The China factor in India–Vietnam relations   127

ASEAN's reluctance to undertake joint initiatives to address the issue was met with a Chinese wall. Of late, ASEAN faced the biggest challenge to its centrality and its capability to bring about regional peace particularly in SCS. As a result, instead of ASEAN member countries addressing their problems in a regional setting, they took recourse to major power security assurances. In the past, there has been cooperation between China, Vietnam and the Philippines when the three countries conducted a Joint Marine Seismic Undertaking, which concluded in 2008.

Given recurrent tensions in the SCS because of Chinese artificial island building and placing dome radars and weapons (including surface-to-air-missiles) on those islands, there might be more tensions and militarization. ASEAN could become increasingly fragmented, as a regional organization gains acceptance when it can give security to its members. ASEAN's centrality has been challenged, and this would give China an opportunity to negotiate bilaterally with each of the claimant countries. The US might seek bases and conduct surveillance and reconnaissance sorties to protect its maritime trade in the region. It might also enter into a strategic partnership agreement with Vietnam. The increasing tensions could see anti-Chinese riots in claimant countries, as witnessed in Vietnam. The claimant parties could explore separate dialogue among themselves to address the issue. After all, the South China Sea is not only about oil and gas, islands and islets, it is about fisheries, ocean resources, freedom of navigation, and commerce. However, the major players would protect their stakes if the situation gets aggravated.

India, Vietnam and the contours of the Silk Road strategy

For India and Vietnam, the issue which germinates is how to make China abide by the internal regulations and accept the international norms. On the other hand, China sees itself as regaining lost pride. The debates about China's rise have gained much academic attention in recent years. However, the problems, both internal and external, that China has been facing have been either swept aside, or there are very few arguments to support that China is fallible. In any academic and multidisciplinary setting, it is natural to audit the strengths and weaknesses of any country. While militarily and economically China has been a rising power, in the past couple of years its rate of economic growth, which had supported China's rise, has come under stress. This was visible during the global financial crisis and also during the current economic outlook provided by different international financial institutions. The IMF report clearly stated that China's economic growth is decelerating and other economies might encroach the captive market that China has been occupying in Europe and the US because of subsidized low-cost production.

The question is – what are the signs of such Chinese slowdown, and what possible options exist for China in the short and long term? The basic premise of economics is to maintain the economies of scale and interlink those emerging markets in the global value addition chain so that production superiority can be

128 *The China factor in India–Vietnam relations*

maintained. China has embarked on such a journey through initiatives such as the Gateway Strategy, opening up its Southern provinces to the markets in Southeast Asia, and its sojourn in Africa to look for resources and minerals that can fuel its economic engine for many decades. However, the resource nationalism and resistance to Chinese projects in countries, such as Myanmar and a few African nations, have forced the Chinese economy managers to revisit their strategy. As a result, the 'One Belt One Road' strategy emerged.

The most important query that emerges at this juncture is – what are the broad contours of such a strategy? Is it a neo-imperialist approach adopted by China to secure its markets and resources? While the usual rhetoric adopted by pro-China scholars is that it is an economic and regional development initiative, anti-China academics counter this by asking how other under-developed and developing economies are going to gain from it.

For China, the largest exporter as well as the manufacturing hub of the globe, the priority is to sustain their manufacturing superiority and economic growth so as to curb any political dissent. However, real wages in China are increasing, and however it may try to control its exchange rate *vis-à-vis* other international currencies, any increase in the value of Chinese currency (Yuan renminbi) *vis-à-vis* the US dollar would erode the low-cost manufacturing advantage of China. As a result, it is trying to integrate itself with low-cost production destinations outside China to manage its low-cost production, and dominate domestic markets in developing countries by weeding out their own individual manufacturing capacities. The OBOR strategy would put stress on the infrastructure sectors of participating economies and would facilitate trade among the countries. However, any infrastructure development would fuel Chinese labour exports to those economies and generate employment for Chinese labour, who are finding employment prospects diminishing within China. Not only would the infrastructure development of the participating economies fuel Chinese exports, but also the development of their ports and harbours. It is a well-known fact that China is facing complaints in the WTO for its dumping of goods and merchandise in many countries. China would need warehousing facilities to retain the market and kill any emerging competition from other low-cost manufacturing economies. Furthermore, it has been seen in the case of Laos and Cambodia that China has not only built ports, roads, and other infrastructure, it has also built Chinese townships to make its labour feel at home. This strategy, from a layman's point of view, is not only economic, but also strategic, as China's OBOR strategy aims to control Asia and Africa through its encirclement strategy, which would benefit China in both the long and short term. The overall objective of China is to control Asia through its cheap exports and also give soft loans to the governments and, in case these governments fail to return these soft loans, then the operating rights of these ports and other related infrastructure would be controlled by China. This can be seen in the case of Gwadar and the ports in Myanmar, as well as in Cambodia.

The China factor in India–Vietnam relations   129

For India, connectivity through highways and railways could play a very positive role in integrating India with her eastern neighbours, including Vietnam. India's needs are twofold: (a) to link India's Manipur with India's main railway corridor, and (b) to re-establish and renovate railway networks in Myanmar. Harmonization of railway tracks in the region is very much essential. Without having a compatible and strong railway system inside Myanmar and Bangladesh, closer communication with the NER and its immediate neighbours will be unfulfilled. The Indian government has come forward and extended a US$ 56 million credit line to the Myanmar government for the upgrading of a 640 km railway system between the Mandalay and Yangon sections. A similar initiative should be taken up for the upgrading of the railway network system in southern (Yangon to Dawei) and northern (Mandalay to Kalay) Myanmar. A possible connection between Myanmar and Thailand could be via Thanbyuzayat and the Three Pagoda Pass, and between India and Myanmar by constructing a new railway line between Tamu and Kalay. On completion of these projects there could be possibilities for a India–Myanmar–Thailand–Malaysia–Singapore rail link, and, finally, a railway system that would connect Delhi with Hanoi.[14] These would facilitate trade with mainland Southeast Asia. Border trade has special significance for the economies of Indian states in the northeast, which share borders with Myanmar, China, Bhutan, and Bangladesh. These states conduct informal trade across borders, and formalization of this border trade would increase merchandise volume and value. Accordingly, measures connected with simplification and facilitation of border trade are being treated as a priority area by the Indian government.

A new counter-narrative to OBOR is also emerging from the US, which sees it pertinent to develop a counter-narrative to the One Belt One Road project. India, Japan, and the US are working on the Indo-Pacific Economic Corridor, and also developing the quadrilateral initiative. The US government has also sanctioned seed money for pilot projects and the conduction of feasibility studies.

Notes

1 Goh, Evelyn. 2006. 'Chapter Two: The Mekong Region', *Adelphi series*, 46(387): 17–18

2 Ratner, Blake D. 2003. 'The Politics of Regional Governance in the Mekong River Basin', *Global Change, Peace & Security*, 15(1): 59

3 Goh, 2006: 22–23

4 Bhattacharyya, Anushree and Chakraborty, Debashis. 2011. 'India's Cross-Border Infrastructure Initiatives in South and Southeast Asia', *The International Spectator*, 46(2): 110

5 Rashid, Harun ur. 'Proposed Diversion of Brahmaputra River by China'. http://www.sydneybashi-bangla.com/Articles/Harun_Diversion%20of%20Brahmaputra%20River%20by%20China.pdf (accessed 6 April 2012)

6 Jha, Hari Bansh. 'Diversion of the Brahmaputra: Myth or Reality?' http://www.idsa.in/idsacomments/DiversionoftheBrahmaputraMythorReality_hbjha_090811 (accessed 5 April 2012)

130 The China factor in India–Vietnam relations

7 Parasher, Sachin. 'Drought-hit China to divert Brahmaputra?' http://articles.timeso findia.indiatimes.com/2011-06-13/india/29652747_1_zangmu-china-dam-brahmaputra (accessed 5 April 2017)

8 'Brahmaputra diversion survey work begins'. http://articles.timesofindia.indiatimes. com/2012-03-21/guwahati/31219714_1_national-water-development-agency-brahma putra-himalayan-component (accessed 6 April 2017)

9 Shirley A Kan et al. 2001. 'China–U.S. Aircraft Collision Incident of April 2001: Assessments and Policy Implications', CRS Report for Congress, October. https:// www.fas.org/sgp/crs/row/RL30946.pdf (accessed 6 April 2018)

10 Misalucha, Charmaine G and Amador, Julio S. 'U.S.–Philippines Security Ties: Building New Foundations?' *Asian Politics & Policy*, 8(1): 52

11 Ibid.: 53

12 Ibid.: 54

13 Ibid.: 54

14 Indian Railways is actively engaged in the harmonization and construction of railway tracks in NER. Considering the projects already sanctioned and under construction, a Diphu–Karong–Imphal–Moreh rail link (on the Indian side) is identified for development, which will link India with ASEAN. Although at present construction work is being carried out in the Diphu–Karong section, linking Karong with Morea via Imphal would link India with Thailand, provided a railway system on the other side (Myanmar) is also developed simultaneously. De, Prabir. 'Infrastructure Development in India'. http://eria.org/research/images/pdf/PDF%20No.2/No.2-pa rt2-4.India.pdf (accessed 19 November 2011)

10 The US factor in Vietnam–India relations

After emerging from the Second World War, the US played a very important role in the world order in the Cold War. In the post-Cold War phase, its hegemony had not yet been challenged. The rise of China made strategists think of a G2 world order, but the dominant role of the US in the world has been recognized at least until the end of the first half of the 21st century. As a leader of the Non-Aligned Movement in the Cold War, and a rising star in the contemporary Indo-Pacific, India is also getting due attention. As an enemy of the US in the Indochina War, Vietnam after the Cold War has attracted the significant attention of the US, because of the former's importance in geopolitical strategy and its growing economic potentials. The Vietnam–US comprehensive partnership, established in 2013, could be seen as a great move in the relations between the two countries. The progress of relations originated from traditional and shared interests in the Asia-Pacific, where the US had strategies such as 'pivot to Asia' and 'Indo-Pacific' to 'defend regional stability' among others.[1] The chapter will examine the US factor in Vietnam–India relations in the different contexts of the Cold War and the post-Cold War.

The US as a threat during the Cold War

The Cold War between two blocs led by the United States and Soviet Union significantly impacted on the foreign policies of many countries in the world, including Vietnam and India. Vietnam and India gained independence in 1945 and 1947 respectively. The Geneva Agreement was signed in 1954, and thereafter the US factor in Vietnam–India relations was inherent. The US, along with the Soviet Union, the People's Republic of China, France, and Great Britain, was a key negotiator at the negotiations. India became a member of the International Control Commission (ICC), an international force established to oversee the implementation of the Geneva Agreements. The US, for its part, decided to get involved in Indochina by 1949, in the context of the North Atlantic Treaty's obligations including France, Chinese communists gaining the upper hand in their war with KMT, and the Soviets' success in exploding an atomic bomb.[2] After France's defeat in Vietnam, the US supported South Vietnam's government, and became deeply engaged within Vietnam in particular

132 The US factor in Vietnam–India relations

and Indochina in general. Anti-imperialism and anti-racialism were the kernel of its foreign policy,[3] but this was profoundly influenced by the modern Indian tradition of idealist political thinking in general.[4] India believed that the US' involvement in South Vietnam could help successfully implement the Geneva Accords. India, for its national interests, sought to develop friendly bilateral relations with the United States by establishing diplomatic relations, seeking American investments and technical knowledge, and developing trade links after initial years of independence.[5]

When the US sent military forces to intervene in the battles in Vietnam, India Gandhi in July 1966 'issued a statement deploring US bombing in North Vietnam and its capital Hanoi. In the latter part of July, in Moscow, she signed a Joint Statement with the Soviet Union demanding an immediate and unconditional end to the US bombing and branding US action in Vietnam as "imperialist aggression".'[6] In the same year, 'Mrs Gandhi developed close links with Nasser of Egypt and Tito of Yugoslavia and began to stress the need for non-aligned countries to cooperate politically and economically in order to counter the danger of neo-colonialism emanating from the U.S. and West European countries.'[7] At the same time, 'India decided to adopt the Green Revolution technology for agricultural development which was backed by the US'.[8]

The Sino-American rapprochement beginning in 1971 and 'the parallel US and Chinese policies on the Bangladesh issue' made India favour the Soviet Union and the latter's friends.[9] 'India defied China and the Western powers hegemony in Asia by recognizing the Heng Samrin regime in Cambodia and coming to the support of Vietnam'.[10]

The US, as a supporter of the development of both Vietnam and India, has tried to enhance ties with both countries, and the major landmark initiatives have been the granting of Permanent Normal Trade Relations (PNTR) with Vietnam, while at the same time lifting sanctions against India, which were imposed because of India's nuclear tests in 1998. The visits of President Obama to Vietnam and India during his second term clearly manifested the strategic role that the US envisaged for the two countries.

The enhanced US–Vietnam relationship

The US became neglected by the Asia-Pacific when it withdrew from the Clark Air Force base and the Subic Bay Naval base in 1991 and 1992. However, in the wake of increasing Chinese influence, the US paid more attention to the region, deploying the 'pivot to Asia' strategy, and the 'Indo-Pacific' strategy. Vice versa, the increasingly important roles of Vietnam since it started to multi-lateralise its foreign policy in 1991, and of India, when it launched its Look East Policy in 1991, have attracted the significant attention of the US.

As mentioned in Chapter 4, after the Cold War in 1991, Vietnam set its foreign policy's objective to be a friend of all countries in the international community and joined ASEAN. The hostile attitude between Vietnam and the

The US factor in Vietnam–India relations   133

United States was scratched out when the US established an office in Hanoi to address the issue of American servicemen missing in the war. Also in 1991, the United States eased travel restrictions on Vietnamese diplomats stationed at the United Nations in New York and on US-organized travel to Vietnam. In 1992, the US lifted restrictions on US telephone service to Vietnam, allowing direct service between the two countries. In the same year, the United States eased some restrictions on US companies doing business in Vietnam. The normalization of the relationship between Vietnam and the US officially took place 1995 when the two countries opened embassies in each other's capitals. Since then, the normalization process has accelerated and bilateral ties have expanded. The most important step toward normalization since 1995 was the signing of a sweeping bilateral trade agreement (BTA), approved by Congress, and signed by President George W. Bush in 2001. Under the BTA, the US extended conditional normal trade relations (NTR) to Vietnam. In return, Vietnam agreed to a range of trade liberalization measures and market-oriented reforms.[11]

In the context of an evolving Asia-Pacific architecture where 'China's rise posed challenges to cooperation and security in the region',[12] Vietnam's foreign policy from 2001 was to actively integrate into the international economy.[13] The full economic normalization between Vietnam and the US was accomplished in December 2006, when President Bush extended Permanent Normal Trade Relations (PNTR) status to Vietnam,[14] and supported Vietnam in their efforts to get access to the World Trade Organization (WTO) in 2007. Thanks to the PNTR, the trade (in goods) relations between the two countries had a strong growth, from US$ 1.189 billion in 2005 to US$ 15.573 billion in 2010 and US$ 52.206 billion in 2016,[15] which made the US the second-largest trading partner (in goods) of Vietnam.

The ties between Vietnam and the US reached a new height when the two countries upgraded their relationship from 'partnership', mentioned for the first time in 2004 during the Vietnamese Prime Minister Phan Van Khai's visit to the US, to a comprehensive partnership. The 'strategic dimension' of Vietnam–US relations was buttressed in 2013, when the Vietnamese President Truong Tan Sang paid a visit to the US. There were five things to take away from the visit. First, in the Joint Statement by President Barack Obama of the United States of America and President Truong Tan Sang of the Socialist Republic of Vietnam in 2013, for the first time, the leaders of the two countries agreed to enhance cooperation at regional and international forums to support peace, stability, cooperation, and development in the Asia-Pacific region. In particular, the two leaders for the first time affirmed their support for the settlement of disputes by peaceful means in accordance with international law, including as reflected in the United Nations Convention on the Law of the Sea; reaffirmed their support for the principle of non-use of force or threat of force in resolving territorial and maritime disputes; underscored the value of full observance of the Declaration of Conduct (DOC) of Parties in the South China Sea, and the importance of launching negotiations to

134   *The US factor in Vietnam–India relations*

conclude an effective Code of Conduct (COC).[16] Second, the respect for each other's political regimes was officially recognised for the first time in 2015, when Vietnam and the US affirmed their comprehensive partnership 'on the basis of respect for the United Nations Charter, international law, and each other's political systems, independence, sovereignty, and territorial integrity'.[17] Third, the last hurdle to the normalization of Vietnam–US relations was removed when the US President Barack Obama announced that the US was fully lifting its embargo on sales of lethal weapons to Vietnam, during his visit to the country in 2016.[18] Fourth, Vietnam was among the countries involved in a five-year Southeast Asia Maritime Security Initiative (MSI) which was launched in 2015, aiming to support a maritime and joint operations centre;[19] improvements in maritime intelligence, surveillance, and reconnaissance (ISR); maritime security and patrol vessel support and sustainment; search and rescue operations support, and participation in multilateral engagements and training.[20] As a result, the US pledged US$ 18 million in 2015 to help Vietnam buy US patrol boats.[21] Ahead of the visit of Vietnamese Prime Minister Nguyen Xuan Phuc to the US in late May 2017, the latter handed over six 45-foot Metal Shark patrol boats to the coast guard of Vietnam, which were said to assist the coast guard in intercoastal patrols and law enforcement in smuggling, illicit trafficking, piracy, and armed robbery against ships, and illegal fishing.[22] Fifth, the USS Carl Vinson aircraft carrier made a port call in Danang, Vietnam, on 5 March 2018, another substantive step in the strategic engagement between the two countries.[23]

Encouraging India to Act East

There were some hurdles facing India–US relations after the US posed an embargo on India in the wake of India's nuclear tests in 1998. However, the ties between the two countries improved after the US President Bill Clinton's visit to India in March 2000. Their relationship was significantly enhanced after the 9/11 incident, since India was one of the first countries to condemn terrorism and raised its voice to support the US in the latter's anti-terrorist war. In the anti-terrorist war in Afghanistan, India supported the US in protecting the American warships passing through the Straits of Malacca.

> Since 2004, Washington and New Delhi have been pursuing a 'strategic partnership' based on shared values and apparently convergent geopolitical interests. Numerous economic, security, and global initiatives, including plans for civilian nuclear cooperation, are underway. This latter initiative, first launched in 2005, reversed three decades of U.S. nonproliferation policy. Also in 2005, the United States and India signed a ten-year defense framework agreement to expanding bilateral security cooperation. The two countries now engage in numerous and unprecedented combined military exercises, and major U.S. arms sales to India are underway.[24]

The US factor in Vietnam–India relations   135

From considering India's important role in the Asia-Pacific, the US has drawn India into conducting joint activities in the region. Recently, in the light of its strategies of pivoting to Asia and the Indo-Pacific, the US has paid more attention to India's role in the region. In September 2010, Kurt Campbell, Assistant Secretary of State for East Asian and Pacific Affairs stated that 'one of the desires of the administration is to take a multi-faceted approach, deeper integration in regional diplomacy, in multilateral institutions, working with India, drawing India in more to the Asian-Pacific region, and working towards consequential diplomacy with China.'[25] Reaffirming the US position of supporting India's increasing engagement in the Asia-Pacific region, and considering India's role in assuring the security and prosperity of the Asia-Pacific, President Obama, in his visit to India in November 2010, highlighted the possibility of forging a truly global US–India partnership, urging India not only to 'Look East' but to 'Act East', because the move would increase the security and prosperity of both the US and India.[26] India's role in democratic propagation was also an important reason for the US to draw India in the region. Secretary of State Hillary Clinton, in her talks at the Council on Foreign Relations in January 2013, stated that the US encouraged India's 'Look East' policy as a way to weave another big democracy into the fabric of the Asia-Pacific.[27]

By acknowledging the importance of each other in the Asia-Pacific, the US and India have shared common views and even conducted joint activities in the region. India and the US, in a Joint Statement in 2014, 'expressed concern about rising tensions over maritime territorial disputes, and affirmed the importance of safeguarding maritime security and ensuring freedom of navigation and over flight throughout the region, especially in the South China Sea'.[28] The two sides also 'called on all parties to avoid the use, or threat of use, of force in advancing their claims' and 'urged the concerned parties to pursue resolution of their territorial and maritime disputes through all peaceful means, in accordance with universally recognized principles of international law, including the United Nations Convention on the Law of the Sea'.[29] The year of 2007 marked a new step in India–US joint naval exercise operations. Instead of deploying joint exercises in the Indian Ocean in the framework of Malabar naval exercises as usual, India and the US conducted a four-day naval exercise in the Philippine Sea in the Western Pacific.[30] The proximity between the Philippine Sea and the South China Sea underlined the significance of the move between India and the US.

In the American approach to the Asia-Pacific region, besides the importance of bilateral mechanisms with its allies in the region, the necessity of the multilateral frameworks in dealing with core issues, such as the South China Sea disputes is also recognised. In the inaugural US–India–Japan trilateral ministerial dialogue, held in New York in September 2015, the three countries 'underscored the importance of international law and peaceful settlement of disputes; freedom of navigation and over-flight; and unimpeded lawful commerce, including in the South China Sea'.[31] In March of 2016, India, the US, and Japan agreed to conduct massive naval exercises by late 2016, off the coast

136 *The US factor in Vietnam–India relations*

of the Philippines, an area close to the East and South China Sea.[32] This move could be seen as the collective effort of India, the US, and Japan to secure stability and freedom of navigation in the region, in the context of China's growing militarization activities in the South China Sea. Retrospectively, India, the US, and Japan conducted joint naval drills in the Western Pacific in April 2007 and in the Bay of Bengal in October 2015.[33]

The US as a security provider in the maritime domain

'At the ending of the Cold War there was a clear shift in the global pattern of relationships with the U.S.A as the sole superpower'.[34] However, since the beginning of the 21st century, while the US, Japan, and the European Union were faced with challenges including slow economic growth, China, India and Russia to some extent have had high economic growth, which has turned the world from unipolar to multipolar order. While the average economic growth of the US in the period 2001–2015 reached only 1.786 per cent, the growth of China and India reached 9.62 per cent and 7.19 per cent respectively in the same period. The Japanese and EU economies gained only 0.74 per cent and 1.267 per cent respectively.[35] As a result, GDP at the constant price of the US increased from US$ 13.094 trillion in 2005 to US$ 17.947 trillion in 2015. Chinese GDP had a great boom, from US$ 2.269 trillion in 2005 (equivalent to 17.33 per cent of the US GDP) to US$ 10.866 trillion in 2015 (equivalent to 60.54 per cent of the US GDP). Indian GDP increased from US$ 834.215 billion in 2005 to US$ 2.074 trillion in 2015. Sadly, Japanese and EU economies had a significant decrease, from their records of US$ 6.151 trillion and US$ 18.321 trillion in 2011 down to US$ 4.383 trillion and US$ 16.229 trillion in 2015 respectively.[36]

Economic scale is one of the most important indicators for manifesting the strength and influence of each country in the world. However, military strength, as shown in military budget annually, is also a key variable. Until 2015, the US had the largest military budget of US$ 595.840 billion. However, Chinese military expenditure grew speedily, increasing from US$ 45.834 billion in 2005 to US$ 215.147 billion in 2015 respectively, equivalent to 9.11 per cent and 36.108 per cent to that of the US. India's military expenditure also increased, from US$ 22.935 billion to US$ 51.643 billion in the same period.[37] In other words, in the first two decades of the 21st century, the world seemed to enter a multipolar era with the emergence of China, India, and Russia. However, with the strong rise of China, both in economic and military fields, there has been a G2 (the US and China) in the making.[38] China's rise has brought both opportunities and challenges.

The world community now finds it difficult to live without Chinese goods, thanks to the cheap prices and diversity.[39] In 2015, China overtook Japan to become the world's second-biggest cross-border investor, after the US, with a record investment of US$ 145 billion abroad.[40] In strategic regions such as Southeast Asia, China is already the top trading partner of most countries, and has almost doubled foreign direct investment in the six largest economies of ASEAN, which has helped China bypass US in terms of investment in the region.[41]

China's military modernization has accelerated lately, in pursuit of the country's urge to become a global military power.[42] Its military modernization has significant implications, including apparent threats to many countries in the Asia-Pacific region. The situation aggravated, especially since China has been increasingly assertive in its action of claiming sovereignty in the South and East China Seas. In order to materialise its sovereign claims, China is believed to have constructed an Anti-Access/Access Denial (A2/AD) system in the far western Pacific Ocean, particularly in and around the East and South China Seas, to control the Sea Lines of Communications (SLOCs) in those seas.[43] China's ambition has posed threats to the freedom of navigation and over-flight in the South China Sea, because China has deployed military assets to the artificial islands in the Spratlys.[44]

China's sovereign claim based on historic rights of the nine-dash line in the South China Sea was officially and legally rejected by the Permanent Court of Arbitration (PCA)'s rulings on 12 July 2016.[45] However, China did not accept the PCA's rulings.[46] Dangerously, although China stated its respect for freedom of navigation and over-flight in the South China Sea,[47] it interprets that the freedom of navigation under the UNCLOS[48] should be the prerogative of the state which controls the maritime zone and territorial sea.[49] This means that the freedom of navigation (and over-flight) in the South China Sea would be forced to comply with the rights and duties as regulated by China, as well as respecting Chinese security interests and sovereign rights as stipulated in the Articles of 21 and 58 of the 1982 UNCLOS.[50]

China's assertive activities in the South China Sea have posed a big threat to the vital interests of Vietnam, India, and other countries with interests attached to SLOCs in the Sea, due to the fact that the growth of their economies depends heavily on sea-borne trade. Vietnam has nearly 3,300 km of coastline, with one million square kilometres of exclusive economic zones in the sea, and its territorial waters that can be exploited are three times larger than the mainland, which helped the country build a new strategy to develop a sea-borne economy, to help foster economic growth, create more jobs, and ensure territorial security.[51] At the same time, 'over 97 per cent of India's trade by volume and 75 per cent by value is sea borne. If one follows the "direction of trade", nearly 50 per cent of Indian trade is east bound and transits through the Straits of Malacca through which over 60,000 vessels transit annually'.[52] Significantly, India and Vietnam recently have been among the top ten exporters-importers of containerized cargo in the world in 2010, 2013, and 2014.[53] Therefore, maintaining peace and stability in the South China Sea is very important to the security and development of both Vietnam and India. The harsh reality for the maintenance of stability and security in the South China Sea is that there are no world police to compel powerful nations to comply with international justice, to make China obey what the PCA awarded on 12 July 2016.[54]

Since China sent the United Nations Secretary General a diplomatic note attached to a map stating its 'cow-tongue line' on 7 May 2009,[55] and then its activities of reclaiming, constructing, and even militarizing in features in the

138   *The US factor in Vietnam–India relations*

Paracels and the Spratlys, the US has directly challenged China's illegal moves. It is only fair to mention here that other countries with interests in the SLOCs in the South China Sea have raised their voices to protect and assure the freedom of navigation and over-flights, and have even conducted naval activities in the international waters in the Sea. However, the US is the only country whose warships have sailed within 12 nautical miles of Chinese-claimed islets and reefs in the Spratlys for the freedom of navigation operations, which took place six times under Obama.[56] The US operations, especially the first one under Trump conducted on May 8, 2017,[57] were clear proof that the US would not abandon its national interests in the South China Sea, which was announced for the first time by the Secretary of State, Hillary Clinton, at the ASEAN Regional Forum in Hanoi in 2010.[58] In other words, the Asia-Pacific in general, and Southeast Asia in particular, constitutes an important region in the US foreign policy.

The US freedom of navigation operations in the South China Sea should be seen as proof of the illegality of the nine-dash line map. In other words, like many countries, the US also supports the PCA's judgement on 12 July 2017. As many have known, Vietnam–India cooperation in exploring oil and gas in Exclusive Economic Zone (EEZ) of Vietnam, especially in offshore blocks 127 and 128, received illegal objections, as well as a warning from China.[59] The Indian warship INS *Airavat* was interrogated by the Chinese Navy when the former was sailing in international waters off Vietnam in July 2011.[60] In the maritime space, Vietnam and India also conducted a joint naval exercise in the South China Sea on 8 June 2013.[61] Besides the PCA's judgement, the US freedom of navigation operations in the South China Sea have contributed to the maintenance of peace and security, and the protection of freedom of navigation and overflight in the South China Sea. Under Obama and Trump's administrations, US warships have conducted freedom of navigation operations by traveling within 12 nautical miles of artificial features in the Spratly Islands, to challenge China's territorial claims in the South China Sea.

The Indo-Pacific context

A free and open Indo-Pacific idea was officially introduced by the US President Donald Trump at the APEC CEO Summit in November 2017 in Vietnam.[62] The Indo-Pacific vision was formalised with the first Australia–India–Japan–US Consultations on the Indo-Pacific, held in the Philippines, in November 2017, on the sideline of the East Asia Summit. In these consultations, the four countries agreed to coordination and cooperation to uphold the rules-based order and respect for international law, as one of measures to ensure a free and open international order in the Indo-Pacific.[63] In the second consultations, held in Singapore in November 2018, Australia, India, Japan and the US reaffirmed their shared commitment to maintain and strengthen a rules-based order in the Indo-Pacific and highlighted their shared support for a free, open, and inclusive region that fosters universal respect for international law, freedom of navigation and overflight, and sustainable development.[64]

The US factor in Vietnam–India relations   139

Interestingly, India is a very important actor in the US Indo-Pacific strategy. In his remarks at the APEC CEO Summit in November 2017 in Vietnam, President Trump acknowledged India as one of the countries outside of APEC making great strides in the new chapter of the Indo-Pacific.[65] The US has strong and growing ties with India, and the US talked about the Indo-Pacific in part because the phrase captures the importance of India's rise, as argued by a senior White House official.[66] In fact, before President Trump introduced the Indo-Pacific in November 2018 in Vietnam, India and the US had already committed themselves as democratic stalwarts in the Indo-Pacific region.[67] At the inaugural US–India 2+2 Ministerial Dialogue, held in September 2018, the US and India committed to working together and in concert with other partners towards advancing a free, open, and inclusive Indo-Pacific region, recognizing ASEAN centrality and promoting respect for sovereignty, territorial integrity, rule of law, good governance, free and fair trade, and freedom of navigation and overflight.[68]

In the context of the Indo-Pacific, Vietnam has been acknowledged as an important player. Vietnam was where President Trump laid out America's vision for a free and open Indo-Pacific. In the US National Security Strategy released in December 2017, Vietnam, along with Indonesia, Malaysia, and Singapore, are named as growing (Southeast Asian) security and economic partners of the US Indo-Pacific strategy.[69] The international rules-based order has been strongly supported by Vietnam and many other countries in the region. Recently, the US has expressed its commitment to deepening cooperation across the Indo-Pacific, to confront common threats to, among others, the safeguarding of navigational rights and freedoms in the East and South China Seas.[70] In the Department of Defence Indo-Pacific Strategy Report released in June 2019, along with Indonesia and Malaysia, Vietnam is one of three key players in ASEAN that the US gives priority to, to develop relationships in its Indo-Pacific strategy.[71]

Thanks to India's Act East Policy and the establishment of Indo-Pacific consultations, India, under Modi's government, has become increasingly engaged in the Asia-Pacific in terms of coordination and cooperation with its Indo-Pacific partners, to ensure peace and security in the region. For instance, India raised its voice to urge parties to fully respect diplomatic and legal processes, particularly at the United Nations Convention on the Law of the Sea 1982 (UNCLOS), in the settlement of disputes in the South China Sea. India also committed to continuing its bilateral investment in oil and gas exploration on the continental shelf and the Exclusive Economic Zone (EEZ) of Vietnam.[72] India's move will contribute more to regional peace, security and prosperity.

For a peace, security and prosperity and a rules-based Indo-Pacific region, the US and other countries in the region have encouraged India to increase its engagement in the region. For its part, India has considered itself to look and act east for its national interests, and Vietnam continues to be an important pillar in the former's AEP and Indo-Pacific calculation. Obviously, the US is a factor partly contributing to the development of Indo-Vietnam relations.

140 *The US factor in Vietnam–India relations*

In short, as a global power, the US has a great influence on the world order. Although India was one leader of the NAM in the Cold War, it took Vietnam's side against the US when the latter sent military force to participate in the battles in Vietnam. The end of the Cold War marked a new chapter in the US relations with Vietnam and India. For its part, India has been making efforts to engage the East in conformity with universally recognised international laws, to protect its national interests. As a country facing many security challenges, including in the maritime domain, Vietnam needs more coordination and cooperation with countries both inside and outside the region to secure, protect and enforce international law. Vietnam–India relations have benefited from the US, since the US has committed to peace, security, and international laws in the region.

Notes

1 Bush, Richard C. 2016. 'America's Alliances and security partnerships in East Asia: Introduction', *Brookings Report*, 13 July. https://www.brookings.edu/research/americas-alliances-and-security-partnerships-in-east-asia-introduction/ (accessed 4 September 2017)
2 Office of Joint History. 2004. *The Joint Chiefs of Staff and The First Indochina War 1947–1954.* Washington DC: Library of Congress Cataloging-in-Publication Data: 33
3 Bandyopadhyaya, Jayantanuja. 1980. *The Making of India's Foreign Policy: Determinants, Institutions, Processes and Personalities.* New Delhi: Allied Publishers Private Limited: 75
4 Ibid.: 71
5 Shrivastava, B K. 1979. 'India and the United States', in Bimal Prasad (ed.), *India's Foreign Policy: Studies in Continuity and Change.* New Delhi: Vikas Publishing House: 38
6 Chandra, Bipal et al. 2008. *India since Independence.* New Delhi: Penguin Books: 282–283
7 Ibid.: 283
8 Ibid.: 193
9 Ayoob, Mohammed. 1990. *India and Southeast Asia: Indian Perceptions and Policies.* London: Routledge: 5
10 Muni, S D. 2016. 'How India is viewed as a regional actor', in Namrata Goswami (ed.), *India's Approach to Asia: Strategy, Geopolitics and Responsibility.* New Delhi: Pentagon Press: 78
11 Manyin, Mark E. 2005. 'The Vietnam–U.S. Normalization Process', *CRS Issue Brief for Congress*, 17 June, Summary
12 Pham, Quang Minh. 2010. *Vietnam's Foreign Policy in the Renovation Period 1986–2010.* Hanoi: World Publishing House: 106
13 Ibid.: 87–117
14 Sarma, Sanghamitra. 2017. 'The US Factor in India–Vietnam Relationship', *IOSR Journal of Humanities and Social Sciences (IOSR–JHSS)*, 22(1), Ver.3, January: 27
15 United States Census Bureau. 2–18. 'Trade in Goods with Vietnam'. https://www.census.gov/foreign-trade/balance/c5520.html#2000 (accessed 4 September 2017)
16 The White House. 2013. 'Joint Statement by President Barack Obama of the United States of America and President Truong Tan Sang of the Socialist Republic of Vietnam', 25 July. https://obamawhitehouse.archives.gov/the-press-office/2013/07/25/joint-statement-president-barack-obama-united-states-america-and-preside (accessed 4 September 2017)

The US factor in Vietnam–India relations 141

17 The White House. 2015. 'United States–Vietnam Joint Vision Statement', 7 July. https://obamawhitehouse.archives.gov/the-press-office/2015/07/07/united-states-%E2%80%93-vietnam-joint-vision-statement (accessed 4 September 2017)

18 Clark, Helen. 2017. 'After Talking to China about China, Vietnam goes to Washington to do it again', *South China Morning Post*, 26 May. https://www.scmp.com/week-asia/politics/article/2095886/after-talking-china-about-china-vietnam-goes-washington-do-it (accessed 4 September 2017)

19 Greintens, Sheena Chestnut. 2016. 'The US–Philippine Alliance in a Year of Transition: Challenges & Opportunities', *Brookings Working Paper*, May. https://www.brookings.edu/wp-content/uploads/2016/11/fp_20160713_philippines_alliance.pdf (accessed 4 September 2017)

20 Paramesrawan, Prashanth. 2016. 'US Kicks Off New Maritime Security Initiative for Southeast Asia', *The Diplomat*, 10 April. https://thediplomat.com/2016/04/us-kicks-off-new-maritime-security-initiative-for-southeast-asia/ (accessed 7 September 2017)

21 Alexander, David. 2015. 'The US is giving Vietnam $18 million for patrol boats to counter China', *Business Insider*, 31 May. https://www.businessinsider.com/r-pentagon-chief-pledges-18-million-for-hanoi-to-buy-patrol-boats-2015-5 (accessed 7 September 2017)

22 'U.S. delivers 6 coastal patrol boats to Vietnam coast guard'. 2017. *ABC News*, 23 May. http://abcnews.go.com/International/wireStory/us-delivers-coastal-patrol-boats-vietnam-coast-guard-47574334 (accessed 7 September 2017)

23 Garamone, Jim. 2018. 'Aircraft Carrier USS Carl Vinson Makes Vietnam Port Call'. The U.S. Department of Defense, 5 March. https://dod.defense.gov/News/Article/Article/1458238/aircraft-carrier-uss-carl-vinson-makes-vietnam-port-call/ (accessed 26 December 2018)

24 Kronstadt, K Alan et al. 2010. 'India–U.S. Relations', *CRS Report for Congress*, 27 October, Summary.

25 'U.S. working to draw India more to Asia Pacific region'. 2010. *The Hindu*, 17 September. https://www.thehindu.com/news/international/U.S.-working-to-draw-India-more-to-Asia-Pacific-region/article15953187.ece (accessed 15 September 2017)

26 Obama, Barack. 2010. 'Remarks to Members of both Houses of Parliament in the Central Hall', New Delhi, 8 November. https://mea.gov.in/in-focus-article.htm?823/Remarks+by+President+Mr+Barack+Obama+to+Members+of+both+Houses+of+Parliament+in+the+Central+Hall (accessed 15 September 2017)

27 Council on Foreign Relations. 2013. 'Hillary Rodham Clinton speaks on U.S. leadership', 31 January. https://www.cfr.org/event/remarks-american-leadership-0 (accessed 15 September 2017)

28 The White House. 2014. 'U.S.–India Joint Statement', 30 September. https://www.whitehouse.gov/the-press-office/2014/09/30/us-india-joint-statement (accessed 15 September 2017)

29 Ibid.

30 Khurana, Gurpreet S. 2014. '"Malabar" Naval Exercises: Trends and Tribulations', *Maritime India*. http://www.maritimeindia.org/CommentryView.aspx?NMFCID=146 (accessed 15 September 2017)

31 Ministry of External Affairs (Government of India). 2015. 'Inaugural U.S.–India–Japan Trilateral Ministerial Dialogue in New York', 30 September. https://www.mea.gov.in/press-releases.htm?dtl/25868/Inaugural+USIndiaJapan+Trilateral+Ministerial+Dialogue+in+New+York (accessed 21 September 2017)

32 Mandhana, Niharika. 2016. 'U.S., India, Japan Plan Joint Naval Exercises Near South China Sea', *The Wall Street Journal*, 3 March. https://www.wsj.com/articles/u-s-india-japan-plan-joint-naval-exercises-near-south-china-sea-1457010828 (accessed 21 September 2017)

33 'India, US, Japan kick off naval drills likely to annoy China'. 2015. *CNBC*, 12 October. https://www.cnbc.com/2015/10/12/india-us-japan-hold-naval-drills-in-bay-of-bengal-china-concerned.html (accessed 21 September 2017)

142 *The US factor in Vietnam–India relations*

34 Malik, Preet. 2012. 'India's Look East Policy: Genesis', in Amar Nath Ram (ed.), *Two Decades of India's Look East Policy: Partnership for Peace, Progress and Prosperity*. New Delhi: Manohar: 31

35 The World Bank. *GDP Growth (Annual %)*. http://data.worldbank.org/indicator/NY.GDP.MKTP.KD.ZG?locations=CN (accessed 21 September 2017)

36 The World Bank. *GDP (Current US$)*. http://data.worldbank.org/indicator/NY.GDP.MKTP.CD (accessed 21 September 2017)

37 The World Bank. *Military Expenditure (% of GDP)*. http://data.worldbank.org/indicator/MS.MIL.XPND.GD.ZS (accessed 21 September 2017)

38 Bush, Richard C. 2011. 'The United States and China: A G-2 in the Making?' *Brookings*, 11 October. https://www.brookings.edu/articles/the-united-states-and-china-a-g-2-in-the-making/ (accessed 25 September 2017)

39 Soller, Kurt. 2007. 'Could you live without China?' *Newsweek*, 15 August. http://www.newsweek.com/could-you-live-without-china-99145 (accessed 25 September 2017)

40 Kim, Kyung-Hoon. 2016. 'China's overseas investment at record high', *RT*, 23 September. https://www.rt.com/business/360397-china-foreign-investment-record-high/ (accessed 25 September 2017)

41 'China embraces Southeast Asia with renewed trade, investment push as US turns inward'. 2016. *South China Morning Post*, 12 December. http://www.scmp.com/news/china/diplomacy-defence/article/2053920/china-embraces-southeast-asia-renewed-trade-investment (accessed 25 September 2017)

42 Gertz, Bill. 2016. 'Report: China's Military Capabilities Are Growing at a Shocking Speed', *The National Interest*, 7 November. http://nationalinterest.org/blog/the-buzz/report-chinas-military-capabilities-are-growing-shocking-18316 (accessed 25 September 2017)

43 Hayton, Bill. 2014. *The South China Sea: The Struggle for Power in Asia*. New Haven and London: Yale University Press. 81–124; Bitzinger, R A. 2016. *Third Offset Strategy and Chinese A2/AD Capabilities*. Washington: Center for a New American Security (CNAS), May

44 Johnson, Jesse. 2017. 'China deploys anti-diver rocket launchers to man-made island in South China Sea: report', *The Japan Times*, 17 May. http://www.japantimes.co.jp/news/2017/05/17/asia-pacific/china-deploys-anti-diver-rocket-launchers-man-made-island-south-china-sea-report/#.WSgBe5LyjMw (accessed 25 September 2017)

45 Permanent Court of Arbitration. 2016. *PCA Case Nº 2013–19 in the Matter of the South China Sea Arbitration between the Republic of the Philippines and the People's Republic of China*. The Hague: Permanent Court of Arbitration, 12 July: 71, 103

46 Yan, Ren and Liu, Xin. 2016. 'S. China Sea verdict "null and void" with no binding force: FM', *Global Times*, 13 July. http://www.globaltimes.cn/content/993909.shtml (accessed 27 September 2017)

47 Ministry of Foreign Affairs (People's Republic of China). 2015. 'Vice Foreign Minister Zhang Yesui Makes Stern Representations to US over US Naval Vessel's Entry into Waters near Relevant Islands and Reefs of China's Nansha Islands', 27 October. http://www.fmprc.gov.cn/mfa_eng/wjbxw/t1310069.shtml (accessed 27 September 2017)

48 Permanent Court of Arbitration, 2016.

49 Yang, Zewei. 2012. 'The Freedom of Navigation in the South China Sea: An Ideal or a Reality?' *Beijing Law Review*, 3: 40

50 Ibid.

51 Maierbrugger, Arno. 2014. 'Vietnam to Expand Sea-Borne Economy', *Investvine*, 7 June. http://investvine.com/vietnam-to-expand-sea-borne-economy/ (accessed 2 October 2017)

The US factor in Vietnam–India relations   143

52 Sakhuja, Vijay. 2012. 'Strategic Dimensions of India's Look East Policy', in Amar Nath Ram (ed.), *Two Decades of India's Look East Policy*. New Delhi: Manohar: 225

53 World Shipping Council. *Trade Statistic*. http://www.worldshipping.org/about-the-industry/global-trade/trade-statistics (accessed 2 October 2017)

54 McGarry, B. 2016. 'Enforcing an Unenforceable Ruling in the South China Sea', *The Diplomat*, 16 July. http://thediplomat.com/2016/07/enforcing-an-unenforceable-ruling-in-the-south-china-sea/ (accessed 2 October 2017).

55 Diplomatic Academy of Vietnam. 2012. *Cow-Tongue line–An Irrational Claim*. Hanoi: Tri Thuc: 171

56 Kilpatrick, Ryan. 2017. 'U.S. Navy Vows to Continue Challenging Beijing's Claims in the South China Sea', *Time*, 9 May. http://time.com/4771767/navy-trump-south-china-sea/ (accessed 3 October 2017)

57 Ibid.

58 Landler, Mark. 2017. 'Trump Hosts Prime Minister Phuc of Vietnam and Announces Trade Deals', *The New York Times*, 31 May. https://www.nytimes.com/2017/05/31/world/asia/vietnam-nguyen-xuan-phuc-trump.html?_r=0 (accessed 3 October 2017)

59 'China to react if India seeks oil in South China Sea'. 2012. *Zee News*, 1 August. http://zeenews.india.com/news/nation/china-to-react-if-india-seeks-oil-in-south-china sea_791100.html (accessed 3 October 2017)

60 Ministry of External Affairs (Government of India). 2011. 'Incident involving INS Airavat in South China Sea', *Media Briefing*, 1 September. http://www.mea.gov.in/m edia-briefings.htm?dtl/3040/Incident+involving+INS+Airavat+in+South+China+Sea (accessed 5 October 2017)

61 Mishra, Rahul. 2014. 'India–Vietnam: New Waves of Strategic Engagement', *ICWA Issue Brief*. New Delhi: Indian Council of World Affairs, January 20: 4

62 Office of Spokesperson (U.S. Department of State). 2018. 'Advancing a Free and Open Indo-Pacific Region', Washington DC, 18 November. https://www.state.gov/ r/pa/prs/ps/2018/11/287433.htm (accessed 25 December 2018)

63 Ministry of Foreign Affairs of Japan. 2017. 'Australia–India–Japan–U.S. Consultations on the Indo-Pacific', 12 November. http://www.mofa.go.jp/press/release/p ress4e_001789.html (accessed 25 December 2018)

64 Ministry of Foreign Affairs of Japan. 2018. 'Japan–Australia–India–U.S. Consultations', 15 November. https://www.mofa.go.jp/press/release/press1e_000099.html (accessed 25 December 2018)

65 The White House. 2017. 'Remarks by President Trump at APEC CEO Summit', Danang, 10 November. https://vn.usembassy.gov/20171110-remarks-president-trump-ap ec-ceo-summit/ (accessed 25 December 2018)

66 "Indo-Pacific" over "Asia-Pacific" reflects importance of India's rise: US official.' 2017. *The Times of India*, 5 November. https://timesofindia.indiatimes.com/india/ indo-pacific-over-asia-pacific-reflects-the-importance-of-indias-rise-us-official/article show/61519942.cms (accessed 25 December 2018)

67 Ministry of External Affairs (Government of India). 2017. 'Joint Statement – United States and India: Prosperity Through Partnership', 27 June. https://www.mea.gov.in/ bilateral-documents.htm?dtl/28560/Joint_Statement__United_States_and_India_Prosp erity_Through_Partnership (accessed 25 December 2018)

68 U.S. Embassy and Consulates in India. 2018. 'Joint Statement on the Inaugural U.S.–India 2+2 Ministerial Dialogue', 6 September. https://in.usembassy.gov/joint-statem ent-on-the-inaugural-u-s-india-22-ministerial-dialogue/ (accessed 25 December 2018)

69 The White House. 2017. 'National Security Strategy of the United States of America', Washington DC, December: 46

70 Office of Spokesperson (U.S. Department of State). 2018. 'Advancing a Free and Open Indo-Pacific Region', Washington DC, 18 November. https://www.state.gov/ r/pa/prs/ps/2018/11/287433.htm (accessed 25 December 2018)

144 The US factor in Vietnam–India relations

71 The Department of Defense (United States of America). 2019. 'Indo-Pacific Strategy Report: Preparedness, Partnerships, and Promoting a Networked Region', 1 July: 36
72 Ministry of External Affairs (Government of India). 2018. 'India–Vietnam Joint Statement during State Visit of President to Vietnam', 21 November. https://www.mea.gov.in/bilateral-documents.htm?dtl/30615/IndiaVietnam_Joint_Statement_during_State_Visit_of_President_to_Vietnam (accessed 24 December 2018)

11 Conclusion

India and Vietnam, two diverse economies and important regional players in South and Southeast Asia respectively, with near identical geopolitical interests, both aspire for peace and prosperity in the larger Indo-Pacific region. The evolving geodynamics in the region, particularly in the context of US–China competition, have elevated their importance as swing states in the Indo-Pacific architecture. While Vietnam survived different colonial powers – France and the US – India wrestled its independence from Britain after more than two centuries of struggle. The important aspect of this bilateral relationship is that the two countries want to maintain their strategic autonomy without compromising on their larger strategic and geopolitical interests.

India's leadership, influenced by the socialist welfare model of development while Vietnam stuck to its communist fundamentals with the Communist Party of Vietnam as the epicentre of political configuration. The closeness of the two countries to the erstwhile Soviet Union facilitated the convergence of ideas between the two sides. However, the relationship has been seen primarily from a strategic, defence point of view, as the economic complementarities have not developed to the expected extent. The dependence on the erstwhile Soviet Union in terms of defence imports and personnel training was seen as a natural binding force between the two countries. The USSR had signed friendship treaties in 1971 with India and 1978 with Vietnam. However, for India, the core foreign policy fundamentals were non-alignment, anti-colonial struggle, and the promotion of unity among the developing countries. The core fundamentals, such as anti-colonial struggles, were reflected in the speeches of illustrious Vietnamese leaders such as Ho Chi Minh and General Vo Nguyen Giap, who have aspired to make Vietnam a strong nation after defeating the three major powers of the world – France, the US, and China – in different phases of their history.

The suffering that Vietnam has weathered, because of US cluster munitions and the use of napalm bombs and Agent Orange (a biochemical agent which destroyed foliage and forest cover), has been reflected adequately in the international media, but the effects of the post-conflict repercussions of such inhumane attacks were not covered in print media. This was primarily due to Vietnam's inclination towards the Soviet bloc. Vietnam's older generation still

146   *Conclusion*

recollects the gory scenes of American napalm bombing and the adverse effects of the bio-agents.

The communist model of development in Vietnam came under duress in late 1980s and so the country embarked on reform processes, known as *Doi Moi*, in 1986. In contrast, India was slowly graduating from an underdeveloped economy to a developing nation, and also adopted economic liberalization in the early 1990s. For India and Vietnam, the trajectory of development under the socialist/communist fundamentals has provided much-needed support to the poor people in both countries. Literacy, knowledge, skills, and building resilient societies were the main aims of the leaderships of both countries. Since the mid-1970s Vietnam, after the unification of the country, achieved a literacy rate of more than 80 per cent, while India was still much below the global average at just above 55 per cent.

Southeast Asia has adopted and assimilated the philosophy and the culture and traditions of the Indic civilization, the remnants of which can still be seen in Vietnam, Cambodia, Indonesia, Malaysia, Thailand, Myanmar, and, more particularly, in the Indonesian island of Bali. The ancient temples of Cham civilization and other architectural influences of Indic civilization are seen in many historical places. The ancient temple complex in My Son near Hoi An city is one such example of ancient ties.

In modern times, India with its multiparty democracy, and Vietnam, with its single-party communist rule, synchronized their relationship to complement each other. However, the two countries, despite being independent, established formal diplomatic ties in the year 1972. It was seen as a move to safeguard their ideological interests. Vietnam was a communist country while India was a leader in the Non-Aligned Movement. Subsequently, the emergence of the two countries as important regional players evolved. Vietnam, which was wary of its northern neighbour China, slowly built its economic and development fundamentals. However, Vietnam's attachment to communist ideals delayed its transformation into a more liberalized economy, while India, because of the post-Gulf War economic crisis, was forced into adopting rapid liberalization measures. To explore newer markets India started looking towards Southeast Asian economies. India and Vietnam became engaged with ASEAN around the same period. This was because ASEAN started projecting itself as an inclusive organisation rather than an anti-communist forum. India and Vietnam entered ASEAN in 1995 as a dialogue partner and a full member respectively. Vietnam, which perceived ASEAN as an anti-communist platform, also started to look into the positive aspects of the regional organization. In 1992, India became a sectoral dialogue partner and thereafter was elevated to a dialogue partner. In 1996, India became a member of the ASEAN Regional Forum, an institutionalized security dialogue mechanism. Over the years, India has worked alongside ASEAN countries and engaged in the institution through processes such as ASEAN plus One summit level meetings, followed by India's participation in the Asia Europe Meeting (ASEM), the East Asia Summit, the ASEAN Defence Ministers Meeting plus (ADMM+), and the Expanded ASEAN Maritime

Forum (EAMF). On the other hand, as Vietnam was a member of ASEAN, India's entry into these institutions was expected.

Given these foundations, both in terms of governments and politics in the two societies, the two countries have done relatively well and are now some of the fastest growing economies in Asia. Development of the manufacturing sector along with increased liberalization has defined new frontiers for growth. While in India, the services sector has grown manifold, Vietnam is looking to emerge as an alternative production centre, and the investment into the Vietnamese economy since 2010 has been a testimony to this. In Vietnam, the FDI has been increasing in critical sectors such as mining, iron and steel, and the construction sector, while in the case of India, the focus has been more on the real estate and services industries, such as insurance and finance, manufacturing, and construction activities. With regard to mining and other related activities, the investment has been very limited. However, the two countries need trade and investment to grow, and in this regard the possibilities of investment from Europe, the US, China, Japan, and Korea are being explored.

The bilateral relationship does have two major factors which have been embedded into the overall strategic and political calculations. For India and Vietnam, the challenge is to maintain an equal distance from both China and the US, while at the same time getting the benefits of better relations with both. The US has remained, and will remain, the primary security guarantor in the Indo-Pacific region. China is trying to establish itself as a great power, but it has not gained global acceptance because its rise is perceived as a threat to global order. Their lack of transparency in both political and economic matters also make it an authoritarian state. China's strong projection as a benign and peaceful rising power dissipated with the more assertive postures adopted in its periphery, which were reflected in maritime transgressions, in the case of South China Sea, and border intrusions, in the case of India. Problems with its neighbours regarding water-sharing and support to rogue regimes, particularly North Korea, have multiplied its issues with ascending to the status which it has envisaged for itself. With regard to India and Vietnam, China will remain a challenge. The maritime disputes with Vietnam about sovereignty over the Paracels and the Spratlys, and its territorial disputes with India would galvanize the two countries to come together both in the strategic sphere and the political space. However, the two countries have been very cautious in making any strong statements with regard to protecting the interests of each other, either in the case of the India–China border or the South China Sea, looking for a flexible space to negotiate with China for their own national interests. China is strongly advocating for bilateral negotiations in the case of the South China Sea, which many other claimants to the South China Sea islands have been hesitantly accepting to safeguard their island territories. The possibility of a bilateral arrangement between claimants is increasing because ASEAN has failed to negotiate with China to protect the interests of the ASEAN countries which are claimants to the Spratlys. Given the increasingly assertive approach of China, the defence and strategic partnership between India and Vietnam are

148   *Conclusion*

likely to grow in the future. However, the importance of their ties with the US might also influence the bilateral relationship between India and Vietnam in the future. Until 2010, American commitment towards Southeast Asia was seen with doubt. Therefore, the then President Obama declared the US' 'Pivot to Asia' policy. This was to reassure the countries in Southeast Asia about US commitment towards the region. India and Vietnam planned to protect their security and strategic interests under this US policy. This was also reflected in US State department documents, and the Joint Statements which were released whenever the leaderships of the two countries (India and US as well as Vietnam and US) visited one another. The Vietnam leadership has been more active in the past, with the visits of the Party General Secretary and political leadership to Washington. India, on its part, also engaged the US in developing an understanding of the larger Indian Ocean and the Asia-Pacific. The development of Indo-Pacific architecture, and the increasing commitment to bilateral trade and investment, as well as developing political a understanding, would create more strategic space between the three countries. One of the elements for future interaction between the three countries would be the development of trilateral dialogue forums, along with Japan and the US, as well as a defence and strategic partnership, the foundation of which has already been established.

The defence and security interactions between the two nations have been predicated on two major factors. Firstly, the comparative weighting given to their respective relations with China, and secondly, the lack of vision as well as commitment towards containing China through bilateral cooperation. On the Indian side, the question has been whether Vietnam would be a cooperating partner, or would confide with its ideological partner, i.e. China. On the other hand, Vietnam was not firm on commitments in terms of engaging India. It was more a relationship of demand and supply. Instead of evolving as strategic partners with a better understanding of one another, their motive was to placate China, and pursue sustainable cooperative development. The pertinent question is whether, when both the nations are developing at a faster rate of growth, they can afford to take sides in the US versus China. To a certain extent, it depends on China's aggressive posture, and whether the US can emerge as a reliable partner. For India and Vietnam, their need is to develop understanding on pressing strategic issues. Apart from building understanding on issues such as politics, defence, and nuclear proliferation, the synergies between the two countries can be explored in multilateral forums, given the commonality of interests reflected in these forums. The level of strategic and defence interactions highlight the importance of any bilateral relationship. This can be seen in the case of the engagements of India and Vietnam with Singapore, Korea, Indonesia, Australia, Japan, and the US. There is a perceptible increase in official interactions among the armed forces personnel of India and US. The increasing defence trade (export or import of weapons and associated systems), have made the US an important source of advanced weapons. Vietnam has also increased armed forces engagement with the US. In the case of Vietnam, frequent diplomatic and political interactions with the US have led to

Conclusion 149

better awareness and understanding. India and Vietnam are also trying to diversify their defence weapon systems, and the US is the most prominent supplier of high-tech systems.

What should be the policy prescriptions for the India–Vietnam defence and security relationship? With the increasing clout of Vietnam in ASEAN, multilateral security organizations need to be strengthened in Southeast Asia. China should also be involved in a constructive manner. India should engage Vietnam because of its low costs and its highly literate population. India should study Vietnamese shipbuilding facilities and look for possible joint ventures. Vietnam's defence equipment is becoming outdated, so India should help in upgrading its military hardware. India might send technicians and fighter pilot trainers to Vietnam in the future. Vietnam and India use the same Russian and erstwhile Soviet platforms, so there is a possibility of selling aircraft spares and engine parts to Vietnam. The two countries can look for an integrated inventory to support each other's military needs. There is a need to create a database of aircraft spares, and for inventories to be shared with Vietnam on a real-time basis. India has conducted bilateral exercises with Vietnam for theatre awareness, as well as engaging the Vietnamese Navy in exercises in the South China Sea. Time and again, Indian exploration interests near the Vietnamese coast have been threatened by China through diplomatic means and through the media, but India must protect its national commercial interests abroad. India should look to export non-lethal military equipment and communication sets to Vietnam. Both countries can look for greater engagement between the Vietnam Marine Police and Indian Coastguards in anti-piracy operations, as well as generally developing coordination.

With regard to economic integration with Vietnam and the ASEAN community as a whole, India started its FTA with Thailand in 2003, which was followed by a Comprehensive Economic Cooperation Agreement with Singapore in 2005, and a Comprehensive Economic Partnership Agreement with Malaysia in 2010. India and Vietnam have implemented the India–ASEAN Free Trade Agreement (2010) and trade volumes have increased considerably. However, over the years India's exports to the region have stagnated, and the major economies of Southeast Asia largely benefited from this FTA, because of their rising exports to India. While India has opened markets for the ASEAN nations, the reciprocal gesture of opening their services market has not been very forthcoming. The Philippines is in the process of ratifying the India–ASEAN Services and Investment Agreement, because India is competing with the Philippines in the services sector, particularly in terms of business processes outsourcing and knowledge process outsourcing sectors. For India, the services sector provides immediate employment to young graduates and technology professionals. Vietnam needs English language expertise to become more integrated into the international market. Furthermore, it needs to evolve as a low-cost manufacturing centre. Vietnam's membership of APEC and the Comprehensive and Progressive Agreement for Trans-Pacific Partnership (CPTPP) has already provided the necessary fundamentals for growth, and a Regional

150 *Conclusion*

Comprehensive Economic Partnership (RCEP) might be signed in future. Therefore, the economic complementarities between India and Vietnam is bound to grow. Further, India has been toying with the idea of expanding BIMSTEC to include the other countries of the CLMV, and strengthening the Mekong India Economic Corridor (MIEC).The Asian highway network and the completion of Trilateral India–Myanmar–Thailand highway project would facilitate industry cooperation, and also develop complementarities between cost-effective economies.

India and Vietnam can collaborate in sectors such as mining, natural resources management, science, technology, and innovation. India has now been focusing more on the CLMV countries (which includes Vietnam). A few other areas which might be of interest include organic cultivation and certification for fruits and vegetables, developing quality systems in manufacturing, small ancillary units particularly related to automobiles, and medium-tech engineering units which could seamlessly integrate under the Mekong–India Economic Corridor. Of late, the concept of the 'blue economy' has gained momentum, and both India and Vietnam need to look into the possibility of exploring the options that are being experimented with by this concept. The sectors which can be viably explored include pharmaceuticals, fisheries, energy, technological development, transport connectivity, tourism, agriculture products and human resource development. Regions such as northeast India have reclaimed their place in India's Act East Policy, and Vietnam needs to work towards developing better connectivity with India, as it will provide the basic platform for integration. One issue which needs to be looked into by both countries is quality assurance and control.

Discourse about the blueprint for Indo-Pacific security architecture is gaining attention and support from the US. India and Vietnam, being strategic partners who also have stakes in the peace and tranquility in the Southeast Asia, have developed an understanding, which is important for regional security. The role of multilateral institutions, as well as the regional security architecture, will be important. India's subscription to the Indo-Pacific is increasing. The geographic expanse of the Act East Policy includes Australia and Japan, which coincides with Indo-Pacific region. For Vietnam, the Asia-Pacific region, which includes India, is preferred as it elevates India to a legitimate stakeholder in the regional security apparatus. Further, one important question which still needs more deliberation and discussion is whether the Indo-Pacific could sustain the proposal of a Quad involving India, Japan, Australia and the US, and, in the case that the Quad undertook maritime security as a major element of cooperation, then whether regional players such as Indonesia, Singapore and Vietnam, or other willing partners, could be considered for a Quad plus arrangement. Given the fact that the US has always supported the 'Hub and Spokes' model for furthering its strategic objectives, it would not be unreasonable to propose that a Quad plus formation might be there to engage formidable regional players. However, it also depends on the maritime capability and the political will of the countries involved. Even if the strategic competition between the US and China becomes intense, India would engage its other major strategic partners Vietnam and Indonesia in Southeast Asia to bring about dialogue between the two major powers.

The bilateral relationship between India and Vietnam in the context of the Indo-Pacific is likely to become more multifaceted. US policies and economic support for the Indo-Pacific would facilitate more synergy between India and Vietnam. The bigger debate which ensued is whether the Indo-Pacific and the Quad are complementary to each other, or would act in separate geopolitical orbits. American interests in the South Pacific and Chinese ingress in Oceania is creating more strategic competition between the two powers. The extension of the competition between the two major powers – the US and China – might get intense in countries such as Papua New Guinea, Fiji, Vanuatu and smaller islands in the Pacific region. This major power competition to protect resources and strategic spaces will pose a challenge to India and Vietnam to maintain their precarious balance and protect their interests. The US and China competition in the Indian Ocean, and the South China Sea would create newer strategic partnerships and possible informal defence arrangements. However, the more nuanced aspects would be the water-sharing, borders (with India) and maritime issues (with Vietnam), which would decide the course of their relations with both the US and China. On the bilateral front, there is still inherent stagnation between the two because of their different economic structures and stages of development. India and Vietnam have different economic growth plans, and therefore there might be challenges in synchronizing their efforts in the regional theatres. With the Indo-Pacific spanning from Africa to the Western Sea Board of the Pacific Ocean, the challenge would be to complement each other's efforts. In this geopolitical matrix, Japan would be a major factor which would help in furthering the involvement of the two countries in this strategic competition. Japan has economic and strategic interests in both countries, and has been investing in India and Vietnam. Given the fact that China's economic trajectory might face challenges in terms of costs and real wages, Japan's reduced investment to China, because of tensions on the East China Sea, would adversely impact Chinese industries. India and Vietnam are yet to match the Chinese exports in terms of costs (as Chinese production is subsidised by the state), but their growing strategic and economic cooperation in the Indo-Pacific will definitely be a challenge for China. In conclusion, one can say that India–Vietnam relations, which have been close in the political domain, would find similar underpinnings in the economic, defence, and regional security domains under the rubric of the Indo-Pacific.

Index

à la carte institution 4
A.B. Vajpayee 33
academic discourse 18, 20
Acharya Kripalani 53
Act East Policy 27, 33, 34, 36, 38, 40,
  45, 46, 47, 48, 53, 58, 61, 69, 98,
  106, 109, 139, 150
Adani 75
adjoining continents and land mass 9
administration 27, 30, 58, 103, 135, 138
ADMM+ *see* ASEAN Defence Ministers'
  Meeting Plus
aerial photography 69
aerospace cooperation 71, 72
Afghanistan 3, 7, 56, 107, 134
African nations 128
Afro-Asian Conference 9, 54
Afro-Asian unity 9, 21
AFTA 25, 94
aid offensive 30
Akash 73, 74
Aksai Chin 34, 58
alliance formation 2, 7
American stance 2
America's Pacific Century 9
America's strategy 22
AMRAAMSKI 68
Andaman & Nicobar 12
animal husbandry 103
Antarctica 11
anthropologists 4
anti-access/access denial (A2/AD) 36,
  46, 77, 79, 137
anti-aircraft guns 78
anti-American 56
anti-China alliance 15
anti-communist 1, 93, 146
anti-dumping 88
anti-imperialist struggle 2

APEC 9, 10, 14, 30, 41, 42, 95, 96, 97, 98,
  100, 101, 138, 139, 149; membership 101
Aquino, Benigno 47
Architecture 2, 10, 15, 53, 59, 94, 112, 116,
  133, 145, 148, 150
Argentina 109
armoured personnel carriers (APCs) 74, 76
artificial island building 127
artificial structures 79
Arunachal Pradesh 34, 35, 39, 58, 121
ASEAN 1–3, 9, 10, 13, 21, 23–26, 29, 30,
  33, 35, 36, 40, 41–47, 56, 58, 61, 67, 70,
  92–94, 96–100, 103, 106–115, 124,
  125–132, 136, 138, 139, 146–149
ASEAN-centred multilateralism 1
ASEAN Community 29, 36, 93, 149
ASEAN consensus 3, 125
ASEAN Defence Ministers Meeting
  (ADMM) 10, 36, 57, 94, 112, 146
ASEAN Defence Ministers' Meeting Plus
  (ADMM+) 10, 36, 97, 112, 146
ASEAN Informal Summit 25
ASEAN Maritime Forum 10, 41, 61, 93,
  94, 112, 124
ASEAN Outlook 112–114
ASEAN plus Six 10, 94
ASEAN Regional Forum 36, 57, 61, 94,
  97, 112, 138
ASEAN wariness 126
ASEAN way 3
ASEAN's centrality 36, 127
ASEAN–India Summit meeting 61
ASEAN–India Summit-level
  partnership 43
ASEAN–India Trade Agreement in Goods
  35, 42
Ashley Tellis 7
Asian and Pacific regions 2
Asian economies 5, 146

Index 153

Asian mainland 39, 43, 46
Asian nations 2, 8, 24, 57, 67, 68, 88, 103, 125
Asian Neighbourhood 33, 40, 46
Asia-Pacific 2, 4–6, 9–15, 20–23, 35–38, 40, 41, 45–49, 53, 56–61, 79, 88, 92, 94, 96, 97, 100, 101, 109, 112–114, 131–135, 137, 139, 148, 150; India's relationships in 12
Association for Southeast Asia (ASA) 2
ASTRA 74
asymmetric conflict 67
Atal Behari Vajpayee 57
Atal Pension Yojana 44
Aung San Suu Kyi 23, 26
Auslin, Michael 22
Australia 2–4, 6, 10, 13, 14, 21, 30, 37, 40–42, 45–47, 66, 93, 97, 99, 100, 109, 110, 112, 113, 114, 124, 138, 148, 150
Australia–India–Japan–US 41, 138
Australian foreign policy 21
authoritarianism 33

balance of power 4, 6, 126
Banking and Financial Sector 90
Bay of Bengal community 4
Bay of Bengal Initiative for Multi-Sectoral Technical and Economic Cooperation (BIMSTEC) 24, 26, 29, 42, 109, 150
BCIM 26
Bilateral Investment Promotion and Protection Agreement (BIPPA) 89
bilateral trade agreement (BTA) 133
BIMSTEC see Bay of Bengal Initiative for Multi-Sectoral Technical and Economic Cooperation
biologists 4
BIST-EC 26
blue economy 28, 150
blue navy 7
Bonism 23
border guards 82, 124
border control 124
botanists 4
Brahmaputra 29, 118, 119, 121–123
Brahmos 70, 73, 74
Brazil, Russia, India, China, and South Africa (BRICS) 4, 26, 31
Britain, 1, 3, 60, 115, 131, 145
British Defence White Paper 3
British forces 3
British Petroleum 82
Buddhist culture 23
buffer state 18

buffer zones 19
Business Advisory Council 58
business-to-business contacts 89
Buzan, Barry 2, 19

Cabinet Secretariat, 116
Cam Ranh Bay 42, 71, 81
Cape of Good Hope 10
capitalism 2
captive market strategies 7
Chagos Archipelago 12
challenge of communism 1
Cham civilization 146
China
China factor 55, 118
China: advantage 5; aggression 66, 124; discourse 122; documents 28; growth story 5; investment 26; military, 5, 22, 94, 136; military modernisation 7, 67; ports 28; Premier 54; reclamation 78; revisionist tendencies, 'assumed' 5; rise 2, 5, 22, 27, 58, 59, 65, 67, 98, 107, 112, 117, 122, 127, 133, 136; security interests 79, 137; and Vietnam 26, 66, 103
civil society 98, 102, 121
Clark Air Force base 132
Classical geopolitics 4, 8
climate change 13,95
CLMV (Cambodia, Laos, Myanmar, Vietnam) 23–30, 89, 150
coastal patrol boats 75
Cocos 13
Cold War 8, 9, 23, 30, 48, 58, 65, 69–71, 74, 80, 108, 111, 119, 121, 130, 143, 144, 148, 151
collective managerial responsibility 11
collective security and alliance systems 9
colour revolutions 45
commercial 3, 6, 60, 67, 75, 82, 84, 88, 89, 91, 92, 96, 99, 149
commodities 35, 90
communism 1, 2
communist insurgents 1
communist party movements 3
Communist Party of Vietnam, 80, 114, 145
Communist Party 3, 61, 73, 91
communist unity 66
community building 2, 3, 45
compliance mechanisms 93, 123
Comprehensive and Progressive Agreement for Trans-Pacific Partnership (CPTPP) 38, 97, 98,113,149

154 *Index*

Comprehensive Economic Cooperation
Agreement (CECA) 35
comprehensive sense of
community 10
Comprehensive Strategic Partnership 40,
47, 57, 60, 62, 74, 83, 114
concentric circles approach 8
Concert of Powers 11
Congress 34, 35, 39, 44, 53, 59,133
constructivist thinking 19
containerized cargo 80, 137
contiguous marine region 4
contiguous strategic importance 9
continental countries 6
continental shelf 47, 62, 78, 82, 84, 139;
outer limit of 75
contrived super-region 2
core area 93, 106, 124
corvettes 76
counter-China strategy 14, 97
counter-insurgency 23, 81, 115
CPTPP *see* Comprehensive and
Progressive Agreement for
Trans-Pacific Partnership
Crimea 37, 45
critical geopolitics 4, 8
critical sea lanes 11, 14
critical technologies 18
cultural and historical links 5
cultural behavioural methods 19
cultural exchanges 5
Customs 25, 88, 101, 106
cyber security 47, 115

Da Nang 70, 81
Dalai Lama 121
dams 118–122
Darwin 13
data reception 116
Dawei 28, 79, 129
de facto 18, 34, 55
Declaration of Code of Conduct 3, 80,
83, 109, 112
defence: acquisitions 12; alliance 2;
diplomacy 66, 67, 70; equipment 24, 67,
149; industries 68; industry workshop
70; planning 12; visits 24
Defence Cooperation Agreement 13, 14,
42, 66, 97
Defence Intelligence Cooperation
Agreement 74
Defence Minister 10, 36, 57, 68, 70, 71, 82,
94, 112, 146
Defence Security Dialogue, 68

Defence White Paper 3, 13, 69
Defense Secretary 30
deferred payment 67
delivery systems 18
democratic fundamentals 1
Democratic Republic of Vietnam (DRV)
54–56, 62
Department of Defense 113
Deputy Prime Minister 59
derived regions 18
Deutsch, Karl 18, 19
Dhanush 74
Dhruv helicopters 74
dialogue partner 3, 36, 47, 67, 92–94, 100,
106, 108, 109, 146
dichotomy 5
Diego Garcia 12
diplomatic blue book 38
diplomatic note 36, 42, 78, 137
dispute resolution 96
division of labour 22
Djibouti 5, 12
Doi Moi 25, 58, 90, 146
Double Taxation Avoidance Agreement
(DTAA), 89, 102
drugs 13, 102
Dutch *see* Netherlands

East Asia Summit (EAS) 10, 14, 21, 33, 36,
41, 45, 57, 61, 94, 95, 112, 124, 138, 146
Ease of Doing Business (World Bank) 34,
44, 99
East Asia: Economic Community 10, 94;
regionalism 25; security 9, 20
East China Sea 2, 11, 28, 67, 93
East of Suez 3
East Sea 13, 45, 46, 61, 62, 80
East Timor crisis 125
e-commerce 100, 116
economic: assistance 5; community 10, 14,
25, 94, 97; diplomacy 5, 98, 99;
interdependence 14, 95, 96; links 23;
preferences 2, 14; zones 3, 14, 80, 137
Egypt V, 132
Eight/Nine-degree Channels 10
electrification programmes 29
electronic warfare 72–74
English Language Training 70, 72
enhanced connectivity 40, 109
environmental degradation 13
equity markets 25, 91
ethnic communities 26
European affairs 3
European neighbours 3

European powers, 11
European Union 10, 35, 45, 97, 99, 113
Exchange Rate Management 90
expeditionary capability 7
Extended ASEAN Maritime Forum 10

facilitating maritime trade 30
Fake Indian Currency Notes (FICN) 115
far seas 7
Farakka 122
fishermen militia 77, 125
Five Power Defence Agreement (FPDA), 1–3
flexible collective security 2
flexible payment 67
Foreign Direct Investment 26, 91, 132
foreign minister 13, 57, 59, 110
four oceans 9
Framework of Comprehensive Cooperation 59, 110
France 1, 12, 53, 54, 60, 70, 107, 115, 131, 145
Francisco System 126
Free and Open Indo-Pacific (FOIP) 30, 38, 112, 113; Vision 38
Free Trade Agreement 14, 23, 25, 40, 88, 92, 95, 97, 99, 100, 106, 113
freedom of navigation 36, 37, 41, 42, 45, 58, 61, 77, 79, 80, 83, 84, 109, 111–114, 135–139; operations (FONOPs) 115
friendly prices 66, 67
friendship treaty 107
Free Trade Agreement of the Asia-Pacific (FTAAP) 14, 82, 95, 97, 100, 101

G20 see Group of Twenty general election 2014 34
General Giap 107
Geneva Agreements 55, 131
geographic space 6
geographical features 3
Geologists 4
geopolitical 2–5, 7, 9, 18, 19, 22, 37, 66, 92, 97, 109, 118, 123, 134, 145, 151; ambitions,4; approaches 19; calculations 5; compulsions 2, 4, 66; imagination 7, 8, 22, 97; interest areas 2; lab 2
geopolitically sensitive 1
geostrategic 7, 9, 19, 20, 93, 121
global commodity prices 91
global financial crisis 13, 127
global financial meltdown 90
global GDP 95
global hegemonic ambitions 7

global hot spot 123
global power struggle 1
global security partnership 30
Global War on Terror 123, 125
Golden Triangle 120
Goldman Sachs 90
governance 2, 21, 71, 88, 95, 112, 113, 116, 121, 139
grading of threat 3
gradual withdrawal 3
great power strategies 19
Greater Mekong sub-region 4
Group of Twenty (G20) 14, 95
Gulf Cooperation Council (GCC) 35
Gulf Sovereign fund 88
Gwadar 28, 128

Hainan Island 72, 125
Hambantota 28
harbours 78, 128
Hatoyama 10, 94
Haushofer, Karl 4, 8
hedging 22
hegemonic power 8
Heng Samrin 57, 108, 132
high level intelligence 111
high mobility vehicles 74
high seas 11, 14, 126
high transactional value 9
high-speed patrol vessels 82
Hindu 23,
Hindustan Aeronautics 68
Ho Chi Minh 54, 66, 68, 79, 81, 98, 107, 120, 145
hostile forces 13
Human Resource Development 25, 150
human rights 98, 115, 125
hydropower 120, 122

ideological conflict 2
ideological underpinnings 2
immigration 3, 13, 45
inclusive and consensus-based organisation 1
inclusive membership 92
independence from British rule 1
India Brand Equity Foundation (IBEF) 99
India Investment Centre 99
India: Air Force 68, 71; Armed Forces 71, 110; army 6, 44, 115; Coast Guard, 68, 70; engagement with Israel 8, 108; interests in the Indian Ocean region 36; Navy, 36, 42, 61, 68, 81, 82; neighbourhood 36, 40, 69; nuclear tests 132,

156 Index

134; President 40, 42, 47, 55, 60, 62, 80, 84; Vice President 41
India–China border 54, 56, 118, 121, 147
India–Japan–US 41, 45, 138; Inaugural Trilateral Ministerial Dialogue 37, 49, 141
India–Republic of Korea: Comprehensive Economic Partnership Agreement (CEPA) 35, 41, 42; strategic partnership 40
India–Malaysia CECA 35, 42
India–New Zealand FTA 42
India–Thailand FTA 42
India–US bilateral documents, 37
Indian Ocean, 4,5,7,9,10,11–14, 18, 20,21,26, 37,38, 45, 46, 57, 58, 67, 69, 79, 80, 109, 114, 135, 148; as 'India's Ocean' 12; and Pacific Oceans 4–10, 12, 13, 22, 23, 41, 92
Indian Peace Keeping Force (IPKF) 67
Indian strategic thinkers 2
Indian sub-continent 23
Indira Gandhi, 46, 56, 108
Indochina, 1, 27; region 25, 28
Indonesia, 1, 3, 6, 10, 13, 21, 23, 25, 40, 42, 45, 46,47,53–55, 58, 66, 88, 91, 103, 108, 109, 111, 118, 123, 125, 139, 146, 148, 150, 151
Indo-Pacific 1–15, 18–22, 24–30, 33–36, 38, 41–47, 53, 55, 56, 60, 65, 68, 70, 88–91, 95, 102, 103, 106, 107, 117–120, 125–128, 131, 132, 135, 138, 145–151; commons 22; as a construct 4, 6, 8, 10, 11, 18, 20, 27, 35, 94; economic corridor 27, 94, 101, 102, 129; Strategy Report 113, 139; Treaty 13
Indus Water treaty 44
industrial conglomerates 33
industrialization 24, 25, 90
Information and Communications Technology (ICT) 25
Information Highways 43
infrastructure development 25, 75, 121, 128; projects 27, 28
Initiative for ASEAN Integration (IAI) 25
inland projects 43
INS *Airavat* 41, 80, 138
INS *Sahyadri* 42
INS *Satavahana* 82
INS *Satpura* 42, 70
INS *Shakti* 42, 70
institute for defence international relations (Vietnam) 70

institutional and governance mechanisms 2
institutional theory 6
integrated supply chains 5
interconnectivity and infrastructure 5
Inter-Continental Ballistic Missiles 18
international discourse 5, 13, 22, 28, 95
international economic discourse 89
International Labour Organization (ILO) 34
international peacekeeping operations 24
international political economy 5, 91
international politics 8
International Relations Conference 33, 46
international security 18
international terrorist groups 34
IORA 9, 20
IPEC vision 101
IR theory 19
Iraq 7, 67
Islamic State 34
island arcs 4, 8
island reclamation activity in South China Sea 5
island territories 12, 147
isolated command economy 5
Israel 8, 18, 73, 108
I-ways 43

JAI 45
Japanese army 11
Joint Command 13
Joint Defence Cooperation Committee 47
Joint Marine Seismic Undertaking 127
joint naval exercise 84, 88, 135, 138
Joint Sub-Commission on Trade 89
Joint Working Group 43, 68
Jungle Warfare School 110, 115

Kaladaan Multi Modal Transport Project 27
Keeling islands 13
Keohane, Robert 19, 90
Kilo-class submarines 71, 82
Kochi Naval air base 72
Konfrontasi (1963–1966) 3

L&T 75, 82
Lakshadweep 12
Lan Do and Lan Tay 82
laser-guided munitions 73
liberal nations 21, 81
Libya 7
Line of Actual Control 44

Lines of Credit 67, 73, 74
Linux-based systems 72, 115
littoral island nations 6
littoral regions 10, 11
logistical chain 91
Lombok 10
Look East Policy 25, 33, 37, 47, 43, 58, 61, 67, 69, 93, 106, 132, 138
low-cost production 28, 119, 128
lower riparian states 119, 120, 123

Mahayana 23, 107
mainland Southeast Asia 23, 30, 129
major powers 1, 18, 20, 23, 58, 59, 61, 75, 100, 103, 128, 132, 145, 151
Malabar series exercises 109
Malacca 9, 10, 20, 36, 79, 80, 137, 139
Malaysia 1–3, 14, 33, 34, 39, 41, 46, 53, 56, 60, 66–69, 73, 75, 90, 91, 93, 96, 99, 112, 113, 117, 126, 128, 131
Maldives 12
Mandalay 129
Manmohan Singh 10, 21, 58, 80
manufacturing base 26
manufacturing capacity 119
Maoist insurgency 34
Marawi 77
marine organisms 4
maritime: borders 19, 69; cargo, 43; commerce 36; emergencies 75; interdiction and patrolling 12; nation 6; strategy 10; surveillance 12, 111, 123; terrorism 80; zone 70, 79, 137
Maritime Security Dialogue 47, 60
Maritime Security Initiative (MSI) 21, 134
Maritime Silk Route 28
Masirah Island 13
Mauritius 12, 45, 102
McKinsey & Company 90
Mearsheimer, John 8
Mekong 4, 24, 27, 29, 118–121
Mekong–Ganga Cooperation (MGC) 24, 27, 43, 45, 47; Business Forum 43; Policy Dialogue 43
Mekong River Commission (MRC) 29, 43, 121, 137
Memorandum of Understanding 30, 68
Menon, Shivshankar 23
Metcalf, Rory 30
MFN 100
Middle East 7, 37, 45
MiG-21s 68
migration 4, 9, 13, 37, 95; patterns 4

military: alliances 1; attaché 68; bases 5; capability 3, 12, 22; commands 3; exchanges 23; installations 68; modernisation 22; strategy 4, 70; strength 18, 136; theatres 3; training 24, 72, 111; trucks 76
minorities 26
Missile Technology Control Regime (MTCR) 70
Modi, Narendra 33–39, 40–43, 46, 47, 53, 54, 73, 82
Mozambique Channel 10
Mukherjee, Pranab 46, 47, 68
multilateral organization 18
multipolarity 7
Mumbai attacks 80
mutual judicial assistance 60
Myanmar 1, 14, 33–39, 47, 53, 54, 68, 77, 83, 108–117, 128, 131, 146, 150; army 24

Napalm 145, 146
Natalgewa, Marty 13
nation's global influence 6
National Defence Authorization Act (NDAA) 21
National League for Democracy 26
national party congress 61
National Technical Research organisation 116
NATO see North Atlantic Treaty Organisation
natural disasters 9, 20, 75, 126
natural strategic landmarks, 19
navy: aviation 24; patrols 123; ships 61, 71, 75, 81, 115
Naval Symposium 11, 14
navigation 3, 8, 36, 37, 41, 42, 45, 48, 53, 61, 77, 78, 81, 89, 100, 101, 103, 106, 107, 109, 111, 121, 123, 124, 125, 127, 135–139
negative balance of trade 5
Nehru, Jawaharlal 9, 21,66, 108; Nehru Award for International Understanding 23; Nehru Museum Library 114; Nehruvian idealism 8
neo-colonialism 56, 132
neo-liberalism 5, 6
neo-realism 8, 19
net provider of security 12
Netherlands 1, 54
new geographic construct 27
New Silk Road (NSR) 27
new strategic order 11

158 *Index*

new terminology 14, 30
New Zealand 3, 21, 42, 47, 97, 100
nine-dash line 61, 77, 78, 137
Non-Aligned Movement (NAM) 9, 21, 36, 93, 131, 146
non-competitive 22
non-tariff barriers 18, 19, 83, 91
non-traditional security 21, 24, 70, 91, 98, 102
non-traditional threats 29
normal trade relations (NTR) 118
North and South Vietnam 1
North Atlantic Treaty Organisation (NATO) 9
North Atlantic 9, 20, 131
Northeast 23, 35, 40, 46, 100; region (NER) 41
northwest Pacific 19
nuclear club 27
nuclear power status 18
nuclear powers 27, 68
nuclear proliferation 27, 132; nonproliferation policy 134
Nye, Joseph 5

Obama administration 58
oceanic features 18
oceanic flavour 5
official statements 13
offshore balancing 7
offshore island arcs 19, 20
oil and gas exploration 43, 54, 67, 68, 80, 81, 82, 127
Oman 24
One Belt One Road (OBOR) 35
ONGC 54, 65, 80, 81, 82
open logistics 106
ordnance 68, 71, 72
organizations 1, 18, 21, 27, 29, 88–91, 98, 109, 132
orientation programme 71
over-flight 61, 77, 79, 113, 137–139
OVL 67, 80

PAC 111
Pacific Alliance 91
Pacific Economic Cooperation Council (PECC) 25
Pacific Islands Forum (PIF) 20, 29, 91
Pacific Ocean 18, 19, 22, 29, 30, 123, 132
Pakistan 14, 27, 39, 40, 46, 53–55, 57, 59, 68, 98, 110
Panikkar 21, 29, 30
Paracels 43, 74, 75, 77, 108, 124, 131

Parliament of India 67
Party General Secretary 44, 132
passive approach 23
peace and stability 1, 14, 81, 83, 124
peacekeeping operations (PKO) 72
People of Indian Origin 39
People's Liberation Army 60, 113
People's Republic of China 56, 75, 77, 78, 113, 117, 123, 124
pepper exchange board 95
per-capita income 33
Permanent Court of Arbitration 56, 74, 75, 77, 81, 103, 111, 123, 124
Permanent Normalization Of Trade Relations (PNTR) 118
Petro Vietnam (PVN) 80
Pham Binh Minh 24, 61
Philippines lawsuit 77
Phnom Penh, 99, 112, 114
phytosanitary 88
piracy 20, 21, 22, 24, 25, 29, 54, 74, 75, 77, 82, 120, 131
policy reforms 89, 93
political commissar 33
political geography 18
political influences 57
political parties 39
port identification 18
Portugal 1
potentially hostile regional powers 19
Potsdam Conferences 56
poverty reduction 40
power and economic configuration 18
Pradhan Mantri Jeevan Jyoti Bima Yojana 44
Pradhan Mantri Suraksha Bima Yojana, 44
principles of international law 47, 55, 67, 78, 81, 82, 103, 121
private-sector competitiveness 36
private-sector initiatives 89
proactive role 24, 113
production centres 19, 83
project aid 121
promoting bilateral investment 65, 81
promoting commerce 38
Promoting Regional Economic Integration 34
promoting tourism 37
protectionism 19, 90
Public Sector Capacity Building 34
Public Security 100, 106
pyrotechnic signalling devices 72

Index 159

QDR 23
Quad 102, 103, 106, 107, 132
Quadrennial Defence Review 23
Quadrilateral initiative 25

Rao, P.V Narsimha 68
Regional Comprehensive Economic
  Partnership (RCEP) 34, 39, 44, 67, 83,
  88–91, 93, 94, 106, 131
regional consensus making 14
regional constructs 18, 19, 20
regional identity 28
regional organization 1, 35, 90, 102, 131
regional security 14, 19, 21, 23, 26, 29, 33,
  68, 88, 89, 98, 99, 101, 102, 106, 110,
  112, 132
regional security architecture 14, 132
regional security convergence 19
regional security organization 14
reincarnating Lamas 34
relations with allies 19
relevance 1, 20, 21, 28, 43, 88
religious imprint 34
renovation 61
Réunion 24
rich natural resources, 42
Richardson, Michael 21
right of passage 47
riparian states: lower 119, 120, 123; upper
  108, 109, 111
Rudd, Kevin 21; proposal 10,94
Russian military equipment 68

SAARC summit 55
Sanya submarine base 67
satellite imagery station 68
satellite tracking centre 106
Scarborough Shoal 75, 77, 112, 114
science and technology 61, 69
sea access 18
Sea Lanes of Control (SLOCs) 74, 75, 78,
  117, 123, 124
sea routes 22
Secretary (East) 39, 46, 56
Secretary of State 20, 38, 106,
  120, 125
sectoral dialogue partner 131
secure resources 21, 29
secure theoretical foundation 19
security: alliances 1, 14, 25, 91, 114; and
  stability 14, 40; communities 27, 28;
  complexes 14, 21, 29; constructs 21, 29;
  environment 33, 88; of Europe 23;
  frontier 14; in the Indo-Pacific

commons 33; regional *see* regional
  security; traditional 21, 25, 29, 89,
  90,91 102
sericulture 96
Seychelles 24
Shangri-La Dialogue 46, 47
ship visits 70, 78
Silk Road Economic Belt 36
Singapore 14, 22, 33, 34, 39, 41, 46, 47,
  53–56, 59, 60, 67, 68, 74, 78, 88, 91, 93,
  96, 99–101, 106, 112, 113, 117, 125, 126,
  131–133
Sino-centric regional order 14
Sino-Indian strategic rivalry 23
Sittwe 36
Six-degree Channel 22
SLOCs *see* Sea Lanes of Control
small powers 28
smart frigates 70
social security 53,54
Socotra Island 21, 29
soft balancing 19
soft power 19
software professionals 106
sophisticated fleet support ship 47
sophisticated technology 102
South and East China Seas 22, 123
South Asia 1, 14, 23, 24, 34, 36, 60
south Asian actor 23
South China Sea 18, 19, 23, 24, 36, 39, 40,
  42, 43, 45, 47, 53, 54, 60, 61, 67, 71–82,
  99, 100, 103, 106–114, 119, 121–127,
  131–133
South China Sea dispute 40, 43, 47, 67, 78
South Korea 14, 38, 53, 91, 100
South Pacific Ocean 14
Southeast Asia 1, 14, 22, 33–39, 42, 43,
  53–60, 67, 68, 78, 83, 88, 89, 95, 99,
  100, 107, 108, 110, 112, 113, 115,
  117–120, 123, 125, 127, 128, 131–133;
  colonies 14; mainland 23, 30, 129
Southeast Asian Treaty Organization
  (SEATO) 14
Southeast 1, 14, 20, 22, 33–39, 42, 43, 46,
  47, 53, 54, 56–60, 67–69, 73, 78, 83,
  88–90, 95, 99, 100, 107–113, 115,
  117–120, 123, 125–128, 131–134
Southern Asia 95
Soviet Union 57, 58, 59, 68, 88, 97, 99,
  100, 117, 128; demise of 7; intervention
  in Afghanistan 14
spatial constructs 27
spatial perspective 19
Spratlys 43, 74, 75, 108, 111, 123, 124, 131

160   *Index*

Sri Lanka 24, 35, 39, 68
staggered method for the inclusion 18
stakeholders and countries 18
standard system 88
standards 34, 88
statecraft 67, 91
stealth frigate 69
Straits of Hormuz 22
Straits of Malacca 21, 29, 43, 77, 78, 120, 124
strategic and defence partnerships 1
strategic communities 25
strategic dialogue 61, 68, 68, 102
strategic framework of reference 19
strategic goals 28
strategic hedge 14
strategic imprint 18
strategic link 34
strategic outlook 34
Strategic Partnership 21, 33, 47, 59, 61, 66–69, 73, 99, 101, 103
strategic periphery 36
strategic point of view 18
strategic priorities 34, 46
strategic prism 19
strategic relations of the nation state 18
strategic space 18, 23, 27, 40, 132
strategic understanding 20, 68
strategic vantage point 18
strategic weapons 79
String of Pearls strategy 42
strong navy 18
structural differences 33
structural power 29
structural reforms of financial institutions 34
structures based on economic priorities 18
Subic Bay Naval base 118
submarine sonar systems 72
Subramanyam, K. 67
sub-regional institutions 18
subscription to US-imposed order 14
Sukhoi-30 70, 71
Sunda 22
supra nationalism 28
swing state 25

Taiwan 43, 75, 112
Tamil movement 39
teacher trainings 37
technicians 70, 71, 131
terrestrial radar systems 73
territorial sea 77, 124

terrorism 20, 24, 40, 55, 75, 78, 82, 89, 101, 120
theoretical framework 27
Theravada 34
think tanks 22, 70
Thomson 28
Tibet 43, 57, 110
TNT explosives 68
Tokyo Declaration 46
totalitarianism 33
Track II 33
trade and cultural routes 19, 20
trade and investment potential 19
Trade in Goods and Services 34
trade linkages 1
trading ports 18
trafficking of weapons 24
trained manpower 34
training of defence personnel 68
trajectory 1, 14, 23, 33, 39, 128, 132
Tran Dai Quang 44, 45, 107
Trans-Pacific Partnership (TPP) 25, 88, 89, 90, 91, 92, 94
Trans-Asian Railways 35
Transatlantic Trade and Investment Partnership (TTIP) 91
transitory arrangement 14
transitory lexicon 29
transnational crimes 24
transport and energy 34
transregional concept 19
transregional construct 22
trilateral highway 35, 37
trilateral ministerial dialogue 121
Trump, Donald 58, 138
Tsangpo 110, 111
Turkey 100

Uighurs 112
Ukraine 44, 68
uncertainties in a region 19
underemployment 33
unemployment 33, 40, 83
unipolar prerogative 19
unipolar world 27, 59
unipolarity 19
United Nations 35, 42, 55, 67, 75, 81, 101, 103, 114, 118, 119, 121, 124, 127
United Nations Convention on the Law of the Sea (UNCLOS), 55, 56, 67, 75, 77, 81, 82, 103, 106, 114, 119, 121, 124, 127
United Nations Economic and Social Commission for Asia and the Pacific, 35

Index   161

United States of America 1, 14, 18, 19,
20, 21, 23, 25, 30, 33–35, 38, 43,
44, 53, 55–61, 65, 67–69, 72, 75, 80,
88–91, 95, 96, 98, 100, 102, 103, 106,
107, 111–128, 131–133, 146, 150;
actions 58; hegemony 19
USAID 35, 95
US–India Joint Declaration 43
US–India 2+2 Ministerial Dialogue 126
US–Soviet–China 59
US–Vietnam War: missing US
servicemen 133

value chain 33, 34, 83, 90
vehicle of convergence 33
Vietnam policy documents 44
Vietnam shipyard 80
Vietnamese Air Force pilots 68
Vietnamese military delegation 67
Vietnamese Sea Police 68
Vietnam-India Business Forum 88
Visa on Arrival 37
visa-free travel 94
Vision for Indo-Vietnam Defence
Relations 72
visiting forces agreement 14

Waever, Ole 29
warship machinery 68
Washington system 89
Washington–Peking–Moscow
triangle 59
water security 70, 108
weapon systems 68, 71, 72, 132
western colonial powers 1
Western Europe 19
Western Pacific 18, 19, 20, 22, 25,
78, 121, 122, 123
Western regionalism 18
white shipping 54
Work Plan 34, 37
World Bank (WB) 40
world population 89
World Shipping Council 77, 124
WTO 34, 83, 88, 91, 94, 115, 119
WTO Doha Round 91
WTO-plus forum 91

Yemen 21, 24, 29
Yugoslavia 58, 117
Yunnan 36, 109

zoologists 1

Printed in the United States
By Bookmasters